D1721637

STARK

WIRTSCHAFTSSCHULE

Abschluss-Prüfungs-
aufgaben mit Lösungen **2008**

Englisch

Bayern
2000–2007

ISBN 978-3-89449-069-0

© 1980 by Stark Verlagsgesellschaft mbH & Co. KG
D-85318 Freising · Postfach 1852 · Tel. (0 81 61) 1790
25. ergänzte Auflage 2007
Nachdruck verboten!

Inhalt

Fortsetzung siehe nächste Seite

Jeweils im Herbst erscheinen die neuen Ausgaben
der Abschluss-Prüfungsaufgaben mit Lösungen.

Autoren:
___

Lösungen der Prüfungsaufgaben 2000 bis 2004, Lernhilfen zur Abschlussprüfung: Peter Ehrl
Hinweise und Übungsaufgabe zur mündlichen Prüfung, Lösungen der Prüfungsaufgaben ab
2005: Chris Riley und Sarah Töpler
Kurzgrammatik: Gabriele Achhammer

Vorwort

Liebe Schülerin, lieber Schüler,

dieses Buch enthält die Prüfungsaufgaben der letzten Jahre, die du als Schüler der Wirtschaftsschule in Bayern im Rahmen deiner Abschlussprüfung bearbeiten musst. Es ist zum Selbststudium gedacht und sollte den schulischen Unterricht ergänzend begleiten.

Für eine erfolgreiche Arbeit mit diesem Buch solltest du die **Lernhilfen** gründlich und in Ruhe durchlesen.

Die **Kurzgrammatik**, die die Schulgrammatik jedoch nicht ersetzen kann, sondern als zusätzliche Arbeitshilfe gedacht ist, solltest du bei der Bearbeitung der Aufgaben zu Rate ziehen. Dann wird es dir leichter fallen, die Abschlussprüfungsaufgaben zu bearbeiten.

Bei der Bearbeitung einer Abschlussprüfung empfiehlt es sich, folgendermaßen vorzugehen:

1. Lies als Erstes den Text gründlich durch.

2. Bearbeite dann die Abschlussprüfung schriftlich, indem du evtl. zuerst die Fragen beantwortest, die dir am leichtesten fallen. Danach setzt du dich mit den restlichen Aufgaben auseinander.

3. Vergleiche anschließend deine Antworten mit den Lösungen und streiche deine Fehler farbig an.

4. Verbessere nun deine Fehler und überlege, warum deine Antwort falsch ist.

5. Schlage unbekannte Wörter im Wörterbuch nach und lerne sie.

6. Bearbeite am nächsten Tag die Aufgaben, die du falsch gemacht hast, noch einmal und vergleiche sie mit der Lösung. So kannst du überprüfen, ob du das Problem tatsächlich verstanden hast.

Übe konsequent! Nur so wirst du in deiner Prüfung erfolgreich sein.

Hinweise zur mündlichen Prüfung

An den Wirtschaftsschulen in Bayern wird eine mündliche Abschlussprüfung eingeführt. Die mündliche Prüfung findet etwa eine Woche vor der schriftlichen Prüfung statt. Die genauen Termine der mündlichen Prüfung werden vom Kultusministerium vorgegeben.

- Die mündliche Prüfung macht 25 % der Gesamtnote der Abschlussprüfung aus.
- In der Regel werden die Schüler zu dritt geprüft. Je nach Schülerzahl werden auch Zweiergruppen gebildet.
- Die Gruppen werden entweder von der Lehrkraft, per Los oder von den Schülern zusammengestellt. Diese Entscheidung bleibt der jeweiligen Schule bzw. der Lehrkraft überlassen.
- Bei jeder Prüfung sind zwei Lehrkräfte anwesend. Eine Lehrkraft stellt den Schülern die Aufgabe, während die andere im Hintergrund mit der Auswertung beschäftigt ist.
- Nach jeder Prüfung entscheiden die beiden Lehrkräfte über die Leistungen der geprüften Schüler.

Folgende Punkte sind an den Tagen der mündlichen Prüfung zu beachten:

- Aufgrund der Fairness dürfen die Schüler, die noch nicht geprüft worden sind, auf keinen Fall mit schon geprüften Schülern zusammenkommen.
- Jeder Schüler muss pünktlich zum vorgegebenen Termin erscheinen.

Prüfungsteile

Die mündliche Prüfung besteht aus drei Teilen und dauert etwa 20 Minuten. Die Rahmenthemen für die jeweiligen Prüfungstage werden vom Kultusministerium vorgegeben.

- Teil 1: „Warm-up" (ca. 1 Minute pro Schüler)
  Jeder Prüfling stellt sich vor und erzählt ein bisschen von sich, seiner Familie, seinen Hobbys, zukünftigen Plänen usw. Es kann auch vorkommen, dass eine Frage zum vorgegebenen Thema gestellt wird, z. B. *What would your dream job be?*
  Da diese Phase als Warm-up gedacht ist, wird sie nicht benotet.
- Teil 2: (1–2 Minuten pro Schüler)
  Dieser Teil der Prüfung bezieht sich auf das vorgegebene Thema. Je nach Thema ist es möglich, dass die Prüflinge Anschauungsmaterial erhalten. Die Lehrkraft stellt jedem einzelnen Schüler eine Frage zum Thema, die dieser allein beantwortet, z. B. *Choose one of the jobs pictured and talk about the advantages and disadvantages of the job.*
- Teil 3: (ca. 7 Minuten)
  In diesem Teil der mündlichen Prüfung führen die Schüler eine Diskussion. Die Lehrkraft stellt lediglich die Aufgabe, z. B. *Discuss whether it is better to stay at school, do an apprenticeship or take a year off to travel.* Ansonsten hält sich die Lehrkraft beim Gespräch weitestgehend zurück. Hier ist es wichtig, dass jeder Schüler sich am Gespräch beteiligt und versucht, in die Diskussion einzugreifen und auf seine Gesprächspartner einzugehen.

Part 1 "Warm-up"

TEACHER: Please come in and sit down. From now on you are only allowed to speak English. To help you relax and warm up, we will ask you to introduce yourselves.
Candidate 1, can you please tell us a little bit about yourself, your family, hobbies and future plans?

CANDIDATE 1: Yes, of course. My name is Markus. I am 16 years old and I live in Happing, a small village near Rosenheim. I have a younger brother who is 14 and an older sister who is 22. At the moment I am doing my final exams at the commercial school in Rosenheim. My hobbies are snowboarding, swimming, going to the cinema and meeting my friends. In September I will start an apprenticeship at an IT company in Raubling.

Part 2

Hinweis: In diesem Beispiel bekommen die Schüler Anschauungsmaterial.

TEACHER: Now we will begin part two of the speaking test. I want you to imagine that you have finished school successfully and are now working for a big company. Your boss wants to send you abroad for a year.
I will give each of you a piece of paper showing the flags of two different countries. Look at your two flags and think about in which of these two countries you would prefer to work. This time we will start with you, Candidate 2. Which two countries do you have?

Australia   France

CANDIDATE 2: I have Australia and France.

TEACHER: Interesting. Please tell us where you would prefer to work and why.

CANDIDATE 2: I would choose Australia because the weather is so nice and I could go swimming every day. Last year we learned about Australia at school.

TEACHER: Oh, what did you learn?

CANDIDATE 2: It's a very big country with a lot of interesting sights, for example, the Outback and the Great Barrier Reef. It would be great to go surfing there. In Australia I would be able to speak English and meet new people. I think there are a lot of pretty girls in Australia, too!

TEACHER: Why wouldn't you want to go to France?
CANDIDATE 2: I have already been to France on holiday. It is too close to Germany and I can go there any time. Anyway, I can't speak French.
TEACHER: So, you would definitely prefer to go to Australia.
CANDIDATE 2: That's right.
TEACHER: Thank you. That's the end of part two.

Part 3

TEACHER: In the next part of the test you have to have a conversation with each other, so please move your chairs so that you are facing each other. You should help each other and try to keep the conversation moving. I will explain the task to you and then will stay out of the conversation as far as possible.
You are all leaving school this summer and have to decide what to do in the future. Please discuss the advantages and disadvantages of: going to another school to continue your education, starting an apprenticeship or taking a year off to travel.
Now, please begin.

CANDIDATE 1: I think starting an apprenticeship is better than going to another school because you earn money when you are doing an apprenticeship.
CANDIDATE 2: That's true, but if I go to another school, I will get a better job later. That means that I will be able to earn more money.
CANDIDATE 3: I don't agree. Money isn't everything. I think that taking a year off, having fun and travelling is important. You have to work your whole life. Why start when you are 16?
CANDIDATE 1: But, if you take a year off, you will find it harder to get a job later. Many employers will think that you are lazy and don't want to work.
CANDIDATE 3: That isn't true! Lots of employers like people who have seen the world. Also, if I go abroad I can learn new languages and practice my English. What do you think? (spoken to candidate 2)
CANDIDATE 2: I think you're right. It's easier to learn a language when you are in the country than at school.
CANDIDATE 1: There is only one problem. Where will you get the money to go travelling?
CANDIDATE 3: That's a good point. Perhaps you could get some money from your parents or …
CANDIDATE 2: Or you could get a summer job and save some money. I'm going to work in a restaurant this summer before I start school.
CANDIDATE 1: I still think that it is much better to start an apprenticeship. I want to earn enough money to get my driving license and buy my own car. Then I will be able to drive to foreign countries to go on holiday.
CANDIDATE 3: Like I've already said, we are all young and should have fun as long as we can.

Part 1 "Warm-up"

TEACHER: Please come in and sit down. Welcome to the speaking part of the final exam. We'd like you to relax and remember only to speak English from now on. Candidate 2, please introduce yourself and tell us what you normally eat for lunch on school days.

CANDIDATE 2: Certainly. My name is Julia Meier and I'm a pupil at the business school in Rosenheim. Rosenheim is a small city between Munich and Salzburg. I live with my mum and my two older brothers. In my free time I like cycling, walking in the mountains and meeting my friends. My mum works full-time, so I often eat something in the city centre before I go home.

TEACHER: What do you usually eat?

CANDIDATE 2: Well, I sometimes buy a sandwich from the bakery, but my favourite thing is a doner kebab.

TEACHER: Thank you, Julia.

Part 2

TEACHER: We'll now start the second part of the test. I'm going to ask each of you the same question. I'll begin with Candidate 3. Do you think it's important for teenagers to learn how to cook? Please give reasons for your answer.

CANDIDATE 3: I think teenagers should be able to cook basic things like eggs, pizza and spaghetti. When I'm hungry and my mum and dad aren't at home, I want something fast. I don't want to work in the kitchen for two hours before I can eat, like my mum does.

TEACHER: That's fine. Do you think you'll want to learn how to cook more complicated things when you leave home?

CANDIDATE 3: Probably not. I would like to get married and I hope that my wife will do most of the cooking.

TEACHER: And what will you do before you find a wife that will cook for you?

CANDIDATE 3: I plan to get a very good job after leaving school, so I'll hopefully earn enough money to eat in restaurants. Not every day, but often. If I have to cook for myself, I'll put a frozen pizza in the oven.

Part 3

Hinweis: In diesem Beispiel bekommen die Schüler Anschauungsmaterial.

TEACHER: Now you are going to have a discussion with each other, so please sit so that you can see each other. In this part you are allowed to help each other. Remember that it is important to keep the conversation going.

You and your friends want to go out to celebrate a friend's birthday. I would like each of you to take one of the sheets, turn it over and briefly describe the type of eating place you see in the picture. Discuss the pros and cons of the three eating places. You should try to convince the other members of the group that your eating place is the best location to celebrate a birthday. Let's begin.

CANDIDATE 1: I have a picture of a group of young people eating pizza. I think they are at an Italian restaurant.

CANDIDATE 2: In my picture I see teenagers at a barbecue. They are grilling sausages and burgers. I think they are at someone's house.

CANDIDATE 3: I can see a group of friends sitting in front of a mountain hut. They are having a good time. Some are drinking beer and one boy is drinking milk.

CANDIDATE 2: A barbecue is the best idea because it is much cheaper than going out to eat. We could buy the food at the supermarket and prepare it ourselves.

CANDIDATE 1: Yes, you're right, but what about people who don't eat meat?

CANDIDATE 2: There is always a lot of salad at a barbecue and you can grill vegetables!

CANDIDATE 3: Salad? Who wants salad at a birthday party? I think we should go up to a mountain hut and eat traditional Bavarian food. How does that sound?

CANDIDATE 1: Sounds boring!! We can eat Bavarian food any time.

CANDIDATE 3: But not with a beautiful view of the mountains. And when we get to the mountain hut, we'll be really hungry so the food will taste great.

CANDIDATE 2: If we get to the mountain hut – not everybody likes hiking. We have friends who aren't fit enough for that.

CANDIDATE 1: In my opinion neither of those ideas are good for a birthday party. We should go to a restaurant in the city, for example a pizzeria. Then it's easier for everybody to get there.

CANDIDATE 3: Perhaps we should go to a restaurant. If we're inside, the weather doesn't matter like at the mountain hut or the barbecue. What do you think? (said to Candidate 2)

CANDIDATE 2: I suppose so. Most people like pizza and it isn't too expensive………

usw.

Lernhilfen zur Abschlussprüfung ab 2003

Part A: Mögliche Aufgabentypen zur Überprüfung des Leseverstehens (Reading Comprehension)

Die unten aufgeführten Aufgabentypen können in der Prüfung gestellt werden. Auf den folgenden Seiten findest du zu vielen dieser Aufgabentypen Beispiele, mit denen du sie üben kannst. In der Prüfung können die Antworten zu den Aufgaben in deutscher oder in englischer Sprache verlangt werden. Dies wird stets in der Fragestellung deutlich gemacht.

- Fragen zum Text, mit denen überprüft wird, ob dieser im Wesentlichen verstanden wurde.

- Wiedergabe bestimmter Textinhalte als Notiz/Memo/Protokoll.

- Freie Wiedergabe der gesamten Textinformation.

- Vorstrukturierte Wiedergabe der gesamten Textinformation.

- Error Spotting: Erkennen von Übersetzungsfehlern.

- Zuordnungsaufgaben
  → Text – deutsche Zusammenfassung oder → Text – englische Überschriften.

- Wiedergabe eines Textes oder Textteils in deutscher Sprache.

Part B: Mögliche Aufgabentypen zur Überprüfung der Sprachfertigkeit (Overall Language Proficiency)

Hierzu gibt es eine besonders große Aufgabenvielfalt. In der Regel werden Textrekonstruktionsaufgaben gestellt, welche die Wortschatz- und Strukturenkenntnisse nicht isoliert testen, sondern in Verbindung mit Lesestrategien:

Lückentexte (Cloze Tests)
- Open Cloze
  Aus einem Text wurden Wörter entfernt, die der Schüler wieder einsetzen muss, um den Text zu rekonstruieren. Der Schüler soll die Wörter aus dem Textzusammenhang ergänzen. Dabei sind z. T. mehrere Lösungsmöglichkeiten denkbar.

- Cloze with initials
  Um die Aufgaben leichter und u. U. eindeutiger zu machen, sind hier die Anfangsbuchstaben (= initials) der fehlenden Wörter angegeben.

- Banked Cloze
  Zur Erleichterung der Aufgabe werden hier die fehlenden Wörter in einer **word bank** mit dem Text angegeben. Allerdings sind sie um eine Reihe von Wörtern erweitert, die nicht in den Textzusammenhang passen und den Schüler „verwirren" sollen.

Auswahlaufgaben (Multiple Choice)

- In einem Text sind an mehreren Stellen für lexikalische oder strukturelle Einheiten verschiedene Lösungsmöglichkeiten vorgegeben. Davon muss jeweils die richtige/beste ausgewählt und gekennzeichnet werden.
- Zu Begriffen aus einem Text werden jeweils verschiedene Wörterbucheinträge vorgestellt. Die Schüler sollen die zutreffenden erkennen und markieren.

Fehlersuche (Error Spotting)

Dazu ist ein kurzer Text vorgegeben, der sprachliche Fehler (im Bereich Rechtschreibung und Grammatik) enthält. Die Fehler müssen gekennzeichnet und verbessert werden.

Erklärungen/Definitionen (Explanation/Paraphrase)

Vorgegebene Begriffe sollen hier in vollständigen Sätzen erklärt werden. Dabei können dir folgende Überlegungen helfen:

- Bei Personen: Was sind typische Eigenschaften oder Tätigkeiten der Person?
  Bei Gegenständen: Wie sieht der Gegenstand aus? Wofür wird er verwendet?
  Bei Adjektiven: Welche Eigenschaft/Welches Gefühl wird damit beschrieben?

- Üblicherweise besteht eine Definition aus einem Hauptsatz, in dem der Begriff eingeengt wird und einem Relativsatz, in dem eine Tätigkeit oder der Verwendungszweck erklärt wird:
  A *customer is somebody/a person* (NICHT: man/woman! Das wäre eine unzulässige Einschränkung.) *who buys something (in a shop/from a company).*
  A *lorry is a big vehicle which is used for transporting heavy/big loads.*

- Verwende niemals zur Erklärung Wörter (z. B. Verben), die von dem Begriff abgeleitet sind.
  NICHT: A *fighter is somebody who fights.*

- Manchmal bietet es sich an, zur Verdeutlichung ein Beispiel anzugeben.
  A *treaty is an agreement between at least two partners on a certain issue, for example the treaty of Maastricht, which established the criteria of the Monetary Union of the EEC.*

Part C: Mögliche Aufgabentypen zur freien Textproduktion (Produktive Skills)

Bei diesem Prüfungsteil können ein gewisser Umfang der Textproduktion (z. B. „Write about 80 words.") und eine bestimmte Anzahl thematischer Aspekte vorgegeben sein. Gemeinsam ist allen möglichen Aufgabentypen, dass es nicht genügt, die vorgegebenen Stichpunkte einfach ins Englische zu übersetzen oder im Text aneinander zu reihen. Sie müssen schon etwas genauer ausgeführt bzw. ausgeschmückt werden. Mögliche Aufgabentypen sind:

- Filling in a form
  Du sollst zu einer vorgegebenen Kommunikationssituation (z. B. Planung einer Reise oder eines Schüleraustausches, Aufnahme in einen Verein) ein Formular ausfüllen, das neben Kurzangaben (zur Person) auch eine zusammenhängende Beschreibung verlangt.

- Personal letter
  Du sollst zu einer vorgegebenen Situation/einem Sachverhalt einen persönlichen Brief verfassen.

- Drawing up a programme
  Du sollst – z. B. für den Besuch von Geschäftsfreunden oder ausländischen Gastschülern – ein Tages- oder Wochenprogramm entwerfen.

- Reporting/Telling a story
  Du sollst zu einem Vorfall einen Bericht anfertigen oder eine Geschichte erzählen bzw. eine unvollständige Geschichte fertig schreiben.

- Formal letter
  Du sollst nach stichpunktartigen Vorgaben in deutscher Sprache ein „Schreiben des öffentlichen Lebens" in Englisch verfassen (Geschäftsbrief, Bewerbungsschreiben, Zeigungsanzeige etc.)

Tipps zum Erfassen von Informationen und zum Lösen der Aufgaben

Lesestrategie und Lesetechnik
Um einem Text Informationen entnehmen zu können, muss man ihn lesen, und zwar strategisch richtig. Präge dir deshalb die folgenden Tipps zur richtigen Lesestrategie und zu wirkungsvollen Lesetechniken genau ein.

1. Lasse den Text als Gesamtheit auf dich wirken (Überschrift – Text – evtl. Bilder)
Schau dir den Text im Überblick an, bevor du mit dem genauen Durchlesen beginnst. Achte auf die Gliederung des Textes und betrachte Illustrationen. Dabei speicherst du bereits unbewusst Informationen. (Beispiel A 4)

2. Den Text diagonal überfliegen (Skimming)
Dabei verschaffst du dir einen Gesamteindruck vom Inhalt und erfasst wesentliche Kernaussagen. Es geht in dieser Phase auf gar keinen Fall um ein detailliertes Textverständnis. (Hilfreich bei den Beispielen A 2, A 3 und A 4)

3. Genaues Lesen, das sich an der Aufgabenstellung orientiert (Scanning)
Lies nun die Aufgabenstellung und anschließend den Text ein weiteres Mal durch und markiere grob die Textstellen, von denen du glaubst, dass sie sich auf die einzelnen Aufgaben beziehen. Zu diesem Zweck notierst du die Nummern der Aufgaben am Textrand. Falls mehrere Textstellen zu einer Teilaufgabe gehören, kannst du sie am Rand mit Bögen o. Ä. verbinden, sodass du beim nächsten Schritt diesen Zusammenhang gleich wieder vor Augen hast.

4. Detailorientiertes Lesen (der markierten Textstellen)
Jetzt sollst du die gekennzeichneten Textpassagen unter Berücksichtigung der genauen Aufgabenstellung sorgfältig durchlesen und die benötigten Informationen markieren. Du kannst sie unterstreichen, farbig anstreichen, einkreisen o.Ä. Entscheidend ist, dass du **nur das Wesentliche** hervorhebst, sonst geht die Übersicht verloren und das Markieren war überflüssig. (hilfreich bei A 1 und A 5)

Zur Vorbereitung sind die Teile A der Abschlussprüfungen der verschiedenen Jahrgänge zu empfehlen, besonders der Jahrgang 1998 *(Flight Attendants)*.

A 1   Traffic jams and smog problems in US cities (aus: *Read On*, September 2002, S. 1)

America, the mobile society, faces serious traffic problems. More than three-quarters of Americans drive to work. The average time it took someone to drive to work in 2000 was 25.5 minutes, up from 22.4 minutes in 1990, according to the US Census Bureau*. Huge traffic jams block the roads in and out of many US cities.

Los Angeles was once famous for its smog, but laws made to improve air quality there have been very effective. LA is no longer the most polluted city in the US. It has been taken over by Houston, Texas and other cities with heavy traffic.

California has a history of introducing innovations in the car industry. The state was responsible for air bags, catalytic converters** and unleaded petrol.

Annotations:
Census Bureau* = statistisches Bundesamt; catalytic converters** = Katalysator

Aufgaben
1. Mark all the correct sentences:

    ☒ Most Americans use their car for going to work.

    ☐ The average time for going to work has decreased from 1990 to 2000.

    ☐ Los Angeles has been the most polluted city in the US for a long time.

    ☑ California has always tried to improve cars.

2. What was the average time an American worker or employee had to spend in his car while driving to and from work in a five-day-working week in 2000?

    He spend his time 127,5 Minutes in his car.

3. Describe the air quality in Los Angeles once and now.

    In Los Angeles there was a smog like smoke were on the street. Now the air have been improved.

4. What was the reason for this change in air quality?

    The laws was the reason.

5. What expects you if you travel to Houston, Texas?

    That there are ver a high pollutan, because of heavy traffic

4

CARSON BROTHERS LTD.
42 New Harbour Rd., Bristol SE 2 2 BE, GB
Tel.: 0138 224 53/54, Fax: 0138 224 55

Gebr. Valtlhauser
Äußere Wiener Str. 22 – 26
93055 Regensburg
Germany

September 8, 2002

Enquiry about Office Equipment Furniture

Dear Sir,

We were very impressed by your office furniture shown at the "Modern Office Exhibition" in Nuremberg in May and we have also seen some of your other products on your web site.

Our company is one of the largest importers and wholesalers of office furniture in the south of the UK and we have excellent business relations with several firms in Germany.

As there is a great demand for high-quality office furniture among our customers, we would appreciate it if you would send us your latest illustrated catalogue as well as your current export price list, including all kinds of discounts you grant. Please also state your terms of payment and delivery. Do you make furniture to specification, too?

You should be able to make delivery within three weeks upon receipt of our order.

We enclose a list of our major business partners in Germany, who will be glad to provide you with any kind of information on our company you may need.

We are looking forward to receiving your reply soon.

Yours sincerely

Jeffrey Carson, jr.
Import Manager

Aufgabe

Herr Muster von der Fa. Valtlhauser hat einen Auszubildenden in seiner Abteilung, der in der englischen Geschäftskorrespondenz noch nicht ganz firm ist. Deshalb stellt der Azubi Herrn Muster Fragen zu der vorliegenden Anfrage, damit er bei deren Beantwortung keinen Fehler macht und das Angebot vollständig ausführt.

Versetze dich in die Lage von Herrn Muster und beantworte die Fragen des Auszubildenden. (Die Antworten müssen nicht lang, aber genau sein.)

1. Was soll das Angebot enthalten und was soll ich ihm beilegen?

2. Hat der Kunde Sonderwünsche?

3. Enthält die Anfrage irgendwelche besonderen Bedingungen?

4. Ist die britische Firma ein interessanter Kunde?

Your situation:
You work in the office of SAM FUGATE Movers and have an enquiry from a German customer living in the USA whose English, however, is not very good.

Tasks (Die deutschen Antworten müssen nicht unbedingt vollständige Sätze sein.)

1. Überzeuge den Kunden, warum er sich gerade für SAM FUGATE entscheiden soll.

   _____

   _____

   _____

   _____

   _____

2. Der Kunde möchte einen Teil seines Hausrats schon vor dem Umzug verpacken, hat aber keine Kisten o. Ä. dafür.

   _____

   _____

   _____

   _____

   _____

3. Der Kunde möche wissen, wer für einen Schaden beim Umzug aufkommt. (Beleg aus dem Text angeben!)

   _____

   _____

   _____

   _____

4. In seiner neuen Wohnung kann der Kunde nicht all seine Möbel unterbringen, er möchte sie aber nicht verkaufen, da er in etwa einem Jahr beruflich wieder an seinen jetzigen Wohnort versetzt wird.

   _____

   _____

   _____

   _____

   _____

The New Georgia Railroad

If your grandpa visited Atlanta 60 years ago he could have taken a ride on this very train, then pulled by our steam engine 750 which made its maiden run in 1910. All of these old-fashioned cars have been restored and are climate-controlled to assure you a comfortable journey.

The New Georgia Railroad is available for: Charter groups up to 900; Saturday excursion rides around Old Atlanta; and excursion trips out to Stone Mountain Village and in the Park where it circles the 5-mile base of the Mountain. These excursion rides are open to the public.

Private parties on the train can be catered but both hot and cold snacks are always available on excursion rides.

The Atlanta Loop trip leaves from the Zero Milepost in the Underground on an 18-mile loop circling the historic district of Atlanta, passing famous old neighborhoods and landmarks. This journey is colorfully narrated and takes approximately 1½ hours, leaving at 10 am, noon, and 2 pm on all Saturdays except those scheduled for Stone Mountain.

These runs are also available for special charter groups. The Village has over 50 specialty shops packed with regional art, crafts and collectibles.

STONE MOUNTAIN VILLAGE

The Mountain rides leave from the Zero milepost at 10 am, and 2 pm. The train is comprised of 21 passenger cars including 4 entertainment lounge cars and several engines — all authentic old-fashioned; a 1917 office car built originally for use by railroad barons. This trip takes about 2½ hours when traveled non-stop, longer if you visit in the Village or Park. For further information call or write:
The Georgia Building Authority
1 Martin Luther King Jr. Dr.
Atlanta, GA 30334
404-656-0769

Ole Clickety Clack Is
Takin' Us Back
All Abooard!

The New Georgia Railroad

Free Parking At 90 Central Avenue

Annotations:
maiden run = Jungfernfahrt; loop trip = Rundfahrt; to narrate = erzählen, erklären

Aufgabe

Mithilfe des Artikels aus einer Fremdenverkehrsbroschüre von Atlanta, Georgia, USA, sollst du ein kurzes informatives Referat über „The New Georgia Railroad" halten. Mache dir dazu ein stichpunktartiges Konzept auf Deutsch.

1. When was the first run of the steam engine 750?

   Die Jungfernfahr fand 1910 statt

2. What makes the journey in the old railroad cars comfortable?

   Sie wurden restauriert und auf Klimaschutz Klima kontrolliert

3. What is the maximum number of people who can travel on "The New Georgia Railroad"?

   Es können 21. Passagiere mitfahren

4. Do they serve food on the trips?

   Heiße und kalte Snakes sind immer verfügbar .

5. How long is the Atlanta Loop trip (distance & time)?

   18 Meilen
   Dauer ca. 1 1/2 Stunden

6. When do these Loop trips usually take place?

7. Where do the Loop trips and the Mountain rides start from?

A 5 **Junk food is making us fat** (aus: *Read On*, September 2002, S. 6, by Chloe Anthony, alterated)

One image of America is that of tanned, slim, blonde beauties, jogging before a day in the office. But the reality is most Americans no longer walk, they sit in the car. Sixty per cent of America's adult population are overweight. Obesity* is the cause of 300,000 deaths per year in America. Twelve per cent of healthcare costs are eaten up by weight problems, which have become more of a problem than drinking or smoking.

It is not only Americans who are becoming fat, many other countries, both rich and poor ones, have this problem. The World Health Organisation found out that 22 million children are overweight.

Malta comes first with the most overweight children, Italy, second, and America, third. In Morocco and Zambia, nearly 20 % of the four-year-olds are too fat. In Mexico, Chile and Peru, one in four children between four and ten years is obese**.

Who is to blame for that? Some experts say it is a question of lifestyle. People do not take enough exercise or eat healthy food. Other experts say it is the fault of the food companies and their marketing. Supermarkets are full of junk food and it is cheap.

Annotations: obesity* = Fettleibigkeit; obese** = Adjektiv von obesity

Aufgabe
Dein Freund hat in der Septemberausgabe 2002 von *Read On* einen Artikel über ungesundes Essen gelesen und schreibt dir darüber. Dabei sind ihm einige Fehler unterlaufen. **Streiche die Fehler durch und verbessere sie.**

~~Eine~~ Vorstellung von Amerika ist die von ~~tannen~~schlanken, blonden Schönheiten, die
Die _____

einen Tag lang vor dem Büro joggen. Aber die Wirklichkeit ist, dass die Amerikaner
_____

meistens nicht mehr gehen, sie sitzen im Auto.
_____

60 % von Amerikas erwachsener Bevölkerung sind übergewichtig. Fettleibigkeit ist die
_____

Ursache für 300 000 Tote pro Jahr in Amerika. Zwölf Prozent der Kosten im Gesund-
_____

heitswesen werden von Gewichtsproblemen ~~aufgegessen~~, die mehr ein Problem bekom-
_____ _verursacht_ _____

men haben als das Trinken oder Rauchen.
_____

Es sind nicht nur Amerikaner, die das Fett bekommen haben, viele andere Länder, beide
_____

reiche und arme, haben dieses Problem. Die Weltgesundheitsorganisation (WHO) fand

heraus, dass 22 Millionen Kinder übergewichtig sind.

Malta kommt an erster Stelle mit den meisten übergewichtigen Kindern, Italien an zwei-

ter und Amerika an dritter Stelle. In der Nähe von Marokko und Sambia sind auch 20 %

der Vierjährigen fett. In Mexiko, Chile und Peru ist eines von vier Kindern zwischen

vier und zehn Jahren fettleibig.

Wer ist dafür zu ~~blamieren~~ verantwortlich? Einige Fachleute sagen, es ist eine Frage des Lebensstils.

Die Leute machen nicht genug Übungen oder essen keine gesunde Nahrung. Andere

Experten sagen, es ist die Schuld der Lebensmittelkonzerne und ihrer Marketingmetho-

den/ihres Marketing. Supermärkte sind voll mit ungesundem Essen, und es ist ~~billig~~ billiger.

Lösungsvorschlag

A 1 Traffic jams and smog problems in US cities

Hinweis: Hierzu ist auf jeden Fall das ‚detailorientierte Lesen' (siehe S. 2) erforderlich, unterstreiche dir beim Lesen die Stellen, die für die Antwort wichtig sind.

1. ☒ Most Americans use their car for going to work.
   ☐ The average time for going to work has decreased from 1990 to 2000.
   ☐ Los Angeles has been the most polluted city in the US for a long time.
   ☒ California has always tried to improve cars.

2. *Hinweis: Bei der Berechnung der Zeit ist zu beachten, dass die Fahrt zweimal täglich anfällt („to and from work").*
   The average time was (about) 255 minutes (= 4 hours and 15 minutes).

3. *Hinweis: Beschreibe hier kurz die zwei Informationen über den Zustand der Luft in LA („… once and now").*
   Once there was smog/the air was very polluted, but now the air quality is much better.

4. *Hinweis: Suche hier den Grund dafür, dass die Luft sich verbessert hat.*
   They made laws to improve the air quality.

5. *Hinweis: Suche hierzu die Informationen im Text, die über Houston im Bezug auf Verkehr und Luftverschmutzung gegeben wird.*
   You will find heavy traffic and the most polluted city in the US.

A 2 Anfrage

Hinweis: Verwende zur Bearbeitung der Aufgabe die Lesetechniken des ‚skimming' und ‚scanning'. Überfliege den Text zunächst und verschaffe dir somit einen Überblick über den Inhalt. Schau dir die Aufgabenstellung genau an und lies dir den Brief daraufhin noch einmal durch. Markiere wichtige Stellen, die du für die Beantwortung der Fragen brauchen wirst. Die Antworten können stichwortartig sein.

1. Das Angebot muss enthalten: Exportpreisliste, mögliche Rabatte, Zahlungs-/Lieferungsbedingungen. Beilegen: Neuesten bebilderten Katalog

2. Ja, Möbelanfertigung nach Maß

3. Lieferung muss innerhalb von drei Wochen nach Auftragseingang erfolgen.

4. Ja, da es sich um einen der größten Importeure und Großhändler von Büromöbeln im UK handelt.

A 3 Movers in the USA

Hinweis: Benutze hier vor allem das ‚skimming'. Da der Werbetext aus Schlagwörtern und Stichpunkten besteht, reicht diese Lesemethode aus, um den Inhalt zu erfassen.

1. SAM FUGATE Movers bietet günstigere Preise als die meisten anderen Spediteure.

2. Kein Problem, SAM FUGATE Movers stellt Umzugskisten und Verpackungsmaterial zur Verfügung.

3. Der Schaden wird durch die Versicherung der Spedition bezahlt.
   (→ Insured for your protection.)

4. Kein Problem, denn SAM FUGATE Movers bietet die Lagerung von Möbeln an.
   (→ Storage)

A 4 The New Georgia Railroad

Hinweis: Bei dieser Aufgabe ist es sinnvoll, sich an die Schritte 1–3 der Lesetechnik zu halten. Zunächst sollte der Inhalt sinngemäß erfasst und mit eigenen Worten wiedergegeben werden. Schau dir die Fragen an und markiere dir daraufhin im Text die entsprechenden Stellen, die für die Beantwortung entscheidend sind. Da es sich um ein Konzept für ein Referat handelt, sollten die Antworten stichpunktartig ausfallen.

1. Jungfernfahrt 1910

2. Eisenbahnwaggons renoviert und mit Klimaanlage ausgestattet

3. 900

4. Ja, für private Gruppen voller Service möglich; auf Ausflugsfahrten immer heiße und kalte Imbisse

5. 18 Meilen, ca. 90 Minuten

6. normal samstags um 10.00 und um 14.00 Uhr

7. Abfahrt vom Zero Milepost

A 5 Junk food is making us fat

Hinweis: Bei dieser Aufgabe verschaffst du dir einen ersten Überblick, indem du den englischen Text und dann die Übersetzung überfliegst. Dabei kannst du schon auffällige Stellen markieren. Beim anschließenden genauen Vergleich des Originaltextes mit der übersetzten Version solltest du vor allem auf Stellen achten, wo englische Begriffe leicht mit deutschen verwechselt werden können, sogenannte „False Friends" (z. B. tanned, most, become, nearly, blame), oder wo ein englisches Wort mehrere Bedeutungen haben kann, evtl. auch in Zusammensetzungen (z. B. both, too, exercise).

Eine Vorstellung von Amerika ist die von ~~tannenschlanken~~, blonden Schönheiten, die *braun gebrannten, schlanken* ~~einen Tag lang vor dem~~ Büro joggen. Aber die Wirklichkeit ist, dass die ~~Amerikaner~~ *vor einem (Arbeits-)Tag im* *meisten* ~~meistens~~ nicht mehr gehen, sie sitzen im Auto. *Amerikaner*

60 % von Amerikas erwachsener Bevölkerung sind übergewichtig. Fettleibigkeit ist die

Ursache für 300 000 ~~Tote~~ pro Jahr in Amerika. Zwölf Prozent der Kosten im Gesund-
Todesfälle

heitswesen werden von Gewichtsproblemen ~~aufgegessen~~, die ~~mehr~~ ein Problem ~~bekom-~~
aufgezehrt / aufgebraucht   eher

~~men haben~~ als das Trinken oder Rauchen.
geworden sind

Es sind nicht nur Amerikaner, die ~~das Fett bekommen haben~~, viele andere Länder, ~~bei-~~
fett geworden sind

~~de reiche und arme~~, haben dieses Problem. Die Weltgesundheitsorganisation (WHO)
sowohl reiche als auch arme

fand heraus, dass 22 Millionen Kinder übergewichtig sind.

Malta kommt an erster Stelle mit den meisten übergewichtigen Kindern, Italien an zwei-

ter und Amerika an dritter Stelle. ~~In der Nähe von Marokko und Sambia sind auch 20 %~~
In Marokko und Sambia sind fast 20 %

~~der Vierjährigen fett~~. In Mexiko, Chile und Peru ist eines von vier Kindern zwischen
der Vierjährigen zu fett

vier und zehn Jahren fettleibig.

Wer ist ~~dafür zu blamieren~~? Einige Fachleute sagen, es ist eine Frage des Lebensstils.
schuld daran / verantwortlich dafür

Die Leute ~~machen nicht genug Übungen~~ oder essen keine gesunde Nahrung. Andere
haben nicht genug Bewegung

Experten sagen, es ist die Schuld der Lebensmittelkonzerne und ihrer Marktingmetho-

den/ihres Marketing. Supermärkte sind voll mit ungesundem Essen, und es ist billig.

B 1   Open Cloze

Fill each gap in the following text with one appropriate word.

Trams return to London (aus: Read On, Juli 2002, S. 2)
Londoners will be _____ to _____ by tram again. The trams will _____
running by 2011, as part of a plan to _____ the capital's traffic problem.
The project, _____ will cost € 750 million, _____ announced _____
Ken Livingstone, London's mayor. Up to 122 million _____ are expected to
_____ the trams every year. The trams will _____ north and south
London and use some of London's best-known roads, including Kingsway _____
Aldwych. They will _____ the Thames _____ Waterloo Bridge. Trams
have not _____ used in London _____ over 50 years.

B 2   Open Cloze

Complete the text with suitable words.

The Golden Jubilee: hit or miss? (aus: Read On, Juli 2002, S. 1)
Last month, Queen Elizabeth II _____ her golden jubilee – 50 _____ on
the British _____. She _____ seen ten Prime Ministers rise and _____
during her _____, and countless heads of state _____ other countries come
and go. Before the parties, ceremonies and parades _____, many Britons were not
_____ that the Queen's long reign was really a cause _____ celebration.
Much had _____ since the young Queen _____ to the throne _____
February 6, 1952. Had the monarchy _____ too unpopular for a big jubilee
celebration?
At the _____ of the year the British press was printing _____ about how
the jubilee was going to flop _____ disorganisation and _____ of public
interest. The royal _____ was _____ by the story about Prince Harry
_____ drugs, but the _____ were sympathetic, portraying Prince
Charles as a caring _____. In the end this bad publicity _____ out to be
_____ publicity. The jubilee office had to _____ more phones to be _____
to _____ all the inquiries _____ the jubilee celebrations.

B 3   **Cloze with initials**

World Cup 2002: Football goes global (aus: Read On, August 2002, S. 1)

It was a World Cup **f**_____ of **s**_____. Senegal beat France, the **w**_____
of the last tournament, South Korea **d**_____ Italy, another **t**_____ European
f_____, the Netherlands **d**_____ not even take **p**_____, Spain only beat
Ireland after a penalty shoot-out, and Argentina, always seen as one of the **b**_____
national teams in **s**_____, did not get past the first **r**_____.

This World Cup, the **f**_____ to be played in Asia, has **c**_____ the **f**_____
of international football. European and South American teams **u**_ _____ to dominate.
Teams from Africa, North America and Asia were seen by many European fans as little
more than a **j**_____.

Not any more. The young US team showed **h**_____ far the game has come **i**_____
a country that still **p**_____ baseball, basketball and American football to soccer. In
the 1998 **c**_____ in France, the American team were beaten 2-0 by Germany
in their first game. They were back on the **p**_____ home **a**_____ just 270
m_____ **t**_____ playing time. What a **d**_____ this time! …

B 4   **Banked Cloze**

Fill each gap in the text with one appropriate word from the word bank. There are more
words in the bank than you need.

word bank: abolish, acceptable, art, as, badest, causes, comfortable, complicated,
depend, do, example, exciting, illegal, in, impossible, inquiry, introduce, kind,
prepared, prevented, protection, sounds, well-paid, worst

More than 350 million children still work (aus: Read On, August 2002, S. 3)

Four years ago, 175 states, members of the International Labour Organisation (ILO),
agreed to _____ child labour. But a new report by the organisation, A Future
Without Child Labour, shows that one in six children aged 5 to 17 – 246 million – are
still working _____ jobs that are harmful to them. A further 106 million are doing
work that is _____ for their age – such _____ working for a few hours in
the family business.

Others – about 170 million – _____ dangerous work like building, mining, working
with chemicals and machinery. The ILO wants children under 15 to be _____
from doing this _____ of work immediately. Young people aged 15–17 should
get more _____ at work.

The ILO is particularly worried about one group of children: the 8.4 million, probably
more, who do the _____ kind of work – as child soldiers, prostitutes, in
pornography, drug dealing and other illegal activities.

Banning child labour is more _____ than it _____. A lot of families
_____ on the money young children earn. In Bangladesh, for _____,
one study found that children earned 30 per cent of the family income.

This leads to the real _____ of child labour. Most parents would prefer to send
their children to school, but poverty, war, natural disaster and diseases such as HIV/
Aids often make this _____.

B 5 Multiple Choice

You are supposed to send an offer to Ms J. Peacock, the purchasing director of OFFICE TODAY in Bristol, UK. In the following draft you will find some alternatives to certain words and structures. Mark the correct one by underlining it. There is always only one solution.

Dear Ms Peacock,

thank you for your letter **drafted/dated/sent** August 22. **Enclosed/Including/ Inside** you will find our **latest/last/recent** offer of laser printers. The export price list is **too/to/also** contained.

Our terms of payment are **how/as/if** follows: our company policy for **initial/import/ immediate** orders require the **openment/opening/offering** of a letter of credit **on/ for/in** our favour, **payment/paying/payable** at Midland Bank, London.

Prepared/Provided/When that sufficient quantities are ordered, we would be happy to **guarantee/promise/grant** you a special company **discount/deduct/decrease** of 5 per cent.

The period of **shipment/consignment/delivery** ranges between one and two weeks.

We hope you will find our conditions **satisfactory/satisfied/satisfy** and look forward to **hear/hearing/heard from/of/by** you soon.

Best wishes/Greetings/Yours sincerely

Charly Simpson

B 6 Aufgabe zu Wörterbucheinträgen

Look up the meaning of the expressions underlined in the sentences and use them to complete the English sentences.

Szene ['stse:nə] *f-, -n* **1.** (*Theat, fig*) scene; (Theat: *Bühnenausstattung*) set. **Beifall auf offener ~** applause during the performance; **hinter der ~** backstage; (*fig*) behind the scenes; **in ~** (*acc*) **gehen** to be staged; **etw in ~ setzen** (*lit, fig*) to stage sth; **sich in ~ setzen** to play to the gallery; **sich in der ~ auskennen** (*sl*) to know the scene. **2.** (*fig: Zank, Streit*) scene. **jdm eine ~ machen** to make a scene in front of sb.

umständlich *adj Arbeitsweise, Methode* (awkward and) involved; (*langsam und ungeschickt*) ponderous; *Vorbereitung* elaborate; *Erklärung, Übersetzung, Anleitung* long-winded; *Abfertigung* laborious, tedious; *Arbeit, Reise* awkward. **sei doch nicht so ~!** don't make such heavy weather of everything!, don't make everything twice as hard as it really is!; **er ist fürchterlich ~** he always makes such heavy weather of everything; **etw ~ machen** to make heavy weather of doing sth; **etw ~ erzählen/erklären/beschreiben** *etc* to tell/explain/describe *etc* sth in a roundabout way; **das ist vielleicht ~** what a palaver (*inf*); **das ist mir zu ~** that's too much palaver (*inf*) or trouble *or* bother.

Made ['ma:də] <-, n> *f* maggot; **madig** *adj* worm-eaten; **jdm etw ~ machen** put s.o. off s.th.; **jdn ~ machen** run s.o. down

1. Es gibt viele Leute, die sich immer <u>in Szene</u> setzen müssen.

   There are many people who must always _____ .

2. Johns Chef hasst <u>umständliche</u> Erklärungen.

   John's Boss hates _____ explanations.

3. Man sollte einen Konkurrenten <u>nicht madig machen</u>.

   You shouldn't _____ a competitor _____ .

18

Translate the words and expressions underlined in the following sentences into German.

snip [snɪp] I. vt schnippen, (ab)schnippeln; schneiden; ~ **off** abschneiden; abzwicken II. vi schnippe(l)n III. s 1. kleiner Schnitt, Einschnitt m 2. Schnipsel, Schnippel m od nt 3. (fam) Schnäppchen nt; **it's a ~ at only £ 100** für nur £ 100 ist es sehr günstig; **have the ~** (fam) sich einer Vasektomie unterziehen

familiar [fə'mɪljəʳ] I adj 1. (usual, wellknown) surroundings, sight, scene gewohnt, vertraut; street, person, feeling bekannt; phrase, title, song geläufig, bekannt; complaint, event, protest häufig. **he's a ~ figure in the town** er ist in der Stadt eine bekannte Gestalt; **his face is ~** das Gesicht ist mir bekannt; **among ~ faces** unter vertrauten Gesichtern; **to be/seem ~ to sb** jdm bekannt sein / vorkommen; **to sound ~** sich bekannt anhören (to sb jdm); **that sounds ~** das habe ich doch schon mal gehört; **to be on ~ ground** Bescheid wissen; **to be on ~ ground with sth** in etw (dat) zu Hause sein.

sunny ['sʌnɪ] adj (+er) place, room, day etc sonnig; (fig) smile, disposition also, answer, face heiter. ~ **intervals** (Met) Aufheiterungen pl; **on the ~ side of the house** auf der Sonnenseite (des Hauses); ~ **-side up** nur auf einer Seite gebraten; **the outlook is ~** (Met) die Wetteraussichten sind gut; (fig) die Aussichten sind rosig; **to look on the ~ side (of things)** die Dinge von der angenehmen Seite nehmen; **to be on the ~ side of forty** noch nicht vierzig sein.

4. This mountain-bike was <u>a snip at only $ 500</u>.

_____

_____

5. In geography he <u>is on familiar ground</u>.

_____

_____

6. You should always <u>look on the sunny side of life</u>.

_____

_____

B 7 Error Spotting

Khalil Kawsaneh

K. K. has been living in GB for quite a time. Although he speaks and reads English quite well, he sometimes makes mistakes when writing. So he asked a colleague to correct the following e-mail before he sends it off. Cross out the mistakes and write the corrections in the space provided.

I am ~~write~~ to complain that we ~~have~~ still ~~not~~ receipt our order ~~from~~ 1 August. The deliv-
    writing   _haven't_   _of_

ery ~~date~~ which we agreed on ~~was~~ 22 August. The parts are urgent needed and I must
date of delivery   _ue was_

insist getting them immediate.

If we ~~not~~ receive the completely order within a week, we ~~would~~ be forced ~~cancelling it~~.
   aren't   _will_   _to cancel_

B 8   Explanation/Paraphrase

Look at the following advertisement of a travel agency.

Christmas on the beach

You are fed up with these cold, awful, rainy winter months without any sun? You like sunshine, the beach, the ocean? Why not spend your Christmas holiday in Australia, where it is summer right now?

Quantas Airlines offer you a special ten-day Christmas arrangement in a four star hotel in Hershey Bay close to a wonderful sandy <u>beach</u>. The arrangement includes a breath-taking <u>outdoor</u> Christmas party with fireworks and boat trips to nearby <u>islands</u>. You will depart from Frankfurt Airport on December 22 and return on January 2. The price for this wonderful arrangement is € 1 599 for an <u>adult</u>. Don't miss it!

Paraphrase or explain the underlined expressions:

1. beach: _Is a mainly to in hot holidayplaces and on the sea_

2. outdoor: _The contrast of indoor_

3. islands: _A land in the middle of the sea_

4. adult: _Older than People who are older than Childrens_

Lösungsvorschlag

Hinweis: Bei der Lösung der Aufgaben B 1–4 kommt es in erster Linie auf die Lesetechniken 1–3 an, da die Lücken nur ergänzt werden können, wenn der Text oder zumindest einzelne Sätze als Ganzes erfasst werden. Insbesondere gilt dies für B 1 und 2. Beim ,skimming' setzt du dich bereits gedanklich mit dem Thema auseinander und reflektierst unbewusst den Wortschatz, der zu diesem Bereich gehört.

B 1   Trams return to London

Hinweis: Da die Wörter allein aus dem Zusammenhang herausgefunden werden müssen, sind auch andere Lösungen denkbar, sofern sie den Text sinnvoll ergänzen.

Londoners will be **able** to **travel** by tram again. The trams will **start** running by 2011, as part of a plan to **solve** the capital's traffic problem.
The project, **which/that** will cost € 750 million, **was** announced **by** Ken Livingstone, London's mayor. Up to 122 million **passengers/travellers** are expected to **use** the trams every year. The trams will **link/connect** north and south London and use some of London's best-known roads, including Kingsway **and** Aldwych. They will **cross** the Thames **at** Waterloo Bridge. Trams have not **been** used in London **for** over 50 years.

B 2   The Golden Jubilee: hit or miss?

Last month, Queen Elizabeth II **celebrated** her golden jubilee – 50 **years** on the British **throne**. She **has** seen ten Prime Ministers rise and **fall/go** during her **reign**, and countless heads of state **from** other countries come and go. Before the parties, ceremonies and parades **started**, many Britons were not **sure** that the Queen's long reign was really a cause **for** celebration. Much had **changed** since the young Queen **came** to the throne **on** February 6, 1952. Had the monarchy **become** too unpopular for a big jubilee celebration?
At the **beginning** of the year the British press was printing **stories/articles** about how the jubilee was going to flop **due to/because of** disorganisation and **lack** of public interest. The royal **image** was **harmed/damaged** by the story about Prince Harry **taking** drugs, but the **media** were sympathetic, portraying Prince Charles as a caring **father**. In the end this bad publicity **turned** out to be **good** publicity. The jubilee office had to **install** more phones to be **able** to **answer** all the inquiries **about** the jubilee celebrations.

B 3   World Cup 2002: Football goes global

Hinweis: Bei dieser Aufgabe sind zusätzlich die Anfangsbuchstaben der zu ergänzenden Wörter vorgegeben. Trotzdem solltest du nicht darauf verzichten, dir einen Überblick zu verschaffen. Der erste Satz dürfte kaum zu lösen sein, wenn du nicht wenigstens den gesamten ersten Absatz überflogen hast.

It was a World Cup **full** of **surprises**. Senegal beat France, the **winner(s)** of the last tournament, South Korea **defeated** Italy, another **top** European **favourite**, the Netherlands **did** not even take **part**, Spain only beat Ireland after a penalty shoot-out, and Argentina, always seen as one of the **best** national teams in **soccer**, did not get past the first **round**.

This World Cup, the **first** to be played in Asia, has **changed** the **face** of international football. European and South American teams **used** to dominate. Teams from Africa, North America and Asia were seen by many European fans as little more than a **joke**. Not any more. The young US team showed **how** far the game has come **in** a country that still **prefers** baseball, basketball and American football to soccer. In the 1998 **competition** in France, the American team were beaten 2-0 by Germany in their first game. They were back on the **plane** home **after** just 270 **minutes total** playing time. What a **difference** this time! ...

B 4 More than 350 million children still work

Hinweis: Diese Aufgabe erfordert ebenfalls ein ‚skimming‘ des Textes. Anschließend suchst du in der ‚word bank‘ nach geeigneten Begriffen, um damit die Lücken zu füllen. Es ist durchaus möglich, dass ein Wort aus der ‚word bank‘ an mehreren Stellen vorkommt. Du darfst es aber nur dann mehrfach verwenden, wenn das betreffende Wort auch in entsprechender Anzahl vorkommt!

Four years ago, 175 states, members of the International Labour Organisation (ILO), agreed to **abolish** child labour. But a new report by the organisation, A Future Without Child Labour, shows that one in six children aged 5 to 17 – 246 million – are still working **in** jobs that are harmful to them. A further 106 million are doing work that is **acceptable** for their age – such **as** working for a few hours in the family business.

Others – about 170 million – **do** dangerous work like building, mining, working with chemicals and machinery. The ILO wants children under 15 to be **prevented** from doing this **kind** of work immediately. Young people aged 15–17 should get more **protection** at work.

The ILO is particularly worried about one group of children: the 8.4 million, probably more, who do the **worst** kind of work – as child soldiers, prostitutes, in pornography, drug dealing and other illegal activities.

Banning child labour is more **complicated** than it **sounds**. A lot of families **depend** on the money young children earn. In Bangladesh, for **example**, one study found that children earned 30 per cent of the family income.

This leads to the real **causes** of child labour. Most parents would prefer to send their children to school, but poverty, war, natural disaster and diseases such as HIV/Aids often make this **impossible**.

B 5 Multiple Choice

Hinweis: Hier wendest du am besten die Schritte 2 bis 4 an, um die richtigen Lösungen aus dem Sinnzusammenhang zu erschließen. Achte auf „False Friends“, die dich in die Irre führen können: Ein typisches Beispiel dazu findest du im vierten Absatz: Alle drei Begriffe (shipment, consignment, delivery) bedeuten im Deutschen ‚Lieferung‘, aber nur „delivery“ steht für die ‚Lieferung‘ als Vorgang.
Einige Lösungen in dieser Aufgabe findest du nur, wenn du einen Satz oder einen festen Begriff als Ganzes betrachtest: So fällt in der ersten Zeile des dritten Absatzes auf, dass es sich vermutlich um einen If-Satz handelt, in dem aber das einleitende „if“ fehlt. Sieht man sich den Satzanfang an, so erkennt man u. a. das Wort „provided“, das mit dem nachfolgenden „that“ als Synonym für „if“ stehen kann. Im fünften Absatz wiederum steht der Ausdruck „to look forward to“: Dabei solltest du dich erinnern, dass danach immer das Gerund (hier: hearing) folgt. Versuche bei diesem Übungsbeispiel für dich selbst Begründungen für die anderen Lösungen zu finden.

Dear Ms Peacock,

thank you for your letter **drafted/<u>dated</u>/sent** August 22. **<u>Enclosed</u>/Including/ Inside** you will find our **latest/last/recent** offer of laser printers. The export price list is **too/to/<u>also</u>** contained.

Our terms of payment are **how/<u>as</u>/if** follows: our company policy for **<u>initial</u>/import/ immediate** orders require the **openment/<u>opening</u>/offering** of a letter of credit **on/ for/<u>in</u>** our favour, **payment/paying/<u>payable</u>** at Midland Bank, London.

Prepared/<u>Provided</u>/When that sufficient quantities are ordered, we would be happy to **guarantee/promise/<u>grant</u>** you a special company **<u>discount</u>/deduct/decrease** of 5 per cent.

The period of **shipment/consignment/<u>delivery</u>** ranges between one and two weeks.

We hope you will find our conditions **<u>satisfactory</u>/satisfied/satisfy** and look forward to **hear/<u>hearing</u>/heard <u>from</u>/of/by** you soon.

Best wishes/Greetings/<u>Yours sincerely</u>

Charly Simpson

B 6 Aufgabe zu Wörterbucheinträgen

Hinweis: Bei der Lösung der Aufgabe solltest du sowohl das ‚skimming‘ als auch das ‚scanning‘ anwenden. Schau dir die einzelnen Wörterbucheinträge genau an und überlege dir, in welcher Bedeutung die unterstrichenen Wörter verwendet werden. Meist ist es nicht die Bedeutung, die als Erstes angegeben wird. Vergleiche die verschiedenen Bedeutungsvarianten mit dem zu übersetzenden Ausdruck.

1. play to the gallery
2. long-winded
3. run ... down
4. sehr günstig für $ 500; ein Schnäppchen für $ 500
5. weiß (er) Bescheid
6. das Leben von der angenehmen Seite nehmen

B 7 Khalil Kawsaneh

Hinweis: Lies dir den Text durch (skimming) und markiere die Fehler, die dir beim ersten Lesen schon auffallen. Du kannst die korrigierte Version auch gleich daneben schreiben. Wenn du weißt, worum es in dem Text geht, lies ihn noch einmal genau und gründlich (scanning). Nun sollten dir auch die anderen Fehler auffallen. Korrigiere sie.

I am ~~write~~ to complain that we have still not ~~receipt~~ our order ~~from~~ 1 August. The deliv-

    writing   *received*   *of*

ery date which we agreed on was 22 August. The parts are ~~urgent~~ needed and I must

                                           urgently

~~insist getting~~ them ~~immediate~~.

insist on getting   *immediately*

If we ~~not~~ receive the ~~completely~~ order within a week, we ~~would~~ be forced ~~cancelling~~ it.

    do not   *complete*   *will*   *to cancel*

Erläuterungen zu den Lösungen:

writing: Nach „I am" muss das Verb als Partizip Präsens „writing" folgen, oder: Stattdessen wird das ‚Simple Present' verwendet: „I write".

received: Man benötigt die Partizip Perfekt-Form des Verbs „received", da es sich hier um ein Teil des Prädikats handelt.

of: „from" wird nur lokal gebraucht, deshalb muss „of" verwendet werden.

urgently: Adverb „urgently", da ein Bezug zu dem Verb „need" besteht.

insist on getting: Nach „insist" folgt die Präposition „on" sowie das Gerund.

immediately: Adverb „immediately", da ein Bezug zu dem Verb „get" besteht.

do not: Hier ist ein Verb im Präsens oder Präteritum mit Umschreibung gefordert; wegen des Kontextes hier Präsens: „do not/don't".

complete: Adjektiv „complete" wegen des Bezugs zu dem Substantiv „order"

will: Entsprechend dem ‚Simple Present' im If-Satz muss im Hauptsatz Future „I will" stehen.

to cancel: Nach „to be forced" steht ein Verb als to-Infinitiv.

B 8 Christmas on the beach

Hinweis: In der Regel kann man die Bedeutung von Wörtern aus dem Textumfeld, dem Kontext, erkennen, da daraus in der Regel der Inhalt klar hervorgeht. Schau dir also die Wörter nicht isoliert an, sondern berücksichtige immer den gesamten Satz, in dem das Wort verwendet wird. Gerade bei Wörtern, die verschiedene Bedeutungen annehmen können, ist eine solche kontextuelle Betrachtung entscheidend für das Verständnis des Satzes.

1. beach: It's the shore of a sea or a lake.
2. outdoor: It means not in a house or a room.
3. islands: An island is a mass/piece of land surrounded with/by water.
4. adult: An adult is a grown-up person who is (at least) old enough to vote.

Die Abschlussprüfungen der vergangenen Jahre enthalten jeweils Beispiele für das Schreiben von Geschäftsbriefen. Deshalb sind hier Beispiele für das Anfertigen von persönlichen Briefen und Berichten zu finden.

C 1 Writing a personal letter

You saw Robbie Williams at Munich Airport. Write a personal letter to a friend about what happened and mention the following items in your letter:
1. When and where exactly did you see him?
2. Who was with him? Describe.
3. What did he look like? What was he wearing?
4. What did he do?
5./6. Find two additional aspects of your own. Write about 120 words.

C 2 Writing a report

You have the task to inform your class about personal ways to protect the environment. Write a report using three of the following prompts and find one additional aspect of your own. Write at least 80 words.

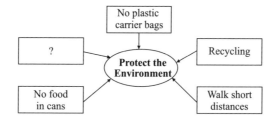

25

C 1 Writing a personal letter

Hinweis: Lies dir zunächst genau die Aufgabenstellung durch. Dabei wird dir auffallen, dass du zwei zusätzliche Inhaltspunkte ergänzen musst und deine Lösung einen bestimmten Umfang haben soll. Letzteres ist aber – wie du bei der Ausarbeitung feststellen wirst – kein Problem.
Grundsätzlich solltest du dich an Formulierungen halten, die du beherrschst. Fehlen dir irgenwo die passenden englischen Begriffe, so überlege dir, wie du den betreffenden Sachverhalt in deiner Muttersprache anders formulieren könntest und übertrage diese dann ins Englische.

At the begining of my last summer holidays I had an exciting experience. I was at Munich Airport with my family and we were waiting at the Lufthansa counter to check in for our flight to Greece, when I suddenly discovered Robbie Williams in the crowd. *[When and where exactly did you see him?]*

There were four other people of his age with him. I think three of them were his bodyguards because they looked very strong, and the fourth person was a fantastic-looking young woman, obviously his girlfriend. *[Who was with him? Describe.]*

Robbie looked great, but a little tired. He was wearing jeans, a T-shirt, a black leather jacket and dark sunglasses. I think he wanted to buy some magazines or newspapers for his flight because he was moving towards a newsstand. *[What did he look like? What was he wearing? What did he do?]*

I was so excited to see one of my favourite singers that I just walked up to him and asked him to sign a music magazine which I had bought before. His bodyguards tried to keep me away from him, but Robbie said it was all right. He was very friendly and asked me for my name and where I came from. Then he wrote on the magazine "To my friend Sandra, ever yours, Robbie Williams". Can you imagine how happy I felt on this special day? *[Two additional aspects.]*

Yours,
Sandra

C 2 Writing a report

Hinweis: Auch bei dieser Aufgabe solltest du zuerst die Angabe genau durchlesen und dir dann überlegen, zu welchen drei der vorgegebenen „prompts" dir genügend Brauchbares einfällt. Dabei genügt es nicht zu schreiben „you should recycle bottles and use no plastic carrier bags", sondern du solltest aufzeigen, warum nicht und eventuell Alternativen erwähnen. Dann erreichst du spielend die geforderte Wortzahl.

Everybody can help to protect the environment in many ways and it doesn't cost you any money, you can even save money. One thing you can do is to use a shopping bag or a basket when you go shopping, so you needn't buy one or more plastic carrier bags to take the things you bought home. You help the environment because these bags are made of valuable resources and it takes a ong time till they get rotten. You should also recycle things like bottles, cans or old papers and magazines instead of throwing them into the trashcan. This helps to produce less waste and to save resources and energy. Another thing everybody can do is to walk short distances instead of using one's car or motorbike. By doing so you help to keep the air cleaner and to save valuable oil. The last thing I'd like to mention is to keep the heating as low as possible and to heat only the rooms in which you stay. This helps to reduce the global warming of the atmosphere.

Adverb – Das Umstandswort

Adverbien dienen zur näheren Bestimmung von **Verben, Adjektiven** und **anderen Adverbien.**
Nach einem Adverb fragt man immer mit „**wie**". Bevor du also ein Adverb bildest, musst du
den englischen Satz analysieren!

Bildung	Anhängen von -**ly** an das **Adjektiv**	slow – slow**ly**
	y → i	happ**y** – happ**ily**
		Ausnahme: shy**ly**
	auf einen Mitlaut folgendes le → ly	simp**le** – simp**ly**
	ic → ically	automat**ic** – automat**ically**
		Ausnahme: pub**licly**
	stummes -e bleibt	extrem**e** – extrem**ely**
		Ausnahmen: fully, wholly, truly

1. Aufgaben des Adverbs

a) Nähere Bestimmung eines Vollverbs

He	**drives**	slowly.
Wie	**fährt** er?	langsam

Beachte: Bildet das Adjektiv mit einem Hilfsverb (Formen von „to be") das Prädikat,
so muss es als Adjektiv erhalten bleiben.

He   is   slow.
⎣__⎦
Prädikat

b) Nähere Bestimmung eines Adjektivs

	He is	**extremely**	**slow.**
Wie **langsam**	ist er?	**äußerst**	**langsam**

c) Nähere Bestimmung eines anderen Adverbs

He drives		**extremely**	slow**ly.**
Wie fährt er?			langsam
Wie **langsam** fährt er?		**äußerst**	(langsam)

Beachte die Stellung, wenn zwei Adverbien im Satz stehen: Dasjenige Adverb (1), das ein anderes Adverb (2) bestimmt, muss vor diesem Adverb, das es bestimmt, stehen.

      1   2
He drives extremely slowly.   (1) bestimmt (2)

2. Attributiver Gebrauch des Adjektivs

Beachte: Du darfst aus einem Adjektiv, das einem Substantiv beigefügt ist, kein Adverb bilden!
He is a **slow** driver.

3. Besonderheiten in der Bildung von Adverbien

a) Endet das Adjektiv bereits auf -ly, so muss das Adverb durch eine Umschreibung mit „**in a ... way**", „**in a ... manner**" gebildet werden.

She asked me **in a friendly way/manner**.

b) Nach bestimmten Verben (**Zustandsverben**, die keine Handlung, sondern einen Zustand beschreiben) darf das Adjektiv **nicht** zum **Adverb** werden, obwohl es das Verb näher bestimmt.

It sounds **good.**

Weitere Zustandsverben:	to become	werden
	to feel	sich fühlen
	to get	werden
	to keep	bleiben, halten
	to look	aussehen
	to remain	bleiben
	to seem	scheinen
	to smell	riechen
	to sound	klingen
	to stay	bleiben, halten
	to taste	schmecken

c) Manche Adverbien haben die **gleiche Form wie Adjektive**, da ansonsten eine **Bedeutungsveränderung** eintritt.

I work **hard.**   Ich arbeite **schwer.**
I **hardly** work.   Ich arbeite **kaum.**

unveränderte Adverbien:	early	früh
	far	weit
	fast	schnell
	hard	schwer
	high	hoch
	late	spät
	long	lang
	near	nahe
Bedeutungsveränderung:	hardly	kaum
	highly	hoch, sehr (abstrakt)
	lately	in letzter Zeit
	nearly	beinahe, fast

d) good → well

She rides very **well**.
Beachte: to be well = gesund sein
I didn't go to work because I wasn't **well** yesterday.

4. Die Steigerung des Adverbs

a) Adverbien auf -ly werden mit „**more**" und „**most**" bzw. mit „**less**" (weniger) und „**least**" (am wenigsten) gesteigert.

He drives **more** (less) slow**ly** than she does.
He drives **most** (least) slow**ly**.

b) Adverbien mit der gleichen Form wie Adjektive (siehe 3 c) werden mit **-er, -est** gesteigert.

fast – faster – fastest;
high – higher – highest;
early – earlier – earliest

He works hard**er** than Tony.
Pupils study hard**est** before a test.

c) unregelmäßige Formen:

well – better   – best
badly – worse   – worst
far   – farther/further – farthest/furthest

G 3

5. Die Stellung des Adverbs

a) Das **Adverb der Art und Weise** steht normalerweise am **Satzende**; es darf nie zwischen Verb und direktem Objekt stehen!

He waited **patiently**.

b) **Gradadverbien** stehen **vor** dem Wort, das sie näher bestimmen; zu den Gradadverbien zählen „extremely, extraordinarily, absolutely, fairly, pretty, rather, quite, very, terribly, especially, really, particularly, much, a bit" usw.

He drives **extremely** carefully.

c) **Häufigkeitsadverbien** wie „often, seldom, rarely, always, never, occasionally, frequently" stehen
  * **vor** dem gebeugten **Vollverb**:
    He **always** reads the newspaper in the morning.

  * **nach** dem **1. Hilfs- oder Modalverb** bei zusammengesetzten Zeiten:
    He has **never** visited the British Museum.

  * **nach „to be"**:
    We are **already** at home.

d) **Adverbien bzw. adverbiale Bestimmungen der Zeit und des Ortes** sowie „in fact, unfortunately, luckily, of course, perhaps, actually" gehören entweder an den **Satzanfang** oder an das **Satzende**.

Three minutes later the boy arrived.
The boy arrived **three minutes later**.

Auxiliaries and their Substitutes –
Hilfszeitwörter und ihre Ersatzformen

Es gibt zwei Arten von Hilfszeitwörtern:
* **primäre** oder **vollständige** Hilfszeitwörter (complete auxiliaries): to be
  to have
  to do
  Mit den vollständigen Hilfszeitwörtern bildet man Fragen, Verneinungen, Kurzantworten und Zeiten.
* **modale** Hilfszeitwörter (modal auxiliaries): Sie drücken aus, dass etwas geschehen kann, muss, darf, soll, könnte etc. Sie werden in Verbindung mit einem Vollverb verwendet, haben aber in der 3. Person Singular kein -s. Sie können auch nicht alle Zeiten bilden und brauchen deshalb **bestimmte Ersatzformen,** deren wichtigste du dir einprägen musst.

1. must

must = to have to = müssen I **don't** have to come.
  Do I have to come?

Die Ersatzform gilt hier als Vollverb und muss deshalb in Frage und Verneinung umschrieben werden.

Simple Present:	I have to come.	I don't have to come.
Simple Past:	I had to come.	I didn't have to come.
Present Perfect:	I have had to come.	I haven't had to come.
Past Perfect:	I had had to come.	I hadn't had to come.
Future I:	I will have to come.	I won't have to come.
Future II:	I will have had to come.	I won't have had to come.

Beachte die Bedeutungsveränderung:
must not (mustn't) = not to be allowed to = nicht **dürfen**

2. can

can = to be able to = können, fähig sein

Simple Present:	I am (not) able to play the piano.
Simple Past:	I was (not) able to play ...
Present Perfect:	I have (not) been able to play ...
Past Perfect:	I had (not) been able to play ...
Future I:	I will (not) be able to play ...
Future II:	I will (not) have been able to play ...

G 5

3. may

may = to be allowed to = dürfen

He ist (not) allowed to come.

4. shall/should/ought to

shall/should/ought to = to be supposed to = sollen
to be expected to
to be to

He **is (not) supposed** to win the match.
He **is expected to** win ...
He **is to** ask the manager.

5. need

need = to have to = brauchen, müssen
needn't = not to have to = nicht brauchen, nicht müssen

You **needn't** come. = You **don't have to** come.

Comparison of Adjectives –
Die Steigerung des Adjektivs

1. Die Steigerung des Adjektivs auf -er, -est

a) Einsilbige Adjektive werden im Komparativ (1. Steigerungsstufe) auf **-er**, im Superlativ (2. Steigerungsstufe) auf **-est** gesteigert.

Grundform:	cheap	billig
Komparativ:	cheap**er**	billig**er**
Superlativ:	cheap**est**	am billig**sten**

b) Zweisilbige Adjektive, die auf **-er, -le, -y, -ow** enden, bilden die Steigerung normalerweise ebenfalls mit **-er, -est**.

clever	cleverer	cleverest	klug	klüger	am klügsten
simple	simpler	simplest	einfach	einfacher	am einfachsten
ugly	uglier	ugliest	hässlich	hässlicher	am hässlichsten
narrow	narrower	narrowest	eng	enger	am engsten

c) Besonderheiten in der Schreibung

stummes -e am Wortende fällt weg	large – larger – largest fine – finer – finest
Konsonant (Mitlaut) am Wortende wird nach einem kurzen, betonten Vokal (Selbstlaut a, e, i, o, u) verdoppelt	hot – hotter – hottest glad – gladder – gladdest
y → i nach einem Konsonanten	happy – happier – happiest sunny – sunnier – sunniest
Beachte: y bleibt nach Vokalen erhalten	gay – gayer – gayest

2. Die Steigerung des Adjektivs mit „more" und „most"

a) Zweisilbige Adjektive, bei denen Regel 1 b nicht in Kraft tritt, bilden den Komparativ mit „**more**" und den Superlativ mit „**most**".

Grundform:		famous	berühmt
Komparativ:	**more**	famous	berühmter
Superlativ:	**most**	famous	am berühmtesten

b) Drei- und mehrsilbige Adjektive werden ebenfalls mit „**more, most**" gesteigert.

difficult	–	**more** difficult	–	**most** difficult
schwierig	–	schwieriger	–	am schwierigsten
comfortable	–	**more** comfortable	–	**most** comfortable
bequem	–	bequemer	–	am bequemsten

3. Unregelmäßige Steigerungsformen

good – better – best	gut – besser – am besten
bad – worse – worst	schlecht – schlechter – am schlechtesten
ill – worse – worst	krank – kränker – am kränksten
much – more – most	viel – mehr – am meisten
many – more – most	viele – mehr – am meisten
little – less – least	wenig – weniger – am wenigsten
far – farther – farthest	weit – weiter – am weitesten
far – further – furthest	weit – weiter – am weitesten
near – nearer – nearest	nah – näher – am nächsten
near – nearer – next	nah – näher – am nächsten
old – older – oldest	alt – älter – am ältesten
old – elder – eldest	alt – älter – am ältesten

Beachte die Bedeutungsunterschiede:

less money	weniger Geld	„less" in Verbindung mit **abstrakten** Substantiven
fewer friends	weniger Freunde	„fewer" in Verbindung mit **zählbaren** Begriffen, die in die Mehrzahl gesetzt werden können
farther south	weiter südlich	„farther" nur in Bezug auf die **räumliche** Entfernung
further information	weitere Information	„further" sowohl im **übertragenen** Sinn mit abstrakten Substantiven als auch im **räumlichen** Sinn
further south	weiter südlich	

the **nearest** pub	das nächste Pub	„nearest" gibt die **räumliche** Entfernung an
the **next** train leaves	der nächste Zug fährt ab	„next" bezeichnet die **Reihenfolge**
my **elder** brother	mein älterer Bruder	„elder" hauptsächlich bei **Verwandtschaftsbezeichnungen**
he is **older** than	er ist älter als	„older" kann **jederzeit** auch bei Verwandtschaftsbezeichnungen verwendet werden
your **last** chance	deine **letzte** Chance	
the **latest** fashion	die **neueste** Mode	

4. Gebrauch der Steigerungsformen im Satz

a) Grundform
(Vergleich von gleichwertigen Dingen)

Our house is as cheap as yours.
Unser Haus ist **so** billig **wie** eures.
Our house is not as beautiful as yours.

b) Komparativ
Signalwort „than" = „als"

Our house is bigg**er than** yours.
Unser Haus ist größ**er als** eures.
Our house is **more** beautiful **than** yours.
Our house is **less** beautiful **than** yours.
... ist **weniger** schön **als** ...

c) Superlativ
Signalwort „the" = „am"

Our house is **the** cheap**est** house (of all).
Unser Haus ist **das** billig**ste** von allen.
Our house is **the most** beautiful of all.
Our house is **the least** beautiful of all.
... ist das **am wenigsten** schöne ...

5. Spezielle Fälle

a) „the ... the" = „je ... desto"

The longer you wait **the** better.
Je länger du wartest, desto besser.

b) „... -er and ... -er",
„more and more" =
„immer ... -er" (zusätzliche
Steigerung)

It's getting cold**er** and cold**er**.
Es wird **immer** kälter.
It became **more and more** interesting.
Es wurde **immer** interessanter.

c) „most" = „very" = „äußerst,
sehr, höchst"

It's a **most** (= very) interesting book.
Es ist ein **höchst** interessantes Buch.

d) Wiederholung des Hilfszeitwortes am Ende des Satzes

Tony is taller than Tom (**is**).
Tony ist größer als Tom.
The book is more exciting than the film (**is**).
Das Buch ist aufregender als der Film.

Gerund – Das Gerundium

Bildung

-ing an die Grundform des Verbs
talk – talking Normalfall
write – writing *Sonderfall:* stummes -e entfällt
run – running *Sonderfall:* Verdoppelung des End-
konsonanten

Verwendung

Es werden nur die üblichen Ausdrücke angeführt; ergänze evtl. anhand
deines Englischbuches.

1. Gerundium als Substantiv (als Subjekt des Satzes)

Swimming is fun. (Schwimmen macht Spaß.)

2. Gerundium nach bestimmten Verben (als Objekt des Satzes)

She can't **give up** smok**ing**.

to admit	zugeben	to keep	weitermachen
to avoid	vermeiden	to mention	erwähnen
to deny	leugnen	to mind	etw. ausmachen
to dislike	nicht mögen	not to mind	nichts dagegen haben
to enjoy	genießen	to miss	verpassen
to feel like	Lust haben zu	to practise	üben
to finish	beenden	to remember	erinnern
to forget	vergessen	to risk	(es) wagen, riskieren
to give up	aufgeben	to stop	aufhören
to go/carry on	weitermachen	to suggest	vorschlagen
to imagine	sich (etw.) vorstellen	to try	probieren

3. Gerundium nach Verb + Präposition

I must **apologize for** be**ing** late.

to agree with	einverstanden sein	to consist of	bestehen aus
to apologize for	sich entschuldigen für	to dream of/about	träumen von
to believe in	glauben an	to feel like	Lust haben auf
to blame for	tadeln wegen	to insist on	bestehen auf
to complain about	sich beschweren über	to look forward to	sich freuen auf

object to	dagegen sein	to talk about	reden über
to prevent from	hindern an	to thank for	danken für
to protect from	schützen vor	to think of	denken an
to rely on	sich verlassen auf	to worry about	sich Sorgen
to succeed in	gelingen, Erfolg haben		machen über

4. Gerundium nach Adjektiv + Präposition

I am **fond of** travel**ling**.

afraid of	(sich) fürchten	sorry about/for	(jdm.) leid tun, dass
famous for	berühmt wegen	tired of/sick of	es satt haben, es leid sein
fond of	mögen	used for	benutzt werden für
good at/bad at	gut/schlecht in	used to	gewohnt
interested in	interessiert an	worried about	besorgt wegen
proud of	stolz auf		

Beachte den Bedeutungsunterschied:

I **am used** to work**ing** hard.   Ich **bin es gewohnt,** schwer zu arbeiten.
I **used to work** hard.   **Früher** arbeitete ich schwer.

5. Gerundium nach einem Substantiv

a) nach Substantiv

Young people often have **trouble** get**ting** a job.

trouble/problem	Schwierigkeiten, Problem(e)
difficulty	Schwierigkeiten
fun	Spaß

b) nach Substantiv + Präposition

She has **difficulty (in)** do**ing** the test.

advantage of	Vorteil von	interest in	Interesse an
chance of	(günstige) Gelegenheit	pleasure in	Freude an
in danger of	in Gefahr	possibility of	Möglichkeit zu
difficulty (in)	Schwierigkeit(en) mit	reason for	Grund für
hope of	Hoffnung zu/auf	trouble in	Schwierigkeiten mit
idea of	Vorstellung, Einfall (zu)	way of	Art und Weise/Weg zu

6. Gerundium nach Präpositionen

Instead of wait**ing** for me he ran away.

after	nach	in spite of	trotz(dem)
apart from	abgesehen von, außer	instead of	anstatt, statt
before	vor	on	gleich nach(dem)
by	dadurch, dass; indem	without	ohne, ohne zu
in	indem		

7. Gerundium nach bestimmten Ausdrücken

This book is **worth** buy**ing**.
It's **no use** ask**ing**.

worth	wert
no use	es hat keinen Sinn
what about/how about	wie wär's mit …

8. Die Übersetzung des Gerundiums

Es ist oft nicht leicht, das „gerund" ins Deutsche zu übersetzen. Dazu bieten sich verschiedene Möglichkeiten an.

a) Substantivierung des Verbs: He can't **give up smoking**.
Er kann **das Rauchen** nicht aufgeben.

b) Eine Infinitivkonstruktion: He was **interested in running** a farm.
Er war **daran** interessiert, eine Farm **zu betreiben**.

c) Ein abhängiger Nebensatz: She overcame her nervousness **by eating** chocolate.
Sie überwand ihre Nervosität, **indem sie (dadurch, dass sie)** Schokolade aß.
These are the new books **worth buying**.
Dies sind die neuen Bücher, **die es wert sind,** gekauft zu werden.

If-Clauses – Bedingungssätze

Bedingungssätze sind Nebensätze, die ausdrücken, dass unter einer bestimmten Bedingung etwas geschehen kann. Sie werden im Deutschen mit „wenn" oder „falls" eingeleitet, im Englischen mit „if". Der „if"-Satz kann vor oder nach dem Hauptsatz stehen; falls er vor dem Hauptsatz steht, muss er durch ein Komma abgetrennt werden.

if-clause (Nebensatz)		main clause (Hauptsatz)
If it rains,		I will take my umbrella.
	oder	
main clause (Hauptsatz)		if-clause (Nebensatz)
I will take my umbrella		if it rains.

Man unterscheidet drei Grundarten von if-Sätzen:

1. Typ 1

Wir verwenden Typ 1, wenn wir über eine Handlung sprechen, die unter einer bestimmten Bedingung in der **Zukunft** geschehen kann. Die **Erfüllung** dieser Bedingung ist **wahrscheinlich**. Dann steht im „if"-Satz das **simple present** und im **Hauptsatz** das **future I**.

If it rains,	I **will** take my umbrella.
Wenn es regnet,	nehme ich meinen Regenschirm.

2. Typ 2

Wir verwenden Typ 2, wenn wir über eine Handlung sprechen, die unter einer bestimmten Bedingung in der **Zukunft** eintreten könnte, aber eher **unwahrscheinlich** ist. Dann steht im „if"-Satz das **simple past** und im **Hauptsatz** das **conditional I**.

If it rained,	I **would** take my umbrella.
Wenn es regnete/regnen würde,	würde ich meinen Regenschirm nehmen.

3. Typ 3

Wir verwenden Typ 3, wenn wir über eine Bedingung in der **Vergangenheit** sprechen, die **nicht mehr erfüllbar** ist. Dann steht im „if"-Satz das **past perfect** und im **Hauptsatz** das **conditional II**.

If it **had rained**,	I **would have taken** my umbrella.
Wenn es geregnet hätte,	hätte ich meinen Regenschirm genommen.

Infinitive – Der Infinitiv

1. Der Infinitiv

Der Infinitiv mit „to" steht nach

a) bestimmten Verben: She **managed to get** a job.

can afford	sich leisten können	to manage	zustande bringen
to agree	zustimmen	to offer	anbieten
to arrange	vereinbaren	to plan	planen
to attempt	versuchen	to promise	versprechen
to choose	wählen	to refuse	verweigern
to decide	entscheiden	to remember	daran denken
to expect	erwarten	to seem	scheinen
to fail	versagen	to try	versuchen
to forget	vergessen	to want	wollen
to hope	hoffen	would like/love	gerne mögen
to learn	lernen		

b) Substantiven: It's a good **idea to visit** London.

c) Adjektiven: It's **easy to find** the way to the post office.

d) Fragewörtern: I don't know **what to do**.

what	where	which	how	who	when	why

2. Objekt + Infinitiv

Im Deutschen wird diese Objekt + Infinitiv-Konstruktion mit einem „dass"-Satz wiedergegeben:

Mary wants **him to come**.   Mary will, **dass** er kommt.
        ↓   ↓
    Objekt   Infinitiv

Diese Objekt + Infinitiv-Konstruktion steht nach

a) folgenden Verben: I persuaded her to come.

to advise	raten	to invite	einladen
to allow	erlauben	to persuade	überreden, -zeugen
to ask	bitten	to remind	daran erinnern
to cause	verursachen	to teach	lehren
to enable	befähigen	to tell	befehlen
to encourage	ermutigen	to want	wollen
to expect	erwarten	to warn	warnen
to force	zwingen	would like/love	gerne mögen
to get	veranlassen	would prefer	vorziehen
to help	helfen		

b) Verb + Präposition: I'm still waiting for him to answer my letter.

to arrange for	vereinbaren, abmachen	to rely on	sich verlassen auf
to count on	rechnen mit	to wait for	warten auf

c) Adjektiv + Präposition: It was kind of her to wait.
It's important for you to learn.

clever of	klug	nice of	nett
dangerous for	gefährlich	normal for	normal
easy/difficult for	leicht/schwierig	possible for	möglich
good of	liebenswürdig	silly of	dumm
important for	wichtig	tactful of	taktvoll
kind of	freundlich	useful for	nützlich
necessary for	notwendig	usual/unusual for	gewöhnlich/ungewöhnlich

d) Substantiv + Präposition: It's a good opportunity for me to see her.

idea for	Idee	chance for/opportunity for	Gelegenheit
mistake for	Fehler	time for	Zeit

e) einem Adjektiv, das durch „too" oder „enough" näher bestimmt wird:

The weather is **too bad for the plane to take off**.
Is the letter **big enough for you to see**?

G 15

Participle Construction – Partizipialkonstruktion

Es gibt zwei Arten von Partizipien:
- **Present Participle** (Mittelwort der Gegenwart/Partizip Präsens)
- **Past Participle** (Mittelwort der Vergangenheit/Partizip Perfekt)

1. Present Participle = Mittelwort der Gegenwart

Bildung			
-ing an die Grundform des Verbs	talk	–	talk**ing**
stummes -e fällt weg	write	–	writ**ing**
Mitlaut nach kurzem, betontem	cut	–	cu**tt**ing,
Vokal wird verdoppelt	stop	–	sto**pp**ing,
	travel	–	trave**ll**ing,
	occur	–	occu**rr**ing

2. Past Participle = Mittelwort der Vergangenheit

a) regelmäßige Verben

Bildung			
-ed an die Grundform des Verbs	talk	–	talk**ed**
y → i	carry	–	carr**ied**
	Ausnahme: pla**yed**
stummes -e fällt weg	live	–	liv**ed**
Mitlaut am Wortende wird	stop	–	sto**pped**,
verdoppelt	travel	–	trave**lled**,
	prefer	–	prefe**rred**

b) unregelmäßige Verben
(musst du auswendig lernen)

Bildung	
die dritte Form	write – wrote – **written**

Das Partizip hat die Aufgabe,
- einen Nebensatz zu verkürzen oder
- Hauptsätze mit demselben Subjekt miteinander zu verbinden.

3. Verkürzung von Nebensätzen durch ein Partizip

As he wanted to win he practised a lot.
Wanting to win he practised a lot.

Gehe dabei in der angegebenen Reihenfolge vor!

a) **Bestimme** als Erstes Hauptsatz (HS) und Nebensatz (NS), denn du darfst nur den Nebensatz verkürzen! **Der Hauptsatz bleibt immer unverändert!**

Nebensätze erkennen wir an folgenden Elementen:

Konjunktion des Grundes	as, because, since
Konjunktion der Zeit	when, while, after, before
Relativpronomen	who (für Personen), which (für Dinge)

b) Als Nächstes prüfst du, um welche **Art von Nebensatz** es sich handelt; bei Partizipialverkürzungen kommen nur folgende Nebensätze infrage:

Nebensatz des Grundes:	die Bindewörter „as, because, since" fallen weg
Nebensatz der Zeit:	die Bindewörter „when, while, before" bleiben erhalten, „after" kann wegfallen
Relativsatz:	die Relativpronomen „who" bzw. „which" fallen weg

	NS		HS		HS		NS
As	he was	ill	he couldn't come.	I saw a man	**who**	cleaned his car.
–	**Being**	ill	he couldn't come.	I saw a man	·	cleaning his car.

c) Dann überlegst du dir, ob HS und NS dasselbe **Subjekt** haben.

- Haben HS und NS **dasselbe Subjekt**, so fällt das Subjekt im NS weg:

	S_1			S_2		
As	**Tony**	was	ill	**he**	couldn't come.	$S_1 = S_2$
–	–	Being	ill	**he**	couldn't come.	

- Haben HS und NS **verschiedene Subjekte,** so müssen beide genannt werden. In den meisten Fällen wird jedoch die Partizipialkonstruktion vermieden.

S_1 S_2
The holidays coming to an end, **the pupils** went back to school. $S_1 \neq S_2$

d) Schließlich musst du noch die **Zeit im NS** beachten.

Present Tense:	he arrives		Present Perfect:	he has arrived
Past Tense:	he arrived		Past Perfect:	he had arrived
	↓			↓ ↓
Present Participle:	arriving		**Perfect Participle:**	**having** arrived

When he	arrives	he takes off his coat.
	↓	
When –	arriv**ing**	he takes off his coat.

After he	had	arrived	he took off his coat.
	↓		
(After) –	hav**ing**	arrived	he took off his coat.

e) Ist der **NS verneint**, so musst du „not" vor das Partizip setzen. Die Umschreibung mit „do, does, did" fällt weg.

As he	**did**	**not**	practise	he failed in the examination.
– –	–	**Not**	practis**ing**	he failed in the examination.

4. Verbindung von Hauptsätzen durch ein Partizip

Dies ist nur möglich, wenn die Hauptsätze **dasselbe Subjekt** haben. Meistens sind sie durch „and" verbunden. Beachte folgende Punkte:

- Ein Hauptsatz, meistens der erste, bleibt unverändert erhalten.
- „and" als Verbindung der Hauptsätze fällt weg.
- Subjekt 2 fällt ebenfalls weg, da es mit Subjekt 1 übereinstimmt.
- Aus dem Verb des zu verkürzenden Hauptsatzes wird das Partizip.

S_1		S_2				
He sat in his chair	and	he	smok**ed**	a pipe.	$S_1 = S_2$
He sat in his chair	–	–	smok**ing**	a pipe.	

5. Auflösung einer Partizipialkonstruktion in einen Nebensatz

a) Als Erstes suchst du das Partizip im Satz und unterstreichst es. Dann überlegst du, um welche **Art von Nebensatz** es sich handeln kann.

- Handelt es sich um einen **NS der Zeit**, so musst du, falls kein Bindewort vorhanden ist, den Nebensatz mit einem passenden Bindewort einleiten, z. B. mit „when, while, after, before."

–	–	**Having**	come home we drank tea.
After we		had	come home we drank tea.

- **Nebensätze des Grundes** musst du mit „as, because, since" einleiten.

–		–	**Talking**	to her	he missed the bus.
As	**(because)**	he	talked	to her	he missed the bus.

- **Relativsätze** müssen mit den Relativpronomen „who" oder „which" beginnen. Du erkennst einen verkürzten Nebensatz

  an einem dem Partizip direkt vorausgehenden Substantiv:

I watched a **man**	–	taking	a photo of his mother.
I watched a **man**	**who**	took	a photo of his mother.

  wenn kein present participle, sondern nur ein past participle im Satz steht (Auflösung durch einen Passivsatz/Signalwort „by"):

He saw a **book**	–		**written by** his friend.
He saw a **book**	**which**	was	written **by** his friend.

b) Als Nächstes suchst du das **Subjekt** im HS und im NS. Ist im verkürzten NS **kein Subjekt** vorhanden, so übernimmst du das Subjekt des Hauptsatzes.

When	–	preparing	supper	I	always listen to the radio.
When	I	prepare	supper	I	always listen to the radio.

c) Schließlich überlegst du dir die **Zeit**, in der der Nebensatz stehen soll. Dabei orientierst du dich an der Zeit des Hauptsatzes.

When	visiting	the Tower they	**saw**	the Crown Jewels.
When they	**visited**	the Tower they	saw	the Crown Jewels.

| When | – | – | coming | to the party you | **will** | meet a lot of friends. |
| When you | **will** | | come | to the party you | will | meet a lot of friends. |

Wird der Nebensatz mit „after" eingeleitet, so solltest du immer past perfect verwenden. (Zeitenfolge NS: past perfect – HS: past tense)

d) Ist der verkürzte **Nebensatz verneint**, so musst du bei der Auflösung mit einer Form von „to do" umschreiben. Ausnahme: wenn ein Hilfszeitwort im Satz steht.

–	–	–	**Not**	having	much practice John failed the examination.
As he	**did**		**not**	have	much practice John failed the examination.
–	–		**Not**	being	good he failed the exam.
As he				**wasn't**	good he failed the exam.

6. Auflösung einer Satzreihe

Ein Partizip kann auch zwei oder mehrere **Hauptsätze** verbinden. Dabei werden immer gleichzeitige Handlungen beschrieben. Beachte deshalb folgende Punkte:

a) Verbinde die Hauptsätze durch „and" oder durch Kommas, falls es mehrere Hauptsätze sind.

b) Ergänze in den aufgelösten Hauptsätzen das Subjekt des ersten Hauptsatzes.

c) Löse das Partizip auf und setze das daraus entstehende Verb in dieselbe Zeit, in der das Verb des ersten Hauptsatzes steht.

He sat in his chair	–	–	**holding**	the newspaper in his hands.
He sat in his chair	**and**	**(he)**	**held**	the newspaper in his hands.
	a	**b**	**c**	

Passive Voice – Das Passiv

Eine Handlung kann im Aktiv oder im Passiv beschrieben werden. Während im Aktiv (Tatform) das Subjekt des Satzes handelt, wird im Passiv (Leideform) mit dem Subjekt etwas gemacht.

Bildung   eine Form von „to   **Aktiv:** Columbus discovered America.
be"+ past participle → **Passiv:** America was discovered by Columbus.

1. Umwandlung vom Aktiv ins Passiv

Beachte bei der Umwandlung vom Aktiv ins Passiv folgende Punkte:

a) Als Erstes bestimmst du **Subjekt und Objekt des Aktivsatzes.** Das Subjekt des Aktivsatzes wird zum Objekt des Passivsatzes, das Objekt des Aktivsatzes wird zum Subjekt des Passivsatzes.

b) Das Objekt im Passivsatz muss mit „by" (im Deutschen: „von") angeschlossen werden.

	S	**P**		**O**	
Aktiv:	They	kick		the ball.	
Passiv:	The ball	**is kicked**	**by**	them.	
	Der Ball	**wird**	**von**	ihnen	**geschossen.**

c) Als Nächstes bestimmst du die **Zeit** des **Aktivsatzes.** Diese verwandelst du dann in die entsprechende Zeit im Passiv.
Lerne für die Umwandlung folgende Tabelle:

	Aktiv:		**Passiv:**	
Simple Present:	I	paint the wall.	It is	painted.
Present Progressive:	I am	painting it.	It is being	painted.
Simple Past:	I	painted it.	It was	painted.
Past Progressive:	I was	painting it.	It was being	painted.
Present Perfect:	I have	painted it.	It has been	painted.
Past Perfect:	I had	painted it.	It had been	painted.
Future I:	I will	paint it.	It will be	painted.
Future II:	I will have	painted it.	It will have been	painted.
Conditional I:	I would	paint it.	It would be	painted.
Conditional II:	I would have	painted it.	It would have been	painted.

d) Sind im Aktivsatz **zwei Objekte** (Objekt im Dativ = O_3/Objekt im Akkusativ = O_4) vorhanden, so kannst du zwei verschiedene Passivsätze bilden, indem du jeweils ein Objekt zum Subjekt des Passivsatzes machst, während du das zweite Objekt unverändert stehen lässt. Beachte allerdings: O_3 muss im Passivsatz mit „**to**" angeschlossen werden.

		O_3	O_4		
Aktiv:	They offered	**him**	a job.		
Passiv:		↓			
1. Mögl.:		**He**	was offered	a job.	
2. Mögl.:				**A job**	was offered **to** him.

Englische Passivsätze werden im Deutschen oft durch einen Aktivsatz mit „man" wiedergegeben.

It **is said** that he earned a lot of money.	**Man** sagt, dass er viel Geld verdient habe.
Nothing **can be done** against it.	**Man** kann nichts dagegen machen.

2. Umwandlung vom Passiv ins Aktiv

a) **Unterstreiche** im Passivsatz das Subjekt und das Objekt, das mit „by" angeschlossen ist. Das Objekt wird im Aktivsatz zum Subjekt, und das Subjekt des Passivsatzes wird zum Objekt des Aktivsatzes.

b) Das „by" aus dem Passivsatz fällt im Aktivsatz weg.

	S				**O**
Passiv:	He	was	asked	by	the teacher.
Aktiv:	The teacher		asked	–	him.

c) Als Nächstes bestimmst du die **Zeit** des Passivsatzes und überträgst sie in den Aktivsatz. Siehe dazu die Tabelle auf S. G 21.

d) Nun überprüfst du, ob das neue Subjekt im Aktivsatz im **Singular** oder im **Plural** steht. Entsprechend musst du die Verbform angleichen.

Passiv:	They	**have**	been	asked	by	the teacher.
		↓				
Aktiv:	The teacher	**has**		asked		them.

e) Ist im Passivsatz **kein Handelnder mit „by"** angegeben, so musst du sinngemäß einen Handelnden ergänzen und zum Subjekt des Aktivsatzes machen. Du kannst dabei **„allgemeine" Subjekte** wie **„people, they, you, we"** verwenden oder ein Substantiv, das inhaltlich passt.

Passiv:	School uniforms	are worn			in Britain .
Aktiv:	Boys and girls	wear	school uniforms	in Britain.

Reciprocal Pronoun – Das Fürwort der Gegenseitigkeit

Das reziproke Pronomen „**each other** = **one another**" bleibt in allen Personen unverändert.

1. Reziproker Gebrauch

Wir verwenden „each other" für das deutsche „sich", wenn **mehrere verschiedene Personen** etwas tun. Im Deutschen kann für „sich" auch „**einander, gegenseitig**" eingesetzt werden. Um Fehler zu vermeiden, solltest du immer die **Einsetzprobe** machen!

She smiles at him. ⎫
⎬ They smile at **each other**.
He smiles at her. ⎭

2. Unterschiede zum Deutschen

Nach bestimmten Verben **entfällt** „each other", auch wenn im Deutschen „sich" steht. Lerne diese Verben!

to meet	sich treffen	to fall in love	sich verlieben
to kiss	sich küssen	to become engaged	sich verloben
to quarrel	sich streiten	to get married	sich (ver)heiraten
to part	sich trennen	to get a divorce	sich scheiden lassen

Unsicherheiten entstehen oft, wenn man sich zwischen „oneself" und „each other" entscheiden soll, da beide Ausdrücke im Deutschen mit „sich" wiedergegeben werden. Merke dir deshalb den wesentlichsten **Unterschied** zwischen „reflexive" und „reciprocal pronoun":

Reflexive Pronoun	bezieht sich auf **ein und dieselbe Person**
Reciprocal Pronoun	**mehrere Personen** sind beteiligt; *Einsetzprobe:* einander, gegenseitig

Reflexive Pronoun – Das rückbezügliche Fürwort

Das Reflexivpronomen im Englischen ist eine Form von „**oneself**". Im Deutschen wird es mit „sich" übersetzt.

Singular:	myself
	yourself
	himself
	herself
	itself
Plural:	ourselves
	yourselves
	themselves

1. Reflexiver Gebrauch

Das Reflexivpronomen darf nur verwendet werden, wenn Subjekt und Objekt im Satz **ein und dieselbe Person** sind. Es heißt eben deswegen „rückbezügliches Fürwort", weil es sich auf das Subjekt im Satz zurückbezieht.

S		O		
Mr. Smith	sees	himself	in the mirror.	**S = O**

2. Unterschiede zum Deutschen

Schwierigkeiten bei der Anwendung ergeben sich dadurch, dass es einige englische Verben gibt, die **keine Form von** „**oneself**" nach sich ziehen, obwohl im Deutschen „sich" steht. Dazu gehören u. a.

to apologize	sich entschuldigen	to lie down	sich hinlegen
to argue	sich streiten	to meet	sich treffen
to change	sich (ver)ändern	to move	sich bewegen
to complain	sich beklagen	to open	sich öffnen
to differ from	sich unterscheiden	to refer to	sich beziehen auf
to feel	sich fühlen	to refuse	sich weigern
to happen	sich ereignen	to relax	sich entspannen
to hide	sich verstecken	to remember	sich erinnern,
to hurry (up)	sich beeilen		sich merken
to imagine	sich (etwas) vorstellen	to wonder	sich fragen
to join	sich anschließen	to worry	sich Sorgen machen

G 24

3. Unterschiedliche Bedeutungen

Es gibt Verben, die als Objekt **sowohl ein Substantiv als auch ein Reflexivpronomen** nach sich ziehen können. Dabei verändert sich allerdings die **Wortbedeutung!** Lerne diese Ausdrücke!

to enjoy	the party	die Party **genießen**
to enjoy	oneself	sich **amüsieren**
to help	a person	jemandem **helfen**
to help	oneself to the milk	sich mit Milch **bedienen**
to occupy	a town	eine Stadt **besetzen**
to occupy	oneself with a book	sich mit einem Buch **beschäftigen**
to control	the traffic	den Verkehr **kontrollieren**
to control	oneself	sich **beherrschen**

4. Verstärkender Gebrauch

Das **verstärkende Pronomen** hat dieselben Formen wie das Reflexivpronomen. Im Deutschen wird es mit „selbst, selber" wiedergegeben. Das verstärkende Pronomen **hebt** das vorausgehende Substantiv oder Pronomen **besonders hervor**.

He prepared this delicious meal **himself**.

Relative Clauses – Relativsätze

Man unterscheidet im Englischen zwei Arten von Relativsätzen: den nicht notwendigen oder nicht bestimmenden (non-defining) Relativsatz und den notwendigen oder bestimmenden (defining) Relativsatz.

1. Nicht bestimmende Relativsätze (Non-defining Relative Clauses)

Nicht bestimmende Relativsätze ergänzen den Hauptsatz durch eine **Zusatzinformation**, die für das Verständnis des Hauptsatzes **nicht** unbedingt **notwendig** ist. Sie müssen durch ein **Komma** vom Hauptsatz abgetrennt werden.

a) Das Relativpronomen bei Personen

Nominativ	Peter, **who** lives in London, visits his uncle.
Genitiv	Peter, **whose** parents are rather old, plays chess.
Präposition + Dativ	Peter, **to whom** Tom owes a lot of money, is angry.
Akkusativ	Peter, **whom** I met yesterday, joined a club.

b) Das Relativpronomen bei Dingen

Nominativ	This room, **which** is our classroom, is new.
Genitiv	This room, **whose** walls are yellow, is rather small.
Präposition + Dativ	This room, **in which** we are, is full of pupils.
Akkusativ	This room, **which** you see, must be tidied.

2. Bestimmende/notwendige Relativsätze (Defining Relative Clauses)

Bestimmende Relativsätze bestimmen den Inhalt des Hauptsatzes näher. Sie enthalten **wichtige Informationen** und sind deshalb notwendig für das Verständnis des Satzes. Sie dürfen nicht durch ein Komma abgetrennt werden.

a) Das Relativpronomen bei Personen

Nominativ	The girl	**who** opens the door **that**		is Mary Parker.
Genitiv	The girl	**whose** bike was stolen		is very sad.
Präposition +	The girl	**for whom**	we are waiting	is late.
Dativ		**whom**	we are waiting **for**	
		who	we are waiting **for**	
		that	we are waiting **for**	
		–	we are waiting **for**	
Akkusativ	The girl	**whom**	we met	is nice.
		who	we met	
		that	we met	
		–	we met	

b) Das Relativpronomen bei Dingen

Nominativ	The book	**which** is red **that**		is from the library.
Genitiv	The book	**whose** cover is red		is very old.
Präposition +	The book	**with which**	we work	is interesting.
Dativ		**which**	we work **with**	
		that	we work **with**	
		–	we work **with**	
Akkusativ	The book	**which**	I bought yesterday	was rather cheap.
		that	I bought	
		–	I bought	

Reported Speech – Indirekte Rede

1. Umwandlung von direkter in indirekte Rede

Eine beliebte Aufgabenstellung im Bereich der Grammatik ist die Umwandlung von der direkten in die indirekte Rede. Grundsätzlich ist bei der Umwandlung von direkter zu indirekter Rede Folgendes zu beachten:

a) Veränderung des Subjekts

Direkte Rede:	He says,	"I ↓	am	tired."
Indirekte Rede:	He says (that)	**he**	is	tired.

b) Veränderung des Possessivpronomens (besitzanzeigendes Fürwort)

Direkte Rede:	He says,	"I	close	**my** ↓	book."
Indirekte Rede:	He says (that)	he	closes	**his**	book.

c) Veränderung der Zeit des Verbs, wenn das „reporting verb" (Verb des Berichtens, z. B. „say") in einer Zeitform der Vergangenheit steht

	Direkte Rede		Indirekte Rede
Verb in	Simple Present	→	Simple Past
	Simple Past	→	Simple Past
	oder	→	Past Perfect
	Present Perfect	→	Past Perfect
	Past Perfect	→	Past Perfect
	Future I	→	Conditional I
	Future Perfect	→	Conditional Perfect

Direkte Rede:	He said,	"I	**shall (will)** ↓	leave."
Indirekte Rede:	He said	that he	**would**	leave.

Beachte: Steht das „reporting verb" in der Gegenwart, so bleibt die Zeit des Verbs erhalten.

Direkte Rede:	He says,	"I	**will (shall)**	leave."
			↓	
Indirekte Rede:	He says that	he	**will**	leave.

d) Veränderung von Adverbien

Direkte Rede:	→	**Indirekte Rede:**
now	→	then
here	→	there
this	→	that
yesterday	→	the day before
tomorrow	→	the next day
next week	→	the following week
ago	→	before
today	→	that day

e) Ein **Befehl** wird in der indirekten Rede als „object + infinitive" wiedergegeben. Das „reporting verb" „say" muss durch „tell" ersetzt werden.

Direkte Rede:	I	**said**	to him,		"Open	the window."
		↓				
Indirekte Rede:	I	**told**	– **him**	**to**	**open**	the window.

f) Ein **verneinter Befehl** erscheint als „object + negative infinitive". Die Umschreibung mit „do, does" fällt weg.

Direkte Rede:	I said	to him	"Do	not		open	the window."
Indirekte Rede:	I told	him	–	**not**	**to**	**open**	the window.

g) Bei der Umwandlung einer direkten in eine indirekte **Frage** musst du Folgendes beachten:

- Ist die Frage mit einem **Fragewort** („who, when, where, what, how ...") eingeleitet, so bleibt dieses erhalten. In der indirekten Frage ändert sich nur die Satzstellung.

Direkte Frage: Prädikat – Subjekt – Objekt (P – S – O)
Indirekte Frage: Subjekt – Prädikat – Objekt (S – P – O)
(Satzstellung wie im Aussagesatz)

		P	**S**	
Direkte Rede:	He asked me, "What	**is**	**your name?"**	
Indirekte Rede:	He asked me	what –	**my name**	**was.**
		S	**P**	

- Ist **kein Fragewort** vorhanden, so musst du die indirekte Frage mit „**if**" oder „**whether**" einleiten.

Direkte Rede:	He asked us,	–	"Are	you	hungry?"
Indirekte Rede:	He asked us	**whether**		we were	hungry.

- Die **Umschreibung** mit „do, does, did" entfällt bei der Umwandlung:

Direkte Rede:	He asked us,	"Why	do	you	leave	the party?"
Indirekte Rede:	He asked us	why	–	we	left	the party.

Ansonsten gelten die Regeln a–d

2. Umwandlung von indirekter in direkte Rede

a) Indirekter Aussagesatz

Hier musst du dieselben Regeln beachten wie bei der Verwandlung in die indirekte Rede, nur in umgekehrter Reihenfolge.
Wichtig ist, dass du als Erstes immer überprüfst, in welcher Zeit das „reporting verb" (Verb des Berichtens) steht. Steht es in der Gegenwart, musst du die Zeit des Verbs beibehalten, steht es in einer Vergangenheitsform, musst du die Zeit des Verbs ändern!

Indirekte Rede:	She said	she	would sell	her	car	the next day.
		↓	↓	↓		↓
Direkte Rede:	She said,	"I	will sell	my	car	tomorrow."
			(shall)			

b) Indirekter Fragesatz

Es gelten die Regeln a–d.

Beachte:
- Das Fragewort bleibt erhalten.
- Ist die indirekte Frage mit „if" oder „whether" eingeleitet, so fällt dieses bei der Rückverwandlung weg.
- Umschreibe mit einer Form von „to do" („do, does, did"), außer wenn ein Hilfszeitwort („is, are, was, were, can, could, must, may ...") im Satz steht.

Indirekte Frage:	She asks	whether	–	he	came	the day before.
Direkte Frage:	She asks,	–	"Did	you	come	yesterday?"

Subject and Object Questions –
Fragen nach dem Subjekt und dem Objekt

Bei den Subjekt- und Objektfragen ist es wichtig, dass du den Satz nach Subjekt (Satzgegenstand im 1. Fall = wer oder was?) bzw. Objekt (Satzaussage im 3. Fall = wem? oder im 4. Fall = wen oder was?) abfragst, damit du die folgenden Regeln anwenden kannst. Auch die Zeit, in der der Satz steht, musst du beibehalten.

1. Fragen nach dem Subjekt: „who" oder „what" = wer oder was?

a) nach Personen

Gegenwart	They visit the Tower. **Who** visit**s** the Tower?	Sie besuchen den Tower. **Wer** besucht den Tower? **1. Fall**: Frage nach dem Subjekt
1. Vergangenheit	They visit**ed** the Tower. **Who** visit**ed** the Tower?	

b) nach Dingen

Gegenwart	The pear-tree grows in our garden. **What** grow**s** in our garden?	Der Birnbaum wächst in unserem Garten. **Was** wächst in unserem Garten? **1. Fall:** Frage nach dem Subjekt
1. Vergangenheit	The pear-tree grew in our garden. **What** grew in our garden?	

Merke: Wenn nach dem Subjekt (Satzgegenstand = 1. Fall) des Satzes gefragt wird, darf **nicht** mit einer **Form von** „to do" umschrieben werden. Das Verb muss gebeugt werden, d. h. in der Gegenwart muss es mit dem -s der 3. Person, in der Vergangenheit mit der Vergangenheitsendung gekennzeichnet werden.

2. Fragen nach dem Objekt: „whom = who" oder „what" = wen oder was?

a) nach Personen

Gegenwart	I know Jenny. (her) Whom/Who do I know?	Ich kenne Jenny. (sie) Wen kenne ich? 4. Fall: Frage nach dem Akkusativobjekt
1. Vergangenheit	I knew Jenny. Whom/Who did I know?	

b) nach Dingen

Gegenwart	She buys a dress. What does she buy?	Sie kauft ein Kleid. Was kauft sie? 4. Fall: Frage nach dem Akkusativobjekt
1. Vergangenheit	She bought a dress. What did she buy?	

Merke: Bei Fragen nach dem Objekt musst du mit „do/does" in der Gegenwart und mit „did" in der 1. Vergangenheit umschreiben.

3. Fragen nach dem Objekt mit Präposition (Verhältniswort): „to whom = who ... to?", „to what = what ... to?"

Viele englische Verben ziehen ein Verhältniswort nach sich, das im Deutschen nicht auftritt, sondern durch den 3. Fall (Dativ) wiedergegeben wird.

a) nach Personen

Gegenwart	This book belongs to me. To whom does this book belong? Who does this book belong to?	Dieses Buch gehört mir. Wem gehört dieses Buch? 3. Fall: im Englischen mit Verhältniswort – Frage nach dem Objekt mit Präposition
1. Vergangenheit	This book belonged to me. To whom did this book belong? Who did this book belong to?	

b) nach Dingen

| Gegenwart | I listen **to** music.
To what do I listen?
What do I listen **to**? | Ich höre der Musik zu.
Wem höre ich zu?
3. Fall: im Englischen mit Verhältniswort – Frage nach dem Objekt mit Verhältniswort |
| **1. Vergangenheit** | I listen**ed** to music.
To what did I listen?
What did I listen **to**? | |

Merke: Bei der Frage nach dem Präpositionalobjekt (Objekt mit Verhältniswort) muss ebenfalls mit „**do/does**" bzw. „**did**" umschrieben werden. Die Präposition kann dabei entweder **vor** dem Fragewort („who, what") oder **am Ende** des Satzes stehen.

G 33

Tenses – Die Zeiten

Im Grammatikteil der Abschlussprüfungen werden oft Einsetzübungen verlangt, bei denen du das Verb in die richtige Zeit setzen musst. Wiederhole daher eigenständig die Bildung der englischen Zeiten und merke dir für ihre Anwendung folgende Grundregel:

So genannte Signalwörter zeigen dir oft an, welche Zeit du verwenden musst. Präge sie dir genau ein!

Für die Bildung bestimmter Zeiten brauchst du z. T. das „present participle" bzw. das „past participle". Zur Bildung und Schreibweise siehe S. G 16.

1. Simple Present/Present Tense

Bildung	entspricht der Grundform (dem Infinitiv) des Verbs	I usually **carry** the parcel to the post office.
	Beachte: Umschreibung mit „**do/does**" in **Frage** und **Verneinung**, wenn das Prädikat aus einem Vollverb besteht	He **doesn't** carry …/I **don't** carry … **Does** he carry …?/**Do** you carry …? **Doesn't** he carry …?/ **Don't** you carry …?
Verwendung	• **Gewohnheiten**, sich wiederholende Handlungen	I read the newspaper **every day.** *Signalwörter:* always, every day, every week, sometimes, usually, often, never
	• **allgemein gültige Aussagen, Wahrheiten**	The sun rises in the east.
	• **Gedanken, Gefühle**, ausgedrückt durch bestimmte Verben	I **think** it's wonderful. *weitere Verben:* to like, to want, to believe, to think, to mean, to know, to understand
	• **Zustände**, ausgedrückt durch bestimmte Verben	This book **belongs to** Tony. *weitere Verben:* to belong, to cost, to own, to need, to seem, to remember, to forget

2. Present Progressive/Present Continuous

Bildung

to be + present participle (am/is/are + -ing-Form)	He **is** just read**ing** a book. He **isn't** read**ing** a book. **Is** he read**ing** a book? **Isn't** he read**ing** a book?

Verwendung

• Handlungen, die **gerade** geschehen	He is **just** reading a book. *Signalwörter:* just, now, at this moment
• Handlungen, die **für die Zukunft** schon fest **geplant** sind	I am flying to New York **next weekend**. I have already got the tickets.

3. Simple Past/Past Tense

Bildung

• **regelmäßige** Verben: -ed an die Grundform des Verbs y → i stummes -e fällt weg Verdoppelung des **Konsonanten** am Wortende nach kurzem, betontem Vokal	I talk**ed** to him yesterday. marry → marri**ed** believe → believ**ed** drop → drop**ped**
• **unregelmäßige** Verben: vgl. die Liste in deinem Schulbuch (2. Verbform)	I **wrote** a letter.
Beachte: Umschreibung mit „**did**" in **Frage** und **Verneinung**	I **didn't** talk to him. **Did** you talk to him? **Didn't** you talk to him?

| Verwendung | • Handlungen, die (in der Vergangenheit) **bereits abgeschlossen** sind | They moved to London **in 1982.** |
| | • Ereignisse einer Erzählung, die **bereits vergangen** sind | They packed their things into suitcases, loaded the car und left for Ireland. *Signalwörter:* yesterday, last week, last year, in 1934, ago, this morning (wenn bereits Nachmittag ist), Fragen mit „when", „what time" |

4. Past Progressive/Past Continuous

| Bildung | was/were + present participle (ing-form) | He **was** (not) writ**ing** a letter. |

| Verwendung | • wenn der **Vorgang** der Handlung interessiert und nicht das Ergebnis | He was reading a book. |
| | • Handlung, die zu einem Zeitpunkt in der **Vergangenheit noch nicht abgeschlossen** war | What were you doing **at 3 o'clock yesterday** afternoon? |

5. Present Perfect

| Bildung | have/has + past participle | I **have** just finish**ed** my homework. |

| Verwendung | • wenn eine Handlung in der Vergangenheit begonnen hat, aber **in der Gegenwart noch andauert** bzw. noch nicht abgeschlossen ist | I haven't met him **since** last Monday. *Signalwörter:* for, how long, since etc. |
| | • wenn das **Ergebnis** einer kürzlich stattgefundenen Handlung **sichtbar** ist | I have **just** washed the cups. They are clean **now.** *Signalwort:* just |

- wenn etwas **schon einmal** oder (bis jetzt) **noch nie** geschehen ist

Have you **ever** been to England?

Signalwörter: already, always, before, ever, yet (immer am Schluss des Satzes), never, not ... yet, often, so far, up till now

- wenn ein Ereignis während eines **noch nicht abgeschlossenen Zeitraums** stattfindet

I haven't seen him **today**.

Signalwörter: this morning/week, today

Beachte den Gebrauch von „since" und „for"

Beide Wörter werden im Deutschen mit "seit" übersetzt!

since
gibt den **Beginn** einer Handlung, einen **Zeitpunkt** an.

I haven't seen him since 1971.
              since last Friday.
              since 3 o'clock.

for
bezeichnet die **Dauer** eines Zustands, den **Zeitraum**.

Beachte: Im Deutschen steht häufig die Gegenwart.

I have known him for 3 years.
              for a long time.
              for some months.

Ich kenne ihn seit 3 Jahren.

6. Present Perfect Progressive

Bildung

have/has + been + present participle (ing-Form)

I **have been** wait**ing** for 3 hours now.

Verwendung

Handlungen, die in der **Vergangenheit begonnen haben** und bis in die **Gegenwart andauern.**

Im Deutschen wird diese Zeit oft durch Präsens wiedergegeben.

Ich warte **schon** seit drei Stunden.

7. Past Perfect

Bildung	had + past participle	I arrived at the station after the train **had left.**

Verwendung	Wenn eine Handlung in der Vergangenheit (1) vor einer anderen Handlung in der Vergangenheit (2) abge-schlossen wurde. Past perfect tritt häufig in Verbindung mit past tense auf.	She had finished her letter (1) when the telephone rang. (2)

8. Past Perfect Progressive

Bildung	had been + present participle (ing-Form)	I had a bad cough because I **had been** walk**ing** in the rain for two hours until I decided to go in.

Verwendung	Handlungen, die bis zu einem Zeitpunkt in der Vergangenheit an-dauerten

9. Future

Es gibt, je nach Absicht, verschiedene Möglichkeiten, die Zukunft auszudrücken.

a) will-future

Bildung	will/shall + infinitive (Grundform des Verbs)	Tomorrow the weather **will be** sunny.

Verwendung	• Ereignisse in der Zukunft, **auf die wir keinen Einfluss** haben	It will be very hot.
	• Handlungen, zu denen wir uns **im Augenblick des Sprechens ent-schließen**	I think I'll (will/shall) watch TV this evening.

b) going-to-future

Bildung	to be going to + infinitive	He **is going to** take part in the football match.

Verwendung	• Handlungen, die man zu tun **beabsichtigt**	I am going to study at Exeter.
	• **Vorhersagen** über die Zukunft aufgrund **äußerer Anzeichen**	Look at these clouds. It's going to rain.

c) Present Progressive

Bildung	to be + present participle (ing-Form)	We **are** watch**ing** the Davis Cup next week. I have already got the tickets.

Verwendung	Handlungen, die für die Zukunft **geplant** sind	*Signalwörter:* tomorrow, next week, next month, soon, tonight, this evening, afterwards

d) Future Progressive

Bildung	will + be + present participle (ing-Form)	**I'll be** read**ing** all evening.

Verwendung	Handlungen, die **zu einem Zeitpunkt** in der Zukunft ablaufen werden	I think I will be travelling to New York next year.

G 39

e) Future Perfect (oder Future II)

Bildung	will have + past participle	He **will have** reached England tomorrow by 9 o'clock.
Verwendung	Handlungen, die **zu einem bestimmten Zeitpunkt** in der Zukunft **abgeschlossen,** vollendet sein werden	*Signalwörter:* by then, before tomorrow, by + bestimmte Zeitangabe

10. Conditional I

Bildung	would + infinitive	He **would take** part in the race.
Verwendung	wenn eine Handlung unter einer bestimmten Bedingung eintreten würde	

11. Conditional Perfect/Conditional II

Bildung	would + have + past participle	He **would have bought** the house.
Verwendung	wenn etwas unter einer bestimmten Bedingung geschehen wäre	

Text Sheet

What Comes Next? An Important Decision Ahead

While you are reading this, thousands of teenagers all over Europe, like you, are sitting their final exams and are about to leave school. All of you are now looking for suitable jobs and are perhaps worried about making the wrong career decisions because of the enormous number of career opportunities to choose from.

5 The obvious place to begin your search for job vacancies is the job pages in the press. However, there's an even better way to find out all that is on offer: the Internet. For people living in Kent in Southern England, for example, there is *Jobline 500*. This is a database of all the latest job vacancies in this region of the country and it is updated daily. So, if you don't have the equipment to go on-line yourself, go to a place that has got it – like
10 your local job centre.

As many employers are not too happy about giving a post to someone who has not had any job before, you should try to get some work experience. Work experience of any kind looks good on your CV. It shows personnel managers that you have initiative and the willingness to invest time and energy in a job.

15 Something that is really worth considering is an apprenticeship, of which there are basically two kinds. The first kind of apprenticeship lasts for about three years and prepares people to become the technicians, clerks or even managers of the future. The training programme usually covers both technical and personal skills. The apprentices learn what they need to know in order to carry out specific tasks at their workplace. But they are also
20 trained in skills such as communication, problem solving and team-work. Apprentices of this kind are trained full-time in companies and – as members of the workforce – they can earn quite good money.

Then there is a different kind of training for a job which takes up to two years to complete. Here the young people – called "trainees" – study for their job qualifications mainly
25 in colleges and spend only short periods of time in a company in order to get some work experience.

Whatever you choose to do, the golden rule is to think carefully, take advice and not rush into something you will regret later. A little bit of time spent beforehand talking to career advisors, friends, relatives – even your parents! – is a very good investment. However,
30 keep in mind that only you can know which job is really the one for you.

(Adapted from: THE TIMES, August 1999)

Work Sheet

Part A: Understanding the text

1   Use the information in the text to choose the correct sentence. Mark the correct sentence with a cross.

1.1   Many teenagers are worried that they will
a) get a job which is not the right one for them.
b) get a job with a low salary.
c) be unemployed.

1.2 *Jobline 500* gives you information on
   a) jobs in the computer industry.
   b) positions in companies which are still open.
   c) dates when you can apply for a job.

1.3 The author thinks that an apprenticeship is
   a) the basis for any kind of job.
   b) the only way to get into a management position later.
   c) a good thing for school-leavers to think about.

1.4 Before you make a career decision you should invest some time and think carefully because
   a) you can be disappointed with a job, if you make your decision too quickly.
   b) it is easier than using the help of a career advisor.
   c) this helps you to find a job more quickly.   (4)

**2   Answer the following questions in complete sentences, using your own words as
   far as possible. (If you copy the text word for word you will lose points.)**

2.1 What does the author tell you to do to find out which jobs are on offer? (2
   items)   (4/4)

2.2 What, according to the author, do young people learn during a three-year
   apprenticeship in a company? (2 items)   (4/4)

2.3 What are the differences between the so-called "trainees" and the other kind of
   apprentices? (Choose 1 item)   (2/2)

3   Additional question (You will not find the answer in the text.)

   Imagine you were invited to an interview. What information would you give
   about yourself? Write at least 35 words.   (4/4)

Part B: Vocabulary

4   Give a synonym or a similar expression for the following words.

4.1 opportunities   (line 4)   (1)
   There are an enormous number of career …
4.2 region   (line 8)   (1)
   Kent is a popular … of England.
4.3 keep in mind   (line 30)   (1)
   There are many things to … when you look for a job.

5   Which words and definitions go together?
                     Fill in:
5.1 suitable (line 2)   ☐   a) a piece of work that must be done

                                  b) right or acceptable
5.2 task (19)   ☐   c) uncles, aunts, cousins etc.

                                  d) a piece of clothing
5.3 advice (27)   ☐   e) in advance

                                  f) something that happens to you
5.4 beforehand (28)   ☐   g) helpful tips to someone about what they
                                     should do

                                  h) all the people you know

2000-2

6   Explain the following words or expressions in a complete sentence.

6.1   teenagers (line 1)   (1/2)

6.2   employers (line 11)   (1/2)

6.3   CV (= curriculum vitae) (line 13)   (1/2)

Part C: Grammar in context

7   Word forms: Fill in the correct form (adjective, adverb, noun, verb, participle) of the words in brackets.

Nowadays some firms receive lots of applications for each position they ... (advertisement) and it's difficult for them to make a ... (choose). Before they can find the ... (succeed) candidate who will be suitable for their firm, they look through CVs, letters and references ... (care). After a lot of discussion they send out ... (invite) for interviews to a number of ... (apply). Then, after the interviews, they ... (final) make their decision.   (7)

8   Verb forms: Complete the text, using the correct form (tenses, infinitive/gerund, active/passive, participles, if-clauses) of the verbs in brackets. Add a preposition where necessary.

Tom Bauer (T. B.) is applying for a job at *Technological Solutions*. This is part of his interview with Lea Solomon (L. S.), the personnel manageress.

L. S.:   Good morning, Mr Bauer. May I begin by ... (ask) why you decided to apply for a post at *Technological Solutions*.   (1)

T. B.:   Well, I ... (read) your brochure ... (promote) your products and you say that you sell for markets in England, Spain and France. As I am very interested ... (learn) languages I thought the post would be just the job for me.   (3)

L. S.:   Well, I must say you are more well-informed than some of the candidates that we ... (interview) since yesterday. But actually, we ... (not speak) much French or Spanish with our customers. Our customers in Europe normally speak English with us. Anyway, from your last school report I ... (see) that English is one of your strong subjects.   (3)

T. B.:   I can write it better than I can speak it but I'm sure that if I ... (have) the opportunity to speak to customers regularly in English I would soon become quite fluent.   (1)

L. S.:   I'm sure you would. And, of course, English courses ... (hold) here in the firm for our colleagues and we expect them ... (attend) these courses.   (2)

Part D: Text production

9   Look at the following jobs:

Secretary, office clerk, lorry driver, bank clerk, medical or dental assistant, tax advisor, taxi driver, hotel receptionist, waiter/waitress, househusband/housewife, travel agent, insurance clerk, shop assistant, nurse, policeman/policewoman, computer operator, hairstylist

Which one would you like to have and which one would you never want to do? In each case, say why! Write 80 to 100 words.

Tip: You can talk about the skills and/or qualifications you need for the jobs, about what's good or bad about them etc. (27)

Part E: Translation

10 **Translate the following letter into German:**

Dear Ms Kronenberg

Order for running shoes

Please find enclosed our order no. 455.

When we studied the catalogue and export price list which you sent us on 12 February, we were pleased to note that your CIF Dover prices include an initial order discount of 5 % for new customers and are also inclusive of packing. We are sure that this will make your products very competitive on the British market.

On receipt of your invoice, the total amount will be remitted to your account in Germany. We would request you to send us the goods within two weeks at the latest.

Please confirm the receipt of this order by fax or telephone and inform us when the goods have been dispatched.

We thank you in advance for your prompt attention to this matter.

Yours sincerely

Mike Tyson
Purchasing Manager (27)

Total: 120

Lösungen

Teil A: Textverständnis

1 **Benutze die Information(en) im Text, um den richtigen Satz auszuwählen. Kennzeichne den richtigen Satz mit einem Kreuz.**

1.1 Viele Teenager sind besorgt, dass sie
a) einen Beruf/Arbeitsplatz bekommen werden, der nicht der richtige für sie ist. (line 3)

1.2 *Jobline 500* gibt einem/dir Informationen über
b) Stellen in Firmen, die noch frei (nicht besetzt) sind. (line 7/8)

1.3 Der Autor glaubt, dass eine Lehre/Ausbildung
c) eine gute Sache ist, über die Schulabgänger nachdenken sollten. (line 15)

1.4 Bevor man eine Entscheidung über den (zukünftigen) Beruf trifft, sollte man etwas Zeit investieren und gründlich überlegen, weil
a) man von einem Beruf enttäuscht sein kann, wenn man sich zu schnell entscheidet. (line 27/28)

2 **Beantworte die folgenden Fragen in vollständigen Sätzen, indem du soweit wie möglich deine eigenen Worte/Formulierungen verwendest. (Wenn du wörtlich vom Text abschreibst, wirst du Punkte verlieren.)**
Du solltest vor der Beantwortung der Fragen aufmerksam die Seite 1 der Lernhilfen durcharbeiten. Bei der Frage 2.3 muss man die zwei Arten von Ausbildungen miteinander vergleichen. Zu den einzelnen Fragen werden zum Teil mehrere Antwortmöglichkeiten bzw. -formulierungen angeboten.

2.1 – You should read the job advertisements/vacancies/pages in the papers.
– You should search in the Internet (to find vacant positions). / You should go on-line.
– You should go to your local job centre where you can use (= can get into) the Internet to find job vacancies.
– If you lived in Kent, you should use the *Jobline 500* database to find possible jobs. (lines 5–10)

2.2 – They learn how to do practical jobs at their workplace./They learn what they have to know for being able to do certain jobs at their workplace. (lines 18/19)
– They also learn how to talk to, get on with and work with other people, and also how to solve problems./They are trained in communication and team-work. (lines 19/20)

Minimalanwort für beide „items" (führt aber mit Sicherheit zu einem Punktabzug):
– They are trained in technical and personal skills.

2.3 – The trainees only train for two years instead of three./The training for trainees takes two years, for apprentices it is three years. (lines 16–23)
– The trainees spend less time in firms/companies than the other apprentices (do)./The trainees spend most of their training time in colleges and only little time in a company. (lines 24–26)
– Trainees don't earn (any) money. (lines 21/22)

3 **Zusatzfrage (Du wirst die Antwort nicht im Text finden.)**
Stell dir vor, du wärst/wurdest zu einem Vorstellungsgespräch eingeladen. Welche Informationen würdest du über dich geben?
Hierzu gibt es sehr viele (und einfache) Möglichkeiten und du wirst schnell feststellen, dass man die geforderte Mindestwortzahl mühelos erreichen bzw. übertreffen kann. Studiere dazu das folgende Beispiel:

My name is Stefan Mustermann and I'm sixteen (years). I live in Musterstadt together with my parents and my two younger brothers. Now I am in my last year of commercial school which I will successfully finish in June .... My favourite subjects at school are data-processing, English and industrial management. My hobbies are .... I'm a member of our local fire brigade and of the youth team of our soccer club.

Teil B: Wortschatz

4 **Gib für die folgenden Wörter ein Synonym oder einen ähnlichen Ausdruck an:**
(Lösungen unterstrichen)

4.1 There are an enormous number of career chances/possibilities.

4.2 Kent is a popular area/district/territory of England.

4.3 There are many things to remember/think about when you look for a job.

5 **Welche Wörter und Definitionen gehören zusammen? Setze ein:**

5.1 suitable (line 2)   B) right or acceptable

5.2 task (line 19)   A) a piece of work that must be done

5.3	advice (line 27)	G)	helpful tips to someone about what they should do
5.4	beforehand (line 28)	E)	in advance
5.5	relatives (line 29)	C)	uncles, aunts, cousins etc.

6   Erkläre die folgenden Wörter oder Ausdrücke in einem vollständigen Satz. (Zum Teil sind mehrere Alternativen angeboten.)

6.1   Teenagers are young people/persons between the age of thirteen and nineteen.

6.2   An employer gives you a job in his/her company. / My employer is the person for whom I work (… who I work for.) / Employers are people who hire other people who work for them in their firm/office etc.

6.3   A CV is a paper or a kind of document in which you inform a possible employer about your qualifications, your education, your job training and your experience. / A CV is a paper which you enclose to an application and which contains important information about yourself, such as name, age, education, job training and work experience. / A CV shows/contains the qualifications and work experience of an applicant. / It's a short written report about one's education and past employment.

Teil C: Grammatik im Textzusammenhang

7   Wortarten: Setze die richtige Form (Adjektiv, Adverb, Nomen, Verb, Partizip) der Wörter in Klammern ein. (Lösungen unterstrichen)

– Nowadays some firms receive lots of applications for each position they <u>advertise</u>/<u>advertised</u>. *(Verb nach Subjekt „they"; vom Textzusammenhang her ist sowohl Simple Present als auch Simple Past möglich)*

– … it's difficult for them to make a <u>choice</u>. *(Nomen nach unbest. Artikel)*

– Before they can find the <u>successful</u> candidate … *(Adjektiv zwischen best. Artikel und Nomen)*

– … they look through CVs, letters and references <u>carefully</u>. *(Adverb, da Bezug auf das Verb „look through")*

– … they send out <u>invitations</u> … *(Nomen, da Objektposition/Plural notwendig, da kein best. oder unbest. Artikel für Singular vorhanden)*

– … to a number of <u>applicants</u>. *(Nomen nach „a number of" zwingend/gleichzeitig deswegen Plural)*

– … they <u>finally</u> make their decision. *(Temporaladverb wg. Textzusammenhang und Bezug aufs Verb)*

8   Verbformen: Vervollständige den Text, indem du die richtige Form (Zeiten, Infinitiv/Gerund, Aktiv/Passiv, Partizipien, If-Sätze) der Verben in Klammern benutzt. Füge eine Präposition hinzu, wo es notwendig ist. (Lösungen unterstrichen)

L.S.:   … May I begin by <u>asking</u> … *(Gerund nach allein stehender Präposition „by")*

T.B.:   Well, I <u>read</u>/<u>have read …</u> *(vom Sinn her Simple Past bzw. Present Perfect möglich = vollendete bzw. gerade vollendete Handlung)*
… your brochure <u>promoting</u>/<u>which promotes</u> your products … *(Relativkonstruktion notwendig, entweder mit Partizip als verkürzter Relativsatz oder mit Relativpronomen und Verb im Simple Present, wg. Allgemeingültigkeit der Aussage)*

L.S.:   … that we <u>have interviewed</u>/<u>have been interviewing</u> since yesterday. *(Present Perfect bzw. Present Perfect Progressive wg. „since" + Zeitangabe)*

But actually, we <u>don't speak</u> much French … *(Simple Present, da Aussage von allgemeiner Gültigkeit; Umschreibung mit „don't", da kein HV im Satz)*
… from your last school report I <u>see</u> that English is one of your strong subjects. *(Simple Present, da allgemein gültige Aussage, außerdem Simple Present im Nebensatz)*

T.B.: … if I <u>had</u> the opportunity … I would soon become quite fluent. *(Simple Past im If-Satz, da im HS Conditional 1 steht)*

L.S.: … English courses <u>are held</u> here in the firm *(Simple Present, da allgemeine Aussage und wg. des Simple Present im 2. HS des Satzgefüges/Passiv wg. Sinn)*
… we expect them <u>to attend</u> these courses. *(to-Infinitiv nach dem Verb „to expect" + Objekt „them")*

Teil D: Textproduktion

9 Zur Aufgabenstellung: Bei dieser Aufgabe soll man anhand von zwei Beispielen aus den aufgeführten „Jobs" einen Wunschberuf und einen ungeliebten Beruf erläutern. Die Konjunktion „and" in der Aufgabenstellung weist darauf hin, dass sowohl ein erwünschter als auch ein wenig begehrter Beruf darzustellen sind. Die angegebene Wortzahl gilt für beide zusammen. Wie du an den folgenden Beispielen sehen kannst, ist diese leicht zu erreichen.

Beispiele:
I would never want to become a hairstylist, and I have several reasons for my decision/attitude: First of all I hate to work indoors all the time and to work on Saturdays when most of my friends don't have to work. I also don't like to touch other people's hair when it is not clean. And above all the pay is not very good in this job.

Am Beispiel „lorry driver" möchte ich sowohl eine negative wie eine positive Einstellung zu diesem Beruf aufzeigen:

I would like to become a lorry driver because I have always been interested in these strong and heavy vehicles. In this job you are independent, your boss cannot control you all the time. What I like about it most of all is that you get to know other cities and countries. And the pay is good.

I would never want to be a lorry driver, because this job is hard and boring. You sit alone in your vehicle most of the week and have nobody to talk to. You must see to arrive at your destinations in time, which is often almost impossible, because the roads and highways are usually crowded and there are lots of accidents. Your family life is poor or doesn't exist at all as you have to work on Saturdays as well. So you also have little time for your friends.

Die ausgeführten Beispiele übertreffen die geforderte Wortzahl, können aber auch entsprechend gekürzt werden.

Teil E: Übersetzung

10 **Übersetze den folgenden Brief ins Deutsche:** (In Klammern findest du Alternativen, mögliche Ergänzungen und Erläuterungen.)

(Betreff:) Bestellung[1] von Laufschuhen (Auftrag über Laufschuhe)

Sehr geehrte Frau Kronenberg,
(Beachte die unterschiedliche Reihenfolge von Anrede und Betreff im Deutschen!)
finden Sie beigefügt[2] unseren Auftrag Nr. 455.

Als[3] wir den Katalog und die Exportpreisliste, die Sie uns am 12. Februar schickten, studierten, waren wir erfreut[4] festzustellen[5], dass Ihre Preise frei[6] (Fracht u. Versicherung) Bestimmungshafen Dover einen Erstauftrags[7]rabatt[8] (Rabatt für Erstaufträge) von 5 % für neue Kunden[9] einschließen[10] und auch[11] inklusive[12] Verpackung[13] sind (... für neue Kunden und auch die Verpackung einschließen). Wir sind sicher[14], dass dies Ihre Erzeugnisse[15] auf dem britischen Markt sehr konkurrenzfähig[16] machen wird. Bei[17] Erhalt[18] Ihrer Rechnung[19] wird die Gesamtsumme[20] auf Ihr Konto[21] in Deutschland überwiesen[22] (werden).
Wir möchten/würden Sie bitten[23], uns die Waren spätestens[24] innerhalb[25] von zwei Wochen zu schicken. Bitte bestätigen[26] Sie den Empfang dieses Auftrags per Fax oder Telefon und informieren Sie uns, wenn[27] die Artikel abgeschickt[28] worden sind.
Wir danken Ihnen im Voraus[29] für die sofortige[30] Erledigung[31] dieser Angelegenheit[32].
Mit freundlichen Grüßen

Mike Tyson
Einkaufsleiter[33]

Anmerkungen

1	order	Bestellung, Auftrag
2	enclosed	beigelegt, beigefügt
3	when	*hier:* als
4	to be pleased	erfreut/glücklich sein, sich freuen
5	to note	bemerken, feststellen, erfahren
6	CIF (= cost, insurance, freight)	frei Bestimmungshafen (der Lieferant zahlt bis dorthin die Seefracht und die Versicherung)
7	initial order	Erstauftrag
8	discount	Rabatt
9	customers	Kunden
10	to include	einschließen, enthalten, einbeziehen
11	also	auch, ebenfalls, ebenso
12	to be inclusive of	einschließen, inklusive/einschließlich ... sein
13	packing	Verpackung
14	to be sure	sicher sein, glauben
15	products	Produkte, Erzeugnisse, Artikel
16	competitive	konkurrenzfähig, wettbewerbsfähig
17	on	*hier:* bei
18	receipt	Erhalt, Empfang
19	invoice	Rechnung
20	total amount	Gesamtsumme
21	account	(Bank)Konto
22	to remit	überweisen
23	to request	bitten, ersuchen
24	at the latest	spätestens
25	within	innerhalb
26	to confirm	bestätigen
27	when	*hier:* wenn (u. U. auch „wann")
28	to dispatch	abschicken, wegschicken
29	in advance	im Voraus
30	prompt	prompt, sofortig
31	attention to	Aufmerksamkeit, Hinwendung, Befassen mit; *hier:* Erledigung
32	matter	Angelegenheit
33	purchasing manager	Einkaufsleiter, Einkaufsdirektor

Text Sheet

The American Love Affair with Guns

It happened in West Paducah, Kentucky, in Jonesboro, Arkansas, in Springfield, Oregon, and in Littleton, Colorado: children and young people armed with guns fired at their schoolmates, injuring or even killing some of them.

5 After every shooting, we have had the usual debate on guns and gun control. There are those who believe that the only way to stop the killing is to have stricter, more effective controls on guns. And there are those who feel they need to defend every American citizen's right to carry a gun.

Guns are part of the American way of life. Forty per cent of US households have a weapon of some kind. Tradition plays a major role in the American gun culture. The US
10 was once a nation of farmers, settling in the wilderness and living at long distances from each other. Therefore guns were useful hunting tools and as such absolutely essential for people to survive.

Today guns are still used for hunting, a perfectly harmless family sport, according to hunters. They say it gets the children out into the fresh air and in touch with nature. Some
15 even argue that hunting and experiencing the death of an animal can actually prevent young people from becoming violent.

Right after the Jonesboro massacre of 1999, in which two teens shot dead 15 of their schoolmates or teachers, there were still many who defended the gun culture. The parents and school, they say, should have looked after their kids properly and not allowed them to
20 wear black trench coats because it was so easy to hide the guns under them.

However, the arguments of the anti-gun lobby are powerful. One of the most impressive is that while gun lovers talk about the safety a gun can give you, 1.2 million kids have guns within easy reach at home. As Hillary Clinton pointed out last year: "More than 35 million households across America have guns and in one home out of three the guns are
25 loaded and unlocked." The First Lady's fear is understandable. Every day in America 13 young people aged 19 and under are killed by guns and in 1993 four per cent of the sixth- to twelfth-graders said they had taken guns to school the year before.

Although new laws are not likely to be a hundred per cent effective, there is still a slight hope in sight; the US Congress is discussing how to keep guns out of the hands of chil-
30 dren and youngsters. But we must not forget that the US gun lobby is still very powerful and really tough laws have no chance of being passed by Congress.

(Adapted from: READ ON, August 1999)

Work Sheet

Part A: Understanding the text

1 **Use the information in the text to say whether these sentences are true or false. Put a cross in the correct box.**

	true	false
1.1 The majority of US homes own weapons.	☐	☐
1.2 Many Americans think that parents should have done more to prevent the Jonesboro massacre.	☐	☐

1.3	About 20 US teens a day are shot dead.	☐ ☐	
1.4	We will probably see really strict US gun control laws in the future.	☐ ☐	(4)

2 **Answer the following questions in complete sentences, using your own words as far as possible. (If you copy the text word for word you will lose points.)**

2.1	What is the typical reaction of the American public to shootings in schools? (1 item)	(2/2)
2.2	Why has it been a tradition for Americans living in the country to own fire-arms? (1 reason)	(2/2)
2.3	What positive influence may hunting have on children? (2 items)	(4/4)
2.4	Where do many children get the guns from? (1 item)	(2/2)

3 **Additional question (You will not find the answer in the text.)**

Many parents buy their children violent videos and computer games. In the light of the recent killings in schools, what do you think of this? Write at least 35 words. (4/4)

Part B: Vocabulary

4 **Complete the sentences with the opposites of the words underlined. Do not simply add "not".**

4.1	Tradition plays a <u>major</u> (line 9) role in the American gun culture, but only a … one in Germany.	(1)
4.2	After the shooting, the pupils said that they were lucky to be still … and not to be among the <u>dead</u> (line 17) schoolmates.	(1)
4.3	It's rather <u>easy</u> (line 20) to obtain guns in the USA. In Europe it is relatively …	(1)

5 **Which words/phrases and definitions go together?**

Fill in:

5.1	to injure (line 3)	☐	a) the feeling of being proud of oneself
			b) to take care of someone
5.2	essential (11)	☐	c) a large amount of
			d) to harm someone very much
5.3	to look after (19)	☐	e) to search for something
			f) little, small
5.4	fear (25)	☐	g) to kill someone without wanting to
			h) very important or necessary
5.5	slight (28)	☐	i) not very interesting
			k) the feeling you have that something terrible may happen (5)

6 **Explain each of the following words or expressions in a complete sentence of your own.**

6.1	tool (line 11)	(1/2)
6.2	massacre (line 17)	(1/2)
6.3	twelfth-graders (line 27)	(1/2)

Part C: Grammar in context

7   Word forms: Fill in the correct form (adjective, adverb, noun, verb) of the words in brackets.

After the ... (terror) shooting in Jonesboro, Littleton and other places, the gun industry in the USA has come under great pressure. Several cities and individuals are taking weapons ... (manufacture) to court. They want them to pay for the cost of policing and ... (medicine) treatment, for example, which the shootings cause. However, it has ... (actual) become more difficult to ... (sale) guns in the USA. That's why some companies are now looking for other possibilities of making money. *Colt,* for example, which used to make millions of dollars with its revolvers now makes other products besides guns. It sells clothing, luggage and even ... (popularity) toys like Sammy the Bear with which it has been ... (enormous) successful.   (7)

8   Verb forms: Complete the text, using the correct form (tenses, participles, infinitive/gerund, if-clauses) of the verbs in brackets. Add a preposition where necessary.

Mary Collins (M. C.) from *Edutoys,* a firm producing educational toys, is talking to Mr Stuart (St.). He is the sales manager of a supermarket chain.

St.:   Good morning, Mrs Collins. John Stuart here. I ... (call) about a very important matter. Last month I ... (order) a number of toys in your *Edutoy* range, but unfortunately I ... (not hear) anything more from you since then. You told us that you would deliver the goods within two weeks, if we ... (place) our order in August.   (4)

M. C.:   I'm terribly sorry, but so many customers now want our *Edutoys* that we haven't succeeded ... (meet) the demand. However, we are giving priority to your order and our manager, Mr Dobbins, tells me that you ... (receive) your toys before the Christmas season begins.   (2)

St.:   Thank you very much. It's really amazing how well your *Edutoys* are selling. Not so many people nowadays seem ... (interest) in buying traditional toys for their children. Last Christmas, for example, we ... (not manage) to get rid of all the toy guns we had in stock.   (2)

M. C.:   Well, I suppose parents ... (shock) by what happened in Jonesboro and they don't want their kids ... (become) fascinated by weapons.   (2)

Part D: Text production

9   As an assistant to the purchasing manager of a German importer you ordered a number of articles from *The Scottish Home Goods Company* in Edinburgh. Your partner in business was a Mr McBurton. After checking the consignment you found that some articles were missing. Write a letter of complaint, using the following prompts:

– Anrede
– Sie bestätigen den Erhalt der Sendung vom 10. Mai bestehend aus: *short-bread, tea* und *marmalade.*
– Sie beschweren sich, dass Sie zwar den *Earl Grey* Tee erhalten haben, noch nicht jedoch den bestellten *Darjeeling.*
– Sie überweisen jetzt den Betrag für die gelieferten Artikel.
– Die Zahlung des Restbetrages erfolgt bei Lieferung der fehlenden Artikel.

– Sie bitten um die Zusendung des neuesten Katalogs und der aktuellen Preisliste so schnell wie möglich.
– Sie beabsichtigen, weitere regelmäßige Aufträge zu erteilen.
– Gruß (27)

Part E: Translation

10 Translate the following text into German:

Shopping by computer

Americans have always shown the world how to shop. They gave the world the supermarket. Shopping centers – those great places with all kinds of shops and entertainment – have also arrived in Europe from across the Atlantic.

Now, once again, Americans have started a new trend in buying – they sit down in front of the computer and buy by mouse click. The trend became particularly clear before Christmas when people went shopping on-line to avoid the crowds in shops.

According to a recent article, around 17 million people bought something from a Web site* last year. During the last few years the total amount of money spent on articles from the Web has more than doubled.

* You need not translate this expression.

(27)

Total: 120

Lösungen

Teil A: Textverständnis

1 Benutze die Information(en) im Text, um auszudrücken, ob diese Sätze richtig oder falsch sind. Setze ein Kreuz in das richtige Kästchen.

		true	false
1.1	Die Mehrzahl der US-amerikanischen Haushalte besitzt Waffen.	☐	☒
1.2	Viele Amerikaner glauben, dass die Eltern mehr hätten tun können, um das Massaker von Jonesboro zu verhindern.	☒	☐
1.3	Jeden Tag werden etwa 20 US-amerikanische Teenager erschossen.	☐	☒
1.4	Man wird wahrscheinlich in der Zukunft in den USA wirklich strenge Gesetze zur Beschränkung von Schusswaffen erleben/bekommen.	☐	☒

2 Beantworte die folgenden Fragen in vollständigen Sätzen, indem du soweit wie möglich deine eigenen Worte/Formulierungen verwendest. (Wenn du wörtlich vom Text abschreibst, wirst du Punkte verlieren.)

Du solltest vor der Beantwortung der Fragen aufmerksam die Seite 1 der Lernhilfen durchlesen. Bei der Zusatzfrage ist zu beachten, dass hier die Eltern ihren Kindern die Videos kaufen, nicht die Kinder selbst. Zu den einzelnen Fragen werden zum Teil mehrere Antwortmöglichkeiten bzw. -formulierungen angeboten.

2.1 The typical reaction is to discuss if it is a good idea to make it more difficult to buy (and sell) guns.

Or: The typical reaction is that the usual discussion on guns and gun control starts again.

Or: A discussion on more effective controls on guns arises/starts. (lines 4–6/7)

2.2 They own firearms because (in the past) they needed them for hunting/for getting their food.

Or: The early settlers were on their own out in the wilderness./… lived in the wilderness far from their next neighbours.

Or: The early settlers needed firearms to protect/defend themselves in the wilderness. (lines 9–12)

2.3 – They get out into the fresh air.
– They get in touch with nature. / They experience nature.
– Seeing/Watching the death of an animal may cause them to take death seriously./… may prevent them from being or becoming violent. (lines 14–16)

2.4 They get the guns from/at home. / They find the guns in their homes (loaded and unlocked). (lines 23–25)

3   Zusatzfrage (Du wirst die Antwort nicht im Text finden.)
Hierzu ist jede vernünftige Stellungnahme zu akzeptieren. Im Folgenden findest du ein Beispiel, das die geforderte Mindestwortzahl übersteigt, aber gekürzt werden kann:

I think the parents shouldn't do this because by watching these videos and playing these games children might get the idea that violence (and killing) is quite normal. They might want to copy one of the actors or characters in a computer game and act violently or try to kill somebody (just to experience the feeling).

Teil B: Wortschatz

4   Vervollständige die Sätze mit dem Gegenteil der unterstrichenen Wörter. Füge nicht einfach „not" hinzu. (Die Lösungen sind unterstrichen.)
Bei Mehrfachnennungen kommen zu Beginn jeweils die besten Lösungen.

4.1 …, but only a <u>minor</u>/<u>small(er)</u> /<u>little</u> one in Germany.

4.2 … they were lucky to be still <u>alive</u> …

4.3 … In Europe it is relatively <u>difficult</u>/<u>hard</u>/<u>tricky</u>/<u>complicated</u>.

5   Welche Wörter und Definitionen gehören zusammen? Setze ein:

5.1	to injure (line 3)	d) to harm someone very much
5.2	essential (line 11)	h) very important or necessary
5.3	to look after (line 19)	b) to take care of someone
5.4	fear (line 25)	k) the feeling you have that something terrible may happen
5.5	slight (line 28)	f) little, small

6   Erkläre jedes der folgenden Wörter oder jeden der Ausdrücke in einem vollständigen, selbst formulierten Satz. (Mehrere Alternativen)

6.1 – A tool is something you use to make or repair things.
– A tool is a useful instrument.
– A hammer or a screwdriver, for example, is a tool.

(Beachte bei der Definition, dass „tools" hier nicht wie im Text im Zusammenhang mit „hunting" steht!)

6.2   – A massacre is an event/a situation where very many people are killed.
      – A massacre is a violent action during which lots of people are killed.
      – A massacre is the merciless killing of a large number of species, usually of people, who have no chance to defend themselves.

6.3   Diese Definition war sehr verzwickt, da man sich hierzu an das amerikanische Schulsystem erinnern und wissen musste, dass „twelfth grade" die letzte Klasse der „Senior High School" ist. Es durfte nämlich weder „grade" noch „twelfth" verwendet werden. Dadurch war es <u>unmöglich</u>, zu schreiben: "They are students of the twelfth class."
      – Twelfth-graders are students/pupils who attend (= are in) their last class at school/at senior high.
      – They are students (who are) in the(ir) second year at senior high school.

Teil C: Grammatik im Textzusammenhang

7   **Wortarten: Setze die richtige Form (Adjektiv, Adverb, Nomen, Verb) der Wörter in Klammern ein.** (Lösungen unterstrichen)

– After the <u>terrible</u> shooting in Jonesboro, … *(Adjektiv vor einem Nomen)*
– Several cities and individuals are taking weapons <u>manufacturers</u> to court. *(Nomen als Teil eines zusammengesetzten Nomens/Verb vom Sinn her nicht möglich; Plural notwendig, da unbest. Artikel im Singular fehlt)*
– They want them to pay for the cost of policing and <u>medical</u> treatment, … *(Adjektiv vor Nomen)*
– However, it has <u>actually</u> *(Adv., da Bezug auf Verb)* become more difficult to <u>sell</u> guns in the USA. *(Verb nach dem Adjektiv „difficult" + to)*
– It sells clothing, luggage and even <u>popular</u> toys … *(Adjektiv vor Nomen)*
– … with which it has been <u>enormously</u> successful. *(Adverb zur näheren Bestimmung des folg. Adj.)*

8   **Verbformen: Vervollständige den Text, indem du die richtige Form (Zeiten, Partizipien, Infinitiv/Gerund, If-Sätze) der Verben in Klammern benutzt. Füge eine Präposition hinzu, wo es notwendig ist.** (Lösungen unterstrichen)

St.:   … I am <u>calling</u>/call about a very important matter. *(Aus der Einleitung „M.C. is talking to Mr St." zu diesem Dialog ergibt sich fast zwangsläufig Present Progressive. Ebenso möglich ist aber auch Simple Present.)*
        Last month I <u>ordered</u> a number of toys … *(Simple Past wg. des Signalworts „last month")*
        … I <u>haven't heard</u>/haven't been hearing from you since then. *(Present Perfect bzw. die entsprechende Progressive-Form wg. des Signalworts „since" + then)*
        … you would deliver the goods within two weeks if we <u>placed</u> our order … *(Simple Past im If-Satz, da im Hauptsatz Conditional 1)*

M.C.:   … we haven't succeeded <u>in meeting</u> the demand. *(Präp. „in" + Gerund nach dem Verb „to succeed")*
        … tells me that you <u>will receive</u>/are going to receive/will have received your toys … *(Futur 1 bzw. Futur 2 ergibt sich aus dem Sinn, evtl. auch wegen „before the Christmas season begins")*

St.:   Not so many people today seem <u>(to be) interested</u> in buying … *(Adj. „interested" leitet sich ab aus der nachfolg. Präp. „in" + Verb als Gerund; „to be" ist nicht notwendig, kann aber ergänzt werden)*
        Last Christmas, for example, we <u>didn't manage</u> *(evtl. auch "<u>couldn't manage</u>")* to get rid of … *(Simple Past wg. „last")*

M.C.: ... parents <u>were shocked</u> by what happened in Jonesboro ... *(Simple Past, da dieses Ereignis in der Vergangenheit liegt; vom Sinn her nicht falsch sind auch „are shocked" u. „have been shocked", vor allem, wenn man „don't want" im folg. Hauptsatz betrachtet)*
... they don't want their kids <u>to become</u> fascinated by weapons. *(to-Infinitiv nach dem Verb „want" + Objekt „their kids")*

Teil D: Textproduktion

9 Der Brief sollte nicht nur aus einer Aneinanderreihung der einzelnen Inhaltspunkte bestehen, sondern er sollte logische Satzverknüpfungen enthalten. Weiterhin ist auf entsprechende Höflichkeitsformen und die Anwendung üblicher „standard phrases" zu achten.

Der folgende Musterbrief ist ein Vorschlag, weitere Möglichkeiten sind durchaus denkbar. Zum Teil sind Alternativen in Klammern angegeben:

Dear Sirs(,) (Gentlemen/Dear Sir or Madam/Dear Mr McBurton,)

We confirm (acknowledge) receipt of your shipment (consignment) of 10 May consisting of (including) shortbread, tea and marmalade (We have received your shipment of ...).

However, we are sorry to have to inform you that we have received the Earl Grey tea but not yet the ordered Darjeeling (Unfortunately your consignment actually only contained the Earl Grey tea but not yet the Darjeeling ordered by us).

Therefore we now only remit the amount of money (the sum) for the delivered articles. Payment of the remainder (remaining sum/outstanding sum/rest) will be made (effected) after (on) delivery of the missing goods.

Please send us your latest catalogue and your current (present) price-list as soon (fast/quickly) as possible (We would appreciate/like you to send us ...).

In spite of the missing articles (the incomplete consignment) we intend (are willing/are prepared/want) to place further regular orders (with you).

Yours sincerely,

Teil E: Übersetzung

10 **Übersetze den folgenden Text ins Deutsche:**
(Zum Teil sind in Klammern Alternativen angeboten.)

Einkaufen per (am) Computer

Die Amerikaner haben der Welt schon immer gezeigt, wie man[1] einkauft. Sie gaben[2] der Welt den Supermarkt. Einkaufszentren – jene[3] großartigen[4] Orte[5] mit allen Arten[6] von Geschäften (Läden) und Unterhaltung[7] – sind auch[8] über den Atlantik[9] nach Europa gekommen.
Nun haben die Amerikaner wieder einmal[10] eine neue Richtung[11] beim Einkaufen begonnen (eingeschlagen) – sie setzen sich[12] vor[13] den Computer und kaufen per „Mouse-Click" (ein). Der Trend wurde[14] vor Weihnachten besonders[15] deutlich[16], als[17] die Leute[18] on-line (im Internet) einkaufen gingen, um den Massenandrang[19] in den Geschäften zu vermeiden[20].

Einem kürzlich veröffentlichten[21] Artikel zufolge[22] (Laut einem aktuellen Artikel …) kauften letztes Jahr etwa[23] 17 Millionen Menschen etwas von einer „Web site" (aus dem Internet/über das Internet). Während[24] der letzten paar[25] Jahre hat sich der Gesamtbetrag an Geld[26], der für Artikel aus dem Web (Internet) ausgegeben[27] wurde, mehr als[28] verdoppelt[29].

Anmerkungen

1	how to (shop)	wie man (einkauft)
2	gave	gaben, brachten, schenkten
3	those	jene
4	great	großartig, herrlich; *aber auch:* groß, riesig
5	places	Orte, Stätten; Plätze
6	kinds	Arten, Sorten
7	entertainment	Unterhaltung
8	also	auch, ebenso, ebenfalls
9	(from) across the Atlantic	über den A., von jenseits des A., von Übersee
10	once again	*hier:* wieder einmal
11	trend	Trend, Richtung, Mode, Entwicklung
12	to sit down	sich setzen (nicht: sitzen!)
13	in front of	vor
14	became	wurde
15	particularly	besonders
16	clear	deutlich, klar
17	when	als (nicht: wenn/wann!)
18	people	die Leute
19	crowds	Menschenmengen, Massen(andrang), Andrang, Gedränge, Gewühl
20	to avoid	vermeiden, entkommen, ausweichen, aus dem Weg gehen
21	(a) recent (article)	kürzlich erschienen/veröffentlicht, aktuell, neuere(r, s)
22	according to	laut, gemäß, zufolge
23	around (+ number)	etwa, ungefähr, circa, rund
24	during	während, in
25	few (years)	paar
26	total amount of (money)	Gesamtbetrag (an Geld), Gesamt(geld)summe
27	spent	ausgegeben (Hier muss der verkürzte Relativsatz ergänzt werden: ... which was spent on ...)
28	(more) than	als
29	to double	verdoppeln, verzweifachen

Text Sheet

People want personal banking

Computers and internet are having an increasing influence on our everyday lives. So it is
no wonder that banks now try to use the internet to handle their business with private
customers. Online banks, however, are having trouble attracting regular users.

Most people don't want to deal with machines all the time, for sometimes they want to
5 discuss their affairs personally. However, machines can only answer the questions that the
programmer thinks they may be asked. Machines cannot talk about personal problems,
customers' wedding plans or new babies. But most important of all: bank clerks who do
not know the answer to a customer's question know where the answer can be found and
they can get it.

10 In a recent survey 50 per cent of the men and 70 per cent of the women stated that they
were happy with the way the bank handled their needs and had no desire to bank online.
More than 50 per cent added that the reason for this was that they preferred to discuss
their affairs face to face. Seven in ten of the thousand people questioned also said they
would not use their mobile phones for banking, even if they had the necessary *WAP* tech-
15 nology.

Big stores also provide customers with their own credit cards to pay for their shopping
and offer them financial services – and they have to face the same problems as banks.
Harrods, for example, is worried about news that people calling up to discuss their *Harrods* store accounts may soon have to do so with someone not in London but in a call
20 centre in Delhi in India. *Harrods'* storecard provider *GE Capital* has decided to use
Indian call centres for part of its UK business because wages are cheaper there. This
means that shoppers will have to discuss all transactions made in their local store with
people who live thousands of miles away.

In their search to cut costs, financial service groups are forgetting the most basic truth
25 about customer relations: Money is an emotional matter and customers like to feel that
they have a personal relationship with the companies looking after their finances. Therefore, many customers are also against the strategy – which a number of banks follow – of
reducing the number of posts for local bank managers. They are worried they will have to
talk to strangers in a regional centre rather than branch staff whose names they know. The
30 closing-down of branches has made the situation even worse for the customers.

When customers start leaving their banks, this cost-cutting may in future turn out to be
very expensive indeed.

(Adapted from an article by Liz Dolan in THE SUNDAY TELEGRAPH, *August 13, 2000)*

Work Sheet

Part A: Understanding the text

1   **Use the information in the text to say whether these sentences are true or false. Put a cross in the correct box.**

                                                                                            true   false

1.1   Banks handle most of their business with private customers mainly using the internet.   ☐   ☐

1.2   At least half the bank customers are not in favour of online banking.   ☐   ☐

1.3   Mobile phones with the latest technology can be used for banking, too.   ☐   ☐

1.4   *Harrods* has opened a new store in Delhi.   ☐   ☐   (4)

2   **Answer the following questions in complete sentences using your own words as far as possible. (If you copy the text word for word you will lose points.)**

2.1   Why do customers prefer a human bank clerk to online banking? (2 items)   (4/4)

2.2   In which way do big stores act as a kind of bank? (1 item)   (2/2)

2.3   What different methods do banks use to reduce their costs? Give at least two.   (4/4)

3   **Additional question (You will not find the answer in the text.)**

    In what situation is it useful to have a mobile phone? Think of some advantages. Write **at least 35 words.**   (4/4)

Part B: Vocabulary

4   **Give a synonym or a similar expression for the following words.**

4.1   <u>trouble</u> (line 3)
    Online banks are having … in attracting regular users.   (1)

4.2   <u>discuss</u> (line 5)
    They want to … their affairs personally.   (1)

4.3   <u>questioned</u> (line 13)
    Seven in ten of the thousand people … said they would not use their mobile phones for banking.   (1)

5   **Which words and definitions go together?**

                 Fill in:

5.1   recent (line 10)   ☐   a) a feeling of wanting something very much

                                             b) letters and parcels

5.2   desire (line 11)   ☐   c) a few days later

                                             d) disliking something

5.3   wages (line 21)   ☐   e) a short time ago

                                             f) the pay you receive

5.4   post (line 28)   ☐   g) nearby

                                             h) a pub far away from your home

5.5   local (line 28)   ☐   i) goods you can buy in a shop

                                             k) a job   (5)

6   Explain each of the following words or expressions in a complete sentence of your own.

6.1   wedding (line 7)   (1/2)

6.2   shoppers (line 22)   (1/2)

6.3   staff (line 29)   (1/2)

Part C: Grammar in context

7   Word forms: Fill in the correct form (adjective, adverb, noun, verb, participle) of the words in brackets.

We are a ... (lead) firm in the field of e-commerce with a ... (strength) financial position. Our operations in France, Italy and Spain are growing very ... (rapid). We are looking for an ... (experience) software specialist to join the staff of the Madrid branch of our firm. The successful candidate must be able to speak Spanish ... (fluency). Please send your ... (apply) to: (6)

Mr James Driscoll
15 Jessam Avenue
Croydon CR8 4QT

8   Verb forms: Complete the text, using the correct forms (tenses, infinitive/gerund, active/passive, participles, if-clauses) of the verbs in brackets. Add a preposition where necessary.

Mr John Dwiar is phoning the firm *Websale*. This is part of the conversation he has with Ms Susan Finch, the personal assistant.

Susan Finch: Good morning, *Websale*. Can I help you?

John Dwiar: Good morning. John Dwiar here. I ... (send) you an order for three
             fax machines four weeks ago, but they ... (not arrive) yet.   (2)

Susan Finch: Oh, I'm very sorry ... (hear) that, Mr Dwiar. We usually suc-
             ceed ... (get) our goods out within a week after ... (receive) the
             order. When ... (you, send) us the letter with your order?   (5)

John Dwiar: Oh, I ... (not write) you a letter. The order ... (send) to you by e-
             mail.   (2)

Susan Finch: Oh, maybe that was the problem. Our mail server was down at the
             beginning of March.

John Dwiar: I see, well in that case, maybe it would be better if I ... (mail) you
             the order again – but by post this time! I ... (ask) my secretary to
             send it first thing tomorrow morning.   (2)

Susan Finch: That'll be fine. Bye for now.

John Dwiar: Bye.

Part D: Text production

9 Describe the situation in the picture and explain what it means to you. Write between 80 and 100 words in complete sentences.

Write your description on the extra paper provided by your school.   (27)

Part E: Translation

10 Translate the following letter into German:

Dear Ms Kohl,

Offer of Portuguese wines

We refer to your advertisement in the latest edition of *Wines of the World* and see that you are a leading importer of wines specializing in Portuguese products. We are a Portuguese wine grower and would like to take this opportunity to draw your attention to a special offer of *Vinho Malachino*. Due to very favourable weather conditions in 1999 we are able to provide you with a wine of outstanding quality at a very competitive price.

We have enclosed our current export price list which grants wholesalers a 30 % discount. In addition we are sending you samples by separate post. This offer is valid for 6 weeks only. We very much recommend you to order soon since stocks are limited.

Yours sincerely, Mato de Fachino

Write your translation on the extra paper provided by your school.   (27)

Total: 120

Lösungen

Teil A: Textverständnis

1 **Benutze die Information(en) im Text, um auszudrücken, ob diese Sätze richtig oder falsch sind. Setze ein Kreuz in das richtige Kästchen.**

		true	false
1.1	Banken erledigen den Großteil ihres Geschäfts mit Privatkunden, indem sie hauptsächlich das Internet benutzen.	☐	☒
1.2	Mindestens die Hälfte der Bankkunden ist nicht für Online-Banking.	☒	☐
1.3	Handys mit der neuesten Technologie können auch für Bankgeschäfte benutzt werden.	☒	☐
1.4	*Harrods* hat in Delhi ein neues Geschäft eröffnet.	☐	☒

2 **Beantworte die folgenden Fragen in vollständigen Sätzen, indem du soweit wie möglich deine eigenen Worte / Formulierungen verwendest. (Wenn Du wörtlich vom Text abschreibst, wirst Du Punkte verlieren.)**
Du solltest vor der Beantwortung der Fragen aufmerksam die Seite 1 der Lernhilfen durcharbeiten. Bei der Frage 2.3 muss man aufpassen, da es sich bei *Harrods* nicht um eine Bank handelt. Zu den einzelnen Fragen werden zum Teil mehrere Antwortmöglichkeiten bzw. -formulierungen angeboten. Achte immer auf die geforderte Anzahl von „items".

2.1 They prefer a human bank clerk because with a person they can discuss business as well as personal problems (enthält 2 „items" Zeile 6/7 und Z. 4)
or: Customers want to talk about their affairs face to face / personally and with a bank clerk they can also talk about personal things / problems. (enthält 2 „items" Zeile 6/7 und Z. 12/13)
or: Bank clerks who can't answer a customer's question at once / right away know where / how to find the answer (but machines don't). (1 „item": Z. 5/6 und Z. 7–9)

2.2 They supply customers with their own credit cards. = They issue credit cards for their customers. (Z. 16)
or: They offer their customers financial services. (Z. 17)
or: They keep accounts for their customers. (Beispiel *Harrods*, Z. 18/19)

2.3 They employ less staff. = They reduce staff / employees. = They reduce the number of bank jobs. (Z. 27/28)
or: They close (down) branches. = They reduce the number of branches. (Z. 29/30)
or: They use the internet for private customers. = They try to attract customers to online banking / internet banking. (Z. 2)

3 **Zusatzfrage (Du wirst die Antwort nicht im Text finden.)**
Es ist wichtig, hierbei die Fragestellung genau zu beachten. Es sind nämlich mindestes zwei Gesichtspunkte zu nennen (Think of some advantages.). Zudem sollten nur Situationen genannt bzw. beschrieben werden, in denen ein Handy nützlich ist, d. h. wenn kein anderes Telefon zur Verfügung steht.

It is useful to have a mobile phone when you are involved in an accident or you get to an accident on a highway / motorway. Then you can quickly call for help / call the police and an ambulance. A handy is also very helpful if you are on the road and your car breaks down or runs out of fuel. Then you can call a garage to get help. With a mobile phone you can easily contact your friends / family wherever you are and they can reach you as well. You can also send them mails. A mobile phone can also be very helpful if you travel abroad, because you can make phone calls without needing foreign currency.

Aus den genannten Bausteinen kannst du welche auswählen, so dass du geforderte Wortzahl erreichst.

Teil B: Wortschatz

4 Gib für die folgenden Wörter ein Synonym oder einen ähnlichen Ausdruck an.
(Lösungen unterstrichen)

4.1 Online banks are having <u>problems</u>/<u>difficulties</u> in attracting regular users.

4.2 They want to <u>talk about</u> their affairs personally.

4.3 Seven in ten of the thousand people (<u>who were</u>) <u>asked</u>/<u>interviewed</u> said they would not use …

5 Welche Wörter und Definitionen gehören zusammen? Setze ein.

5.1	recent (line 10)	e)	a short time ago
5.2	desire (line 11)	a)	a feeling of wanting something very much
5.3	wages (line 21)	f)	the pay you receive
5.4	post (line 28)	k)	a job
5.5	local (line 28)	g)	nearby

6 Erkläre die folgenden Wörter oder Ausdrücke jeweils in einem vollständigen Satz.
(Zum Teil sind mehrere Alternativen angeboten.)

6.1 Wedding is the ceremony, day, celebration or party when two people get married/marry.
or: The ceremony when two people get married is called wedding.

6.2 Shoppers are people/persons who buy something in a shop/store.
or: Shoppers are the customers of a shop/store.

6.3 The staff are the employees of a company/firm.
or: The staff are the people working/who work for a company/who are employed in a company.

Teil C: Grammatik im Textzusammenhang

7 Wortarten: Setze die richtige Form (Adjektiv, Adverb, Nomen, Verb, Partizip) der Wörter in Klammern ein.
(Lösungen unterstrichen)

We are a <u>leading</u> firm in the field of e-commerce … (Adjektiv in Partizipform zur näheren Bestimmung des nachfolgenden Nomens)

… with a <u>strong</u> financial position. (Adjektiv nach unbest. Artikel zur näheren Bestimmung eines zusammengesetzten Nomens)

Our operations in France, Italy and Spain are growing very <u>rapidly</u>. (Adverb, da Bezug auf das Verb „to grow")

We are looking for an <u>experienced</u> software specialist to join … (Adjektiv in Partizipform nach einem unbest. Artikel zur näheren Bestimmung eines zusammengesetzten Nomens)

The successful candidate must be able to speak Spanish <u>fluently</u>. (Adverb, da Bezug auf das Verb „to speak")

Please send your <u>application</u> to: (Nomen nach Possessivpronomen/vom Sinn her nur „application" möglich!)

8 Verbformen: Vervollständige den Text, indem du die richtige Form (Zeiten, Infinitiv/Gerund, Aktiv/Passiv, Partizipien, If-Sätze) der Verben in Klammern benutzt. Füge eine Präposition hinzu, wo es notwendig ist.

(Lösungen unterstrichen)

JD: … I <u>sent</u> you an order … (Simple Past wegen des Signalworts „ago") but they <u>haven't arrived</u> yet. (Present Perfect wegen des Signalworts „not … yet")

SF: Oh, I'm very sorry <u>to hear</u> that … (to-Infinitiv nach „to be sorry")
We usually succeed <u>in getting</u> our goods out … (Präp. „in" + Gerund nach dem Verb „to succeed") … within a week after <u>receiving/having received</u> the order. (Partizipialkonstruktion nach „after"/vom Sinn her wäre auch „receipt of" möglich, was allerdings eine Wortart darstellt.)
When <u>did you send</u> us …? (vom Textzusammenhang geht nur Simple Past/da es sich um eine Frage handelt und kein Hilfsverb vorhanden ist, muss mit „did" umschrieben werden.)

JD: Oh, I <u>didn't write</u> you a letter. (Simple Past, da Antwort auf vorherige Frage, die im Simple Past steht.)
The order <u>was sent</u> to you by e-mail. (Passiv wg. „by-agent" + Objekt/Simple Past wie im Satz vorher.)

JD: …, maybe it would be better if I <u>mailed</u> you the order … (Simple Past im If-Satz, da im HS Conditional I steht)
I <u>will ask/am going to ask</u> my secretary to send it first thing tomorrow morning. (Future I wg. des Signalworts „tomorrow")

Teil D: Textproduktion

9 Beschreibe die Situation auf dem Bild und erkläre, was es für dich bedeutet.

Schon durch diese Anweisung wird klar, dass es hier mehrere Möglichkeiten gibt, wie man Inhalt und „Message" auffassen kann. Man sollte sich aber das Bild genau betrachten, da der Inhalt vielleicht auf den ersten Blick nicht ganz klar wird.

Nachfolgend findest du zwei Lösungsmöglichkeiten zu diesem Aufgabenteil, wie sie in ähnlicher Weise von Schülern formuliert wurden:

1. In the picture you can see a scene in a kitchen. In the foreground there is a man who is washing the dishes. Next to the man you can still see a big pile of dirty plates, cups and pots. He looks angry because of the work he has to do. Behind him you can see a woman who carries a big and heavy waste-bin/garbage can full of junk. She looks angry, too. On the left there is a teenage girl who smiles at her parents. She carries a huge (cassette recorder) guitar amplifier in her right hand and wears headphones around her neck. On her right you can see a guitar. (Probably she is just saying something to her parents.)
The message of the picture is that teenagers only want to have fun/often give parties at home, but they don't want to do anything in the household.

2. The picture shows a scene in a family's kitchen. There are three people/persons. The man in the centre washes up/cleans the dishes. There is a lot of foam in the sink and close to it you can see lots of dirty dishes. On the left there is a teenage girl who carries (a ghettoblaster) a guitar amp in her right hand and has headphones round her

neck. Next to her a guitar is leaning against the wall. On the right you can see the girl's mother carrying a big dustbin. She sweats, so the rubbish must be very heavy. The woman and her husband both look very angry. Their daughter, however, just stands at the door and watches her parents work.
The message of the picture is that kids expect their parents to do everything for them. They never think of helping in the household, having fun is more important for them. (Message: I think the picture shows an everyday situation which you can find in lots of families: The parents aren't strong enough to educate their children and set limits. Consequently the adults have to do all the work and the children do what they want. So the kids never learn what it means to be part of a community in which everyone has to do his job.)

Teil E: Übersetzung

10   Übersetze den folgenden Brief ins Deutsche:
(In Klammern findest du Alternativen, mögliche Ergänzungen und Erläuterungen.)

(Betreff:) Angebot über portugiesische Weine

Sehr geehrte Frau Kohl, *(Beachte die unterschiedliche Reihenfolge von Anrede und Betreff im Deutschen!)*

wir beziehen[1] uns auf Ihre Anzeige[2] in der letzten[3] Ausgabe[4] von *"Wines of the World"* und entnehmen daraus[5], dass Sie ein führender Importeur von Weinen sind, der sich auf portugiesische Produkte spezialisiert (hat)[6]. Wir sind portugiesische Weinanbauer[7] und möchten diese Gelegenheit ergreifen[8], um Ihre Aufmerksamkeit auf ein Sonderangebot von *Vinho Malachino* zu lenken[9]. Wegen[10] sehr günstiger[11] Wetterbedingungen[12] im Jahr 1999 können wir Sie mit einem Wein von hervorragender[13] Qualität zu einem sehr günstigen[14] Preis beliefern[15].

Wir haben unsere derzeitige[16] Exportpreisliste (Preisliste für den Export) beigelegt[17], die Großhändlern[18] einen Rabatt[19] von 30 % gewährt[20]. Außerdem[21] senden wir Ihnen mit getrennter[22] Post (einige) Proben[23] (Muster). Dieses Angebot gilt[24] nur für sechs Wochen. Wir empfehlen[25] Ihnen sehr (= dringend), bald zu bestellen, da[26] die Vorräte[27] begrenzt[28] sind.

Mit freundlichen Grüßen

Mato de Fachino

Anmerkungen

[1]	to refer to	sich beziehen auf/Bezug nehmen auf
[2]	advertisement	Anzeige/Annonce/Inserat/Werbung
[3]	latest	letzte/neueste
[4]	edition	Ausgabe/Nummer
[5]	to see that	*hier:* daraus entnehmen/erfahren
[6]	specializing in	hier ist es wichtig, auf die Auflösung der Partizipialkonstruktion zu achten
[7]	grower	Anbauer/-bauer (Züchter)
[8]	to take the opportunity	die Gelegenheit ergreifen/nutzen
[9]	to draw one's attention to	jds. Aufmerksamkeit lenken auf/jdn. darauf aufmerksam machen
[10]	due to	wegen/aufgrund
[11]	favourable	günstig/vorteilhaft
[12]	conditions	Bedingungen/Voraussetzungen

[13]	outstanding	hervorragend/ausgezeichnet/erstklassig
[14]	competitive	günstig/konkurrenzfähig/vorteilhaft
[15]	to provide with	versorgen mit/beliefern mit
[16]	current	derzeitig/augenblicklich/neueste (r, n)/gültig
[17]	to enclose	beifügen/beilegen
[18]	wholesalers	Großhändler
[19]	discount	Rabatt
[20]	to grant	gewähren/geben/einräumen
[21]	in addition	außerdem/daneben
[22]	separate	getrennt/extra
[23]	samples	Muster/(Waren)Proben
[24]	to be valid	gültig sein
[25]	to recommend	empfehlen/raten
[26]	since	*hier:* da/weil
[27]	stocks	Vorräte/Lagerbestände
[28]	limited	begrenzt/beschränkt

Text Sheet

Green – Greener – Olympics 2000 – what Sydney can teach us

Although the Olympic Games 2000 in Sydney, Australia, have been over for nearly a year now, they will be unforgotten because they were the first "Green Games". These were the results of a close co-operation between the Australian Olympic Committee and Australia's Greenpeace Movement. This teamwork led to strict rules, aiming at reducing waste,
5 water and energy consumption considerably.

Some of the most spectacular items should be mentioned: Solar panels provided all the energy which was required for the heating of the Olympic Village. Rainwater was collected from roofs and squares and used for watering lawns and football fields. In addition, the Olympic Stadium had no PVC plastics in its 110,000 seats and saved electricity by
10 cutting air-conditioning down to a minimum. Air pollution was also minimised because spectators had to use public transport when travelling to the Olympic Park.

No wonder that Greenpeace was quite proud of these first "Green Olympics" and awarded them a bronze medal. Blair Palese, their Olympic spokeswoman, said: "What counts most are the Olympic environmental rules established for the first time ever. I hope that Sydney
15 has set standards for all future Olympic events."

It was not long, however, before critics made it clear that this opinion was not shared by all Australians.

Greenpeace leaders, they believed, had clearly forgotten that a large part of the Olympic Park had been used as a chemical factory for as long as a generation. Moreover, there
20 were reports that the factory had dumped toxic waste in their backyard a short time after they had gone out of business. "The Olympic competitors are sitting safely in their armchairs at home now," a person from Sydney commented angrily, "but we are here to stay – and we're sitting on a chemical time bomb."

Heavy criticism also came from the native Australians, who are great friends of the earth.
25 "It's us who have been living in harmony with Mother Earth for ages," says Brian Mazhuen, a member of a protest group. "For the first time since Whites arrived here, they have tried to treat Mother Earth in the way our ancestors did – and they would like to take all the praise for it. This is simply not fair."

What's more, many native Australians weren't happy with the part they played in the
30 Games. As Mr Mazhuen pointed out: "In the opening ceremony we were simply used to add an exotic touch to this world-wide TV show. We weren't allowed to paint ourselves with all our traditional colours and patterns. And the clothes we wore were the clothes of the white man. I looked like Goofy in a Disney theme park."

Work Sheet

Part A: Understanding the text

1 Use the information in the text to choose the correct sentence. Put a cross in the correct box.

1.1 The Olympics' soccer events were played on grass which was
   a) grey – as it never rains in Southern Australia in September. ☐
   b) watered by the local fire brigade in summer. ☐
   c) kept green by the use of rainwater. ☒

1.2 The Sydney Olympics will always be remembered because they
   a) didn't pollute the environment at all. ☐
   b) were given a prize by an environmental group. ☒
   c) were the first Olympics outside Europe and the Americas. ☐

1.3 Ticket holders were unable to reach the sport sites
   a) in private vehicles. ☒
   b) because of the long distance. ☐
   c) because there were too many cars on the motorways. ☐

1.4 In Sydney, people fear that a chemical firm perhaps
   a) will have to fire its workers when it goes out of business. ☐
   b) has competitors in its backyard. ☐
   c) has illegally thrown away dangerous materials. ☒

(4)

2 Answer the following questions in complete sentences, using your own words as far as possible. (If you copy the text word for word you will lose points.)

2.1 Why were the 2000 Olympics awarded a medal by Greenpeace? (1 item) (2/2)

2.2 How did the organisers of the Games 2000 manage to keep energy costs down? (2 items) (4/4)

2.3 Why are the native Australians unhappy about the Games? Give two reasons. (4/4)

3 Additional question (You will not find the answer in the text.)

What do you personally do to save energy and/or raw materials? Your answer must contain two or more ideas in complete sentences. Write **at least 35 words.** (4/4)

Part B: Vocabulary

4 Complete the sentences with the opposites of the underlined words.

4.1 reduce (line 4)
People must try to reduce waste and not … it. (1)

4.2 saving (line 9)
Saving and not … energy is important for the environment. (1)

4.3 future (line 15)
All future Olympic Games should be "green" – not like the Olympic Games of the … (1)

2001-11

5 **Which words and definitions go together?**
    Fill in:

5.1 considerably (5)   [k]   a) pleased or satisfied with something

                                    b) a shipment of goods

5.2 lawn (line 8)   [d]   c) sad and unhappy about something

                                    d) an area in a garden or park that is covered
                                       with short grass

5.3 public transport (11) [g]   e) rules you have to keep to

                                    f) someone who gives his opinion about the
                                       good and bad qualities of something

5.4 proud (line 12)   [a]   g) buses, trains, trams etc. which everyone can
                                       use

                                    h) the act of giving your opinion

5.5 critic (line 16)   [f]   i) just a little bit

                                    k) very much, a lot   (5)

6   **Explain each of the following words or expressions in a complete sentence of your own.**

6.1 co-operation (line 3) to agree with the other   (1/2)
6.2 factory (line 19) a firm which produce something   (1/2)
6.3 Olympic <u>competitors</u> (line 21)   (1/2)

Part C: Grammar in context
                                                              Participle

7   **Word forms: Fill in the correct form (adjective, adverb, noun, verb, participle) of the words in brackets.**

Dear Sirs,

We are very pleased to tell you that the BT51 footballs we received from you are extremely popular with a large number of our customers. In fact we are having some 1.. (difficult) in meeting the enormous demand. For this reason we 2.. (requirement) another 150 BT51 footballs. As the football season is now beginning, we hope that you will be 3. (ability) to send the order within a week. We would also be grateful for further 4. (inform) about other products in your BT51 range and the terms of 5. (pay) and delivery.

We hope that you will deal with this matter 6.. (prompt).   (6)

Yours faithfully,
Ian Boyle

8   **Verb forms: Complete the text, using the correct forms (tenses, infinitive/gerund, active/passive, participles, if-clauses) of the verbs in brackets. Add a preposition where necessary.**

Mr Lewis is interviewing Ms Rebecca Henry, the successful founder of a chain of shops: *The Sporting Life.*

Mr Lewis: I would like to thank you … (find) time to talk to me, Ms Henry. I
            know how busy you are.   (2)

Ms Henry: Oh, it's a pleasure. After all, it's all good publicity for our shops!

Mr Lewis:	Well, to start with: When ... (you/set) up your first shop?	(1)
Ms Henry:	About five years ago and since then, we ... (open) branches in four other major towns.	(1)
Mr Lewis:	How do you explain your great success?	
Ms Henry:	Well, many people know that they can greatly improve their health by ... (do) more sport in their spare time and, of course, many people nowadays have more spare time than they did in the past. We've managed ... (attract) many of these people with our wide range of sports articles.	(2)
Mr Lewis:	But there are many other shops ... (sell) sports articles.	(1)
Ms Henry:	That's true, but we also do something which other shops ... (not do).	(1)
Mr Lewis:	What's that?	
Ms Henry:	We run special courses for skiing, athletics and gymnastics. And those people who buy sports articles in our shops ... (give) a reduced price for these courses.	(1)
Mr Lewis:	There is one last question that I would like ... (you/answer).	(1)
Ms Henry:	Please go ahead ...	
Mr Lewis:	If I buy 8 rackets for myself, my wife and my six children, ... (you/give) me a discount?	(1)

Part D: Text production

9   **Sie sind Mitarbeiter/Mitarbeiterin der Sport & Mode GmbH, Kümmersbrucker Straße 30, 92224 Amberg, und haben die unten abgebildete Rechnung erhalten. Ihre Abteilungsleiterin hat handschriftlich zwei Anmerkungen angebracht:**

<table>
<tr><td colspan="4" align="center">Joshua Carter Ltd
Chapel-on-le-Frith
Buxton DE2 3RS</td></tr>
<tr><td colspan="4">Sport & Mode GmbH
Kuemmersbrucker Str. 30
D-92224 Amberg</td></tr>
<tr><td colspan="4" align="right">5. April 2001</td></tr>
<tr><td colspan="4">Invoice # 4678
Your order # 512, of 2 March 2001</td></tr>
</table>

Item #	Item	Qty	Unit Price €	Total €	
DC-S-XL	Dovedale Cardigans	40	22.50	900.00	
SL-S-S	Scardale Leggins	40	28.50	1 140.00	Summe falsch
KSJ-S-L	Kinder Scout Jumpers	30	25.50	765.00	20 % Rabatt fehlt
			Net Total	2 905.00	
			VAT	508.38	
			Total	3 413.38	

Ihre Aufgabe ist es, für Ihre Vorgesetzte eine unterschriftsreife Antwort nach folgenden Vorgaben zu erstellen:
- Anrede
- Beziehen Sie sich auf Ihre Bestellung # 512 vom 2. März dieses Jahres.
- Die Warensendung ist ohne Mängel angekommen, jedoch 15 Tage nach dem vereinbarten Liefertermin.
- Bei künftigen Geschäften ist es unbedingt notwendig, dass Lieferungen pünktlich erfolgen.
- Bei der Prüfung der Rechnung wurde ein Fehler bei der Summe festgestellt.
- Außerdem wurde anscheinend vergessen, den vereinbarten Rabatt abzuziehen.
- Bitten Sie die Firma Joshua Carter Ltd. um Überprüfung.
- freundlicher Schluss
- Gruß

Write your letter on the extra paper provided by your school. (27)

Part E: Translation

10 **Translate the following text into German:**

As computer skills become more and more important in business, firms are thinking up new ways to help their employees to get essential skills.

A famous US car firm based in Michigan recently announced that they would provide all their employees with computers, colour printers and unlimited access to the internet at home. They will have to pay just $5 a month for the package.

This plan, which will cost the company about $300 million over the next three years, was agreed on between the car firm and the unions last year. There will be no checks on how long the employees use the internet.

The carmaker believes that the programme will keep the company ahead of its competitors in e-business and information technology by helping employees to improve their ability to work with computers.

Write your translation on the extra paper provided by your school. (27)

Total: 120

Lösungen

Teil A: Textverständnis

1 Benutze die Information(en) im Text, um den richtigen Satz auszuwählen. Setze ein Kreuz in das richtige Kästchen.

1.1   Die olympischen Fußballspiele wurden auf Rasen ausgetragen, der
       c) durch die Verwendung von Regenwasser grün gehalten wurde. (Zeile 7/8)

1.2   An die Olympischen Spiele von Sydney wird man sich immer erinnern, weil ihnen
       b) von einer Umweltschutzgruppe ein Preis verliehen wurde. (Z. 12/13)

1.3   Karteninhaber konnten die Sportstätten nicht
       a) mit Privatfahrzeugen erreichen. (Z. 11)

1.4   In Sydney befürchten die Menschen, dass eine Chemiefirma vielleicht
       c) illegal gefährliche Materialien/Stoffe entsorgt hat. (Z. 19–23)

2 Beantworte die folgenden Fragen in vollständigen Sätzen, indem du soweit wie möglich deine eigenen Worte/Formulierungen verwendest. (Wenn du wörtlich vom Text abschreibst, wirst du Punkte verlieren.)
Du solltest vor der Beantwortung der Fragen aufmerksam die Seite 1 der Lernhilfen durchlesen. Zu den einzelnen Fragen werden zum Teil mehrere Antwortmöglichkeiten bzw. -formulierungen angeboten.

2.1   The 2000 Olympics were awarded a medal by Greenpeace because the organisers/the Olympic Committee set up special rules/established strict environmental rules. (Z. 12/13 und 4/5)
      or: The 2000 Olympics got a bronze medal from Greenpeace because the organisers found many (different) ways to protect the environment.

2.2   They managed to keep energy costs down/to reduce energy costs by using solar panels to supply energy (= which provided all the energy) for the heating of the Olympic Village/to heat the O.V.
      or: Besides/Moreover they used very little electricity/energy for air-conditioning/they cut down air-conditioning enormously/they ran air-conditioning at a very low level only. (Z. 6/7 und 9/10)

2.3   The native Australians/The Aborigines were unhappy about the Games for two reasons: Firstly/First of all they say that they have always treated nature/the environment/Mother Earth well/with respect, but the whites did so only for the first time during the Olympic Games and want to get all the praise/honour/appreciation for it.
      or: The Aborigines say it's unfair that the whites claim all the praise for treating the environment well although they only did so for the first time during the Games while the Aborigines have always lived in harmony with nature/Mother Earth.
      Secondly the Aborigines were forbidden/were not permitted to paint their bodies/themselves in their traditional ways/in their traditional colours and patterns.
      or: Secondly they were not allowed to wear their own/traditional clothes
      or: They were unhappy because they had to wear the clothes of the white man.

3   Zusatzfrage (Du wirst die Antwort nicht im Text finden.)
Hier ist zu beachten, dass mindestens zwei verschiedene Gedanken ausgeführt werden mussten. Man könnte sich auf das Einsparen von Energie oder Rohstoffen beschränken oder aber auf beide Aspekte eingehen.
Du kannst also aus den nachfolgenden Möglichkeiten nach Belieben mehrere auswählen, bis die geforderte Wortzahl erreicht ist. Der einleitende Satz zu Beginn jedes Blocks ist nicht unbedingt notwendig.

There are several things I do to save energy:
– I always have a shower instead of a bath, this saves energy as well as water. Apart from that I prefer cold showers in summer.
– I never put my TV set or video cassette recorder on stand-by when I don't use them.
– I switch off the lights in my room when I watch TV at night.
– I walk or cycle to school.
– I don't use my car/motor-bike for short distances.

There are also several ways to save raw materials:
– I collect and use rainwater for watering plants/the garden.
– When I go shopping I take a shopping basket or shopping bag to carry the products, so I don't need any plastic bags.
– I transport/carry the food for my break in a special container/in a lunch box, so I need no paper or foil to wrap it (up).
– I always take materials like papers/magazines, empty cans and bottles, plastic cups/containers etc. to the recycling department/station of our town.

Teil B: Wortschatz

4   Vervollständige die Sätze mit dem Gegenteil der unterstrichenen Wörter.
Die Lösungen sind unterstrichen. Bei Mehrfachnennungen steht am Anfang jeweils die beste Lösung.

4.1   People must try to reduce waste and not <u>increase/produce</u> it.

4.2   Saving and not <u>wasting/using too much</u> energy is important …

4.3   All future Olympic Games should be "green" – not like the Olympic Games of the <u>past</u>.

5   Welche Wörter und Definitionen gehören zusammen? Setze ein.

5.1   considerably (line 5)   k) very much, a lot

5.2   lawn (line 8)   d) an area in a garden or park that is covered with short
                                         grass

5.3   public transport (line 11)   g) buses, trains, trams etc. which everyone can use

5.4   proud (line 12)   a) pleased or satisfied with something

5.5   critic (line 16)   f) someone who gives his opinion about the good and bad
                                         qualities of something

6 **Erkläre jedes der folgenden Wörter oder jeden der Ausdrücke in einem vollständigen, selbstformulierten Satz.** (Mehrere Alternativen)

6.1 Co-operation means working together (on a common project).
or: Co-operation is the willingness to work together.
or: When you need someone's co-operation you need his support/help.

6.2 A factory is a large building or a group of buildings where goods are produced, especially in great quantities by machines.
or: A factory is a place where products are made (in great numbers) often by using
machines.

6.3 Olympic competitors are people/athletes who take part in (the) Olympic sport events.
or: A sportsman who is allowed/who is good enough to take part in the Olympic
Games is an Olympic competitor.

Teil C: Grammatik im Textzusammenhang

7 **Wortarten: Setze die richtige Form (Adjektiv, Adverb, Nomen, Verb, Partizip) der
Wörter in Klammern ein.** (Lösungen unterstrichen)

In fact we are having some difficulty/difficulties in meeting the enormous demand.
(Nomen, da vorher unbestimmtes Numerale „some"/auch ableitbar vom nachfolgenden
Gerund mit Präposition)
For this reason we require another 150 BT51 footballs. (Verb nach Subjekt; Simple
Present ergibt sich aus dem Kontext; denkbar wäre u. U. auch Future I)
… we hope that you will be able to send … (Adjektiv ergibt sich aus der Konstruktion/
dem Kontext)
We would also be grateful for further information about … (Nomen wg. des Kontexts
und der Objektposition)
… and the terms of payment and delivery. (Nomen wg. Kontext/feststehender Begriff
„terms of …")
We hope that you will deal with this matter promptly. (Adverb, da Bezug auf das Verb
„deal")

8 **Verbformen: Vervollständige den Text, indem du die richtige Form (Zeiten,
Infinitiv/Gerund, Aktiv/Passiv, Partizipien, If-Sätze) der Verben in Klammern
benutzt. Füge eine Präposition hinzu, wo es notwendig ist.** (Lösungen unterstrichen)

Mr L: I would like to thank you for finding time … (Präposition + Gerund nach „to
thank")

Mr L: … When did you set up your first shop? (Simple Past ergibt sich aus dem
Zusammenhang; Umschreibung mit „did" notwendig, da kein HV im Satz)

Ms H: About five years ago and since then, we have opened branches in four other
major towns. (Present Perfect wg. des Signalworts „since then"/Beachte: „ago"
bezieht sich auf die vorherige Frage)

Ms H: … can greatly improve their health by doing more sport … (Gerund nach der
Präposition „by")
We have managed to attract many of … (to-Infinitiv nach „to manage")

Mr L: But there are many other shops selling/which sell sports articles. (Partizip als
Verkürzung eines Relativsatzes oder Relativpronomen u. Verb im Simple Pre-
sent/Zeit wg. Allgemeingültigkeit)

Ms H: … do something which other shops don't do. (Simple Present analog zur Zeit
des Hauptsatzes)

Ms H: And those people who buy sports articles in our shops <u>are given</u> a reduced price … (Passiv wg. des Sinns/Simple Present wg. der Zeit im Relativsatz)

Mr L: … that I would like <u>you to answer</u>. (to-Infinitiv nach „would like" + Objekt „you")

Mr L: If I buy …, <u>will you give/are you going to give/would you give</u> me a discount? (Future I im Hauptsatz, da im If-Satz Simple Present steht; Conditional I ist ebenfalls möglich, da die Antwort ungewiss, d. h. ein „ja" also nur „möglich" ist)

Teil D: Textproduktion

9 Der Brief sollte nicht nur aus einer Aneinanderreihung der einzelnen Inhaltspunkte bestehen, sondern er sollte logische Satzverknüpfungen enthalten. Weiterhin ist zu achten auf entsprechende Höflichkeitsformen und die Anwendung üblicher „standard phrases". Die Vorgabe „freundlicher Schluss" ist nicht zu verwechseln mit dem Schlussgruß. (siehe *!)

Der folgende Musterbrief ist ein Vorschlag, weitere Möglichkeiten sind durchaus denkbar. Zum Teil sind Alternativen in Klammern angegeben:

Dear Sirs, (Gentlemen/Dear Sir or Madam)

Our order # 512 of March 2, 2001
(Referring to our order # 512 of March 2, 2001 we would like to …)

We would like to inform you that your shipment (consignment) has arrived without any faults, however, 15 days after the date of delivery we agreed on. We must point out that it is absolutely essential (necessary) for future business transactions that delivery is made punctually (in time).

While checking the invoice (When we checked the invoice) we found (discovered) a mistake in the net total. Apart from that (in addition/besides) you obviously (apparently) forgot to deduct the discount we agreed on. Please check the invoice and send us a new and correct one (We ask you to check …).

We are sure that you will handle the matter to our full satisfaction and wait for your immediate answer.* (We wait for your early reply and we are sure that errors like these or delays will not occur again as we have always been content with the way you executed our orders.)* (Of course, we intend to place further orders with you, if errors like the ones mentioned above do not occur again and if there are no further delays in delivery.)*

Yours sincerely,

Teil E: Übersetzung

10 Übersetze den folgenden Text ins Deutsche.
(Zum Teil sind in Klammern Alternativen angeboten.)

Da Computerkenntnisse[1] im Geschäftsleben[2] immer[3] wichtiger werden, denken sich Firmen neue Möglichkeiten[4] aus[5], um ihren Angestellten[6] (dabei) zu helfen, die notwendigen[7] Fertigkeiten[8] zu bekommen. Eine bekannte US-amerikanische Autofirma mit Sitz in[9] in Michigan kündigte[10] kürzlich[11] an, dass sie all ihre Mitarbeiter zu Hause mit Computern, Farbdruckern und unbeschränktem[12] Zugang[13] zum Internet ausstatten[14] werde (würde). Sie werden nur[15] $5 pro Monat für das Paket[16] (Pauschalangebot) bezahlen müssen.

Dieser Plan (Dieses Vorhaben), der (das) die Firma während[17] der nächsten drei Jahre ungefähr[18] 300 Millionen Dollar kosten wird, wurde letztes Jahr zwischen der Autofirma und den Gewerkschaften[19] vereinbart[20]. Es wird keine Kontrolle (keine Überprüfung) geben, wie lange die Mitarbeiter das Internet nutzen.

Der Autohersteller glaubt, dass dieses Programm (diese Maßnahme) der Firma einen Vorsprung vor ihren Konkurrenten[21] im „e-business" und in der Informationstechnologie sichern[22] wird, indem[23] es den Mitarbeitern hilft, ihre Fähigkeit[24], mit Computern zu arbeiten, zu verbessern[25].

Anmerkungen

1	computer skills	Computerkenntnisse
2	in business	im Geschäftsleben, in der Wirtschaft
3	more and more	immer mehr
4	ways	Wege, Möglichkeiten
5	to think up	sich etwas ausdenken
6	employees	Angestellte, Beschäftigte, Mitarbeiter
7	essential	wichtig, notwendig
8	skills	Fähigkeiten, Fertigkeiten, Können, Kenntnisse
9	based in	mit Sitz in
10	to announce	ankündigen
11	recently	kürzlich, vor kurzem
12	unlimited	unbeschränkt
13	access	Zugang
14	to provide with	*hier:* versorgen mit, ausrüsten/ausstatten mit
15	just	*hier:* nur
16	package	Paket/Bündel; *hier auch:* Pauschalangebot
17	over (the next years)	während (der nächsten Jahre)
18	about	*hier:* ungefähr
19	unions	*hier:* Gewerkschaften
20	to agree on	vereinbaren
21	competitors	Konkurrenten, Mitbewerber
22	to keep ahead of	einen Vorsprung sichern vor
23	by	indem
24	ability	Fähigkeit, Können
25	to improve	verbessern

Text Sheet

Teenage driving in the USA

When it comes to driving, American teenagers are much luckier than young Germans. Many of them can start driving when they are just 15 – if there is an adult driver in the passenger seat – and they can drive on their own when they are 16. Learning to drive is much easier and cheaper than in Germany, too, with high schools offering driver's educa-
5 tion classes.

In contrast to Germany, driver education is not even required in some states in the USA either, although you can get cheaper insurance if you have had it. In many cases all you need is to get a certain amount of practice – with your parents, for example – before you take your test and get a full driver's license.

10 However, for many families, the trouble starts when teenagers get behind the wheel. Parents worry that their children will not drive carefully enough, or might even drive after drinking. They are also worried about the effect on the family finances when teenagers start using the family car and burning up expensive gas.

A recent article looked at ways of dealing with these problems by making a "teenage
15 driver contract". In this contract teenagers should agree
  – not to drive after drinking,
  – to make sure they and their passengers use safety belts,
  – not to use a mobile phone while driving,
  – not to let friends borrow the car except in a real emergency.
20 If teenage drivers do not keep to these rules, they have to face the consequences.

Parents can also promise the use of the car to get kids to try harder at school and behave better at home. Families can agree on school grades that the youngsters have to get in their subjects. Or teens have to do certain household duties if they want to use the car. Young drivers can also agree to pay a part of the costs for gas, insurance and servicing.

25 The author says that having a written contract makes life easier for everyone. Parents – and kids – just have to point to the contract when there is an argument.

Many American parents will be pleased that states are also – at last – getting stricter with teenage drivers. Many states now have "graduated licensing" for young people. In most cases, this means that before getting their licenses teens must have six months of driving
30 experience, including 50 hours of practice with a qualified co-driver such as one of their parents. In addition they have to attend driver's education classes at school. Many states do not allow teens to drive at night. Others limit the number of teenage passengers in a car. Some states, such as Florida, use licenses to make sure kids go to school: If teens do not attend school, they run the risk of losing their licenses!

35 States that have "graduated licensing" are very pleased with the results. In North Carolina, for example, accidents involving 16-year-old drivers dropped by 26 per cent between 1997 and 1999. Deaths and serious injuries dropped by 29 per cent.

(Adapted from: Read On, Nov. 2000)

Work Sheet

Part A: Understanding the text

1 **Use the information in the text to say whether these sentences are true or false. Put a cross in the correct box.**

                                                                                            true   false

1.1 Teenagers should never lend the car to others. ☐ ☐

1.2 Some US states have introduced special laws for teenage drivers. ☐ ☐

1.3 "Graduated licensing" has not had any influence on the accident rate. ☐ ☐   (3)

2 **Answer the following questions in complete sentences using your own words as far as possible. (If you copy the text word for word you will lose points.)**

2.1 Getting a driver's license in the USA is different from getting one in Germany. Describe two differences. (4/4)

2.2 What are parents worried about when their kids start driving? (2 items) (4/4)

2.3 How can parents use their car to influence their children's behaviour? (2 items) (4/4)

3 **Additional question (You will not find the answer in the text.)**

3.1 Would you like to have your own car as soon as you get your driver's license? Give reasons for your answer. Write at least 35 words. (4/4)

Part B: Vocabulary

4 **Give a synonym or a similar expression for the following words.**

4.1 <u>required</u> (line 6)
Driver's education is not ... in some states. (1)

4.2 <u>certain</u> (line 23)
Or teens have to do ... household duties if they want to use the car. (1)

4.3 <u>dropped</u> (line 36)
In North Carolina accidents ... by 26 per cent. (1)

5 **Which words and definitions go together?**

                            Fill in:

5.1 to deal with (14) ☐   a) to visit

5.2 contract (15) ☐   b) a heated discussion, quarrel

5.3 argument (26) ☐   c) like, an example of something

5.4 such as (33) ☐   d) to go to, to be present at

5.5 to attend (34) ☐   e) something that follows as a result

                                                          f) to trade with

                                                          g) the knowledge or skill you get from seeing or doing something

                                                          h) an agreement between two people or groups of people

                                                          i) as well as

                                                          k) to handle, to find an answer to   (5)

6   **Explain each of the following words or expressions in a complete sentence of your own.**

6.1   adult driver (line 2)   (1/2)

6.2   ... when teenagers get behind the wheel. (line 10)   (1/2)

6.3   serious injuries (line 37)   (1/2)

Part C: Grammar in context

7   **Word forms: Fill in the correct form (adjective, adverb, noun, verb) of the words in brackets.**

The following is an extract from a brochure from *Reedway Air Helpers.*

Dear Customers,

"Where can I make a hotel ... (reserve)?"   (1)

"Will the ... (fly) leave on time?"   (1)

"How can I get through customs as ... (quick) as possible?"   (1)

"Where's the ... (depart) lounge?"   (1)

"Do I have to ... (declaration) my camera?"   (1)

These and thousands of other questions are asked by customers of *Reedway Air* every day. We're here to answer your questions and ... (assistance) you.   (1)

So don't forget: If you have any questions just look for one of our *Reedway* helpers. You'll find that they are very ... (help).   (1)

8   **Verb forms: Complete the text, using the correct form (tenses, infinitive/ing-form, active/passive, if-clauses) of the verbs in brackets. Add prepositions where necessary.**

Hans Meier wants to get his driving licence in England, so he is enquiring at the Conway Driving School in Croydon.

8.1   Receptionist: Good morning, sir. What can I do for you?

        Hans Meier: Good morning. I'd like ... (take) some driving lessons,
                       please. I come from Germany so I ... (not know) much
                       about ... (get) a driving licence in England.   (3)

8.2   Receptionist: Well, if you wait here, I ... (go) and ask Mr Stuart, the head
                       of our driving school, ... (give) you some information.   (2)

8.3   Mr Stuart: Ah, good morning, young man. Ms Adams tells me you're
                       interested ... (learn) to drive in our school.   (1)

        Hans Meier: That's right.

        Mr Stuart: Well, tomorrow night we start our course on the "Highway
                       Code".

        Hans Meier: That's funny. We have a theory exam in Germany but I
                       thought there wasn't one in England.

8.4   Mr Stuart: I'm afraid there is. It ... (introduce) by the government five
                       years ago and since then it ... (be) an important part of our
                       exam.   (2)

8.5   Hans Meier: I see. By the way, how old ... (I, have to be) before I can get
                       a driving licence in England?   (1)

        Mr Stuart: Seventeen.

8.6   Hans Meier: Great. If I took the exam in Germany I ... (have) to wait
                       until I was 18.   (1)

Part D: Text production

9 Describe the situation in the picture and explain what it means to you. Write between 80 and 100 words in complete sentences.

(27)

Part E: Translation

10 Translate the following letter into German

Dear Mr McDonald,

We are writing to you to complain about the consignment of "Rose Garden" china, which we received on 16 May 2002.

On opening the ten wooden chests we discovered that the cups and plates had several cracks on them. Moreover – probably due to an error in packaging – none of the teacups fit the saucers you have sent us.

As we plan to reopen our hotel on 13 June 2002, you will understand that this is a matter of great disappointment for us, and we hope you will deal with the problem without delay.

We would also like your sales representative to visit our hotel at any time that is convenient for him so that we can show him the defective items.

As time is pressing we would appreciate immediate replacement of the damaged articles.

Yours sincerely
Graham Jones

(24)
Total: 120

Lösungen

Teil A: Textverständnis

1 **Benutze die Information(en) im Text, um auszudrücken, ob diese Sätze richtig oder falsch sind. Setze ein Kreuz in das richtige Kästchen.**

	true	false
1.1 Teenager sollten ihr/das Auto niemals anderen leihen.		X
1.2 Einige US-Bundesstaaten haben besondere Gesetze für jugendliche Autofahrer eingeführt/erlassen.	X	
1.3 „Graduated Licensing"* hatte keinen Einfluss auf die Unfallquote. (*= stufenweises Erteilen der Fahrerlaubnis)		X

2 **Beantworte die folgenden Fragen in vollständigen Sätzen, indem du soweit wie möglich deine eigenen Worte/Formulierungen verwendest. (Wenn Du wörtlich vom Text abschreibst, wirst Du Punkte verlieren.)**
Du solltest vor der Beantwortung der Fragen aufmerksam die Seite 1 der Lernhilfen durcharbeiten. Zu den einzelnen Fragen werden zum Teil mehrere Antwortmöglichkeiten bzw. -formulierungen angeboten. Achte immer auf die geforderte Anzahl von „items".

2.1 Possible items:
– In some of the US states no driver education is required/no driving instructions are required. (Z. 6/7)
– In the USA you can learn to drive with your parents. (Z. 7/8)
– In the USA you can drive at the age of 15 if a qualified driver/an adult driver is in the car with you/accompanies you. (Z. 2/3)
– In the USA you can drive on your own/alone when you are 16. (Z. 3)

2.2 Possible items:
– They are worried/They fear that their kids don't drive carefully (enough).
– They are worried/afraid that their kids might drive after drinking alcohol.
– They fear that they will have to pay a lot of money for the gas/fuel their children use (while driving around just for fun). (Z. 10–13)

2.3 Possible items:
They can use their car
– to make their kids work harder at school.
– to make their children do housework/do household jobs/help in the household/help with the housework.
– to get their kids to behave better at home. (Z. 21–23)

3   Zusatzfrage (Du wirst die Antwort nicht im Text finden.)
Hier solltest du dich für eine Möglichkeit entscheiden und Gründe dafür anführen.

Of course, I would like to have my own car as soon as I get my driver's license, because most of my friends have a car and for young people a car is a symbol for being grown up. If you have your own car you are independent, you can go/travel wherever you want. You don't have to ask your parents, your brother or a friend to take you to the disco or to a concert. You don't have to call your parents after midnight to pick you up at the disco and you do not have to be a nice guy all the time to get the family car when you need it.

No, I wouldn't. An important reason for this decision is that a car costs quite a lot of money. It's not only the money for buying, but the money you need every month to run your car. You must pay for the insurance which is especially expensive for young drivers and for the tax. Then you need a lot of money for the service, for repairs and above all for the fuel which is very expensive. All my friends would expect me to pick them up for the disco but nobody would support me with the costs. You also have great responsibility when there are other people in your car. Their lives are in your hands and if you get involved in an accident as a young inexperienced driver you might be responsible for the death of a friend.

Aus den genannten Bausteinen kannst du welche auswählen, so dass du die geforderte Wortzahl erreichst.

Teil B: Wortschatz

4   Gib für die folgenden Wörter ein Synonym oder einen ähnlichen Ausdruck an.
(Lösungen unterstrichen)

4.1   Driver's education is not <u>needed</u> / <u>necessary</u> / <u>compulsory</u> / (<u>essential</u>) in some states.

4.2   Or teens have to do <u>specific</u> / <u>special</u> / <u>particular</u> household duties if they want to use the car,

4.3   In North Carolina accidents <u>fell</u> / <u>went down</u> / <u>decreased</u> / <u>were reduced</u> by 26 per cent.

5   Welche Wörter/Ausdrücke und Definitionen/Begriffe passen/gehören zusammen?

5.1	to deal with (line 14)	k) to handle, to find an answer to
5.2	contract (line 15)	h) an agreement between two people or groups of people
5.3	argument (line 26)	b) a heated discussion, quarrel
5.4	such as (line 33)	c) like, an example of something
5.5	to attend (line 34)	d) to go to, to be present at

6   Erkläre die folgenden Wörter oder Ausdrücke jeweils in einem vollständigen Satz.
(Zum Teil sind mehrere Alternativen angeboten.)

6.1   An adult driver is a person who is old enough to drive.
or
An adult driver is someone who is also old enough to vote and who has some driving experience.

6.2   … when teenagers get behind the wheel they begin to drive/start driving.

6.3   When somebody has serious injuries it means that he/she got hurt/was harmed very badly.
or
When somebody has serious injuries from an accident he may be in danger of losing his life.

Teil C: Grammatik im Textzusammenhang

7   Wortarten: Setze die richtige Form (Adjektiv, Adverb, Nomen, Verb) der Wörter in Klammern ein. (Lösungen unterstrichen)

– Where can I make a hotel <u>reservation</u>? (Nomen als Teil eines zusammengesetzten Nomens, vorher unbest. Artikel ohne nachfolg. Adjektiv)
– Will the <u>flight</u> leave on time? (Nomen nach best. Artikel/kein Adjektiv nach dem Artikel)
– How can I get through customs as <u>quickly</u> as possible?

(Adverb, da Bezug auf das Verb "get")
– Where's the <u>departure</u> lounge? (Nomen nach best. Artikel)
– Do I have to <u>declare</u> my camera? (Verb nach HV "have to")
– We're here to ... <u>assist</u> you. (Verb nach to/to be here to)
– You'll find that they are very <u>helpful</u>. (Adjektiv als prädikative Ergänzung zu "to be")

8   Verbformen: Vervollständige den Text, indem du die richtige Form (Zeiten, Infinitiv/Gerund, Aktiv/Passiv, If-Sätze) der Verben in Klammern benutzt. Füge eine Präposition hinzu, wo es notwendig ist. (Lösungen unterstrichen)

8.1 I'd like <u>to take</u> some driving lessons ... (to-Infinitiv nach "would like")
I come from Germany, so I <u>don't know</u> ...(Simple Present, da gleiche Zeit wie im Hauptsatz vor dem Komma)
... <u>getting</u> a driving license in England. (Gerund, da Gebrauch als Objekt)

8.2 Well, if you wait here, <u>I'll/I will</u> go and ... (Future I, da im If-Satz Simple Present steht) ... ask Mr Stuart, ..., <u>to give</u> you ... (to-Infinitiv nach Verb "ask" + Objekt "Mr Stuart")

8.3 ... you are interested <u>in learning</u> to drive ... (Präposition "in" + Gerund nach "to be interested")

8.4 It <u>was introduced</u> by the government five years ago ... (Simple Past wg. des Signalworts "five years ago"; Passiv wg. des "by-agent") ... and since then it <u>has been</u> ... (Present Perfect wg. des Signalworts "since then")

8.5 ... how old <u>do I have to be</u> ... (Simple Present wg. des Textzusammenhangs und der Zeit im Nebensatz, Umschreibung mit "to do" bei "have to" üblich/notwendig)

8.6 If I took the exam in Germany, I <u>would have</u> to wait ... (Conditional I, da im If-Satz Simple Past steht → "took")

Teil D: Textproduktion

9   Beschreibe die Situation auf dem Bild und erkläre, was es für dich bedeutet/was es dir sagt.
Schon durch diese Anweisung wird klar, dass es mehrere Möglichkeiten gibt, wie man Inhalt und „Message" auffassen kann. Du solltest das Bild genau betrachten, damit die Aussage vollkommen klar wird. Die nachfolgende Lösung ist etwas umfangreicher als verlangt, könnte aber noch gekürzt werden.

In the centre of the picture you see a little boy of about five or six years. He sits on a *swivel-chair** at/in front of a huge desk. On this desk there are a computer and two books. The boy is working on/at the (computer) keyboard and is watching the monitor/

screen in absolute concentration. The screen shows him the development of the Siemens *share prices**. On the wall in front of the boy you can see three (wall) *charts/ diagrams** showing the development of the Dax, the Dow Jones and FT-SE 100. Behind the boy you can see lots of his toys like teddybears, balls and musical instruments lying on the floor. Obviously the boy hasn't played with them for a long time as they are covered with *cobwebs (= spiders' webs)**.

Message: (Hier findest du einige Alternativen, die nicht unbedingt in voller Länge dargestellt werden müssen (siehe 3!) Du kannst sie auch mit „I think …" einleiten)

1. The computer-mania has already reached children at elementary school age. They are more interested in working with computers and surfing in the internet/getting information from the internet than in playing with their toys.

2. During the last few years lots of people got crazy about buying and selling shares at the *Stock Exchange** and making a lot of money. Now this mania has obviously reached children's rooms as well.

3. In our computerized world even kids are influenced by real life and business at a very early age. So they don't have a happy unspoilt childhood which may have serious consequences for their development.

*Anmerkung: Die Bildbeschreibung ist kaum ohne die mit * gekennzeichneten Wörter zu bewerkstelligen. Diese sind allerdings eher nicht im Unterricht verwendet worden.*

Teil E: Übersetzung

10 Übersetze den folgenden Brief ins Deutsche. (In Klammern findest du Alternativen, mögliche Ergänzungen und Erläuterungen.)

Sehr geehrter Herr McDonald,

Wir schreiben Ihnen, um uns über die Lieferung[1] von „Rose Garden" Porzellan[2] (= Porzellan der Marke „Rose Garden") zu beschweren[3], die wir am 16. Mai 2002 erhielten.

Beim Öffnen (Als wir die … öffneten) der zehn Holzkisten[4] entdeckten (= sahen) wir, dass die Tassen und Teller mehrere Sprünge[5] (an sich) hatten. Außerdem[6] – wahrscheinlich[7] wegen[8] eines Irrtums (= Fehlers) beim Verpacken[9] – passte(e)[9] keine der Teetassen zu den Untertassen[10], die sie uns schickten/uns geschickt haben.

Da wir planen, unser Hotel am 13. Juni 2002 wieder zu eröffnen[11], werden Sie verstehen, dass dies eine große Enttäuschung[12] (= eine Sache[13] von großer Enttäuschung) für uns ist, und wir hoffen, dass Sie sich umgehend[14] mit dem Problem befassen[15] werden.

Wir möchten auch, dass Ihr Vertreter[16] zu jeder[17] Zeit (= zu jedem Termin), die günstig[18] für ihn ist, unser Hotel besucht, so dass wir ihm die fehlerhaften[19] (= mangelhaften) Artikel[20] zeigen können.

Da[21] die Zeit drängt[22], würden wir einen sofortigen Ersatz[23] für die beschädigten[24] Artikel zu schätzen wissen[25].

Mit freundlichen Grüßen
Graham Jones

Anmerkungen

[1]	consignment	(Waren) Lieferung
[2]	china	Porzellan
[3]	to complain	sich beschweren
[4]	chest	*hier:* Kiste
[5]	cracks	Risse, Sprünge
[6]	moreover	außerdem
[7]	probably	wahrscheinlich
[8]	due to	wegen, aufgrund
[9]	to fit	passen
[10]	saucer	Untertasse
[11]	to reopen	wieder eröffnen
[12]	disappointment	Enttäuschung
[13]	matter	Sache, Ding, Angelegenheit (matter of disappointment *auch:* Tatbestand der Nichterfüllung eines Vertrags, Vertragsverletzung, Vertragsbruch)
[14]	without delay	umgehend, sofort, unverzüglich, ohne Verzögerung
[15]	to deal with	*hier:* sich befassen mit, sich kümmern um
[16]	sales representative	(Handels) Vertreter
[17]	at any time	jede(r), jegliche(r), beliebig(e/r)
[18]	convenient	günstig, passend, angenehm
[19]	defective	fehlerhaft, mangelhaft
[20]	item	Artikel, Ware, Posten, Gegenstand
[21]	as	*hier:* da, weil
[22]	to press	*hier:* drängen
[23]	replacement	Ersatz
[24]	damaged	beschädigt
[25]	to appreciate	schätzen, zu schätzen wissen

Text Sheet

It is official: In Britain girls do better in exams

Last year for the first time in the 49-year history of the A-level exams*, girls got more grade A's than boys did. To many, this came as no surprise, as GCSE** results also show that girls do better on average. Their results improve from year to year, while boys' performance stays the same. Are girls really more intelligent than boys, or could there be
5   other reasons for the difference? This question is at the centre of a heated debate in Britain.

A study of the 13 to 19-year-old school boys showed that 17 percent hated school so much that they did not pass even a single exam. More boys than girls leave school without any qualifications. They have great difficulty in finding jobs and become frustrated as a
10   result.

The government is now looking into this problem in order to find ways to improve the performance of the male pupils. One reason for their poor results seems to be that boys are afraid of competing with girls, because they don't want to be seen losing. Boys believe they are better than girls, and when they find out they are not, they feel hurt. Con-
15   sequently, fields where girls are good become taboo for boys.

Moreover, many of them are afraid that the other boys in their class will look down on them if their marks are "too good". They do not want to be seen trying hard in class, so they try to get attention and prestige in other ways such as by being noisy and disturbing lessons. The boys' ideal is the lazy genius who does well in exams without working
20   much. In contrast, girls do not have image problems when working hard at school and doing their homework neatly and regularly. And with more and more mothers going out to work, girls start thinking of career opportunities at an early age. They also see an increasing number of women in politics and top jobs. The housewife and mother who stays at home all day is therefore no longer a role model for such girls.

25   But how can boys be helped to become more successful at school?

Some people argue that boys could do better, if they were taught separately in single-sex-classes. Then they would not mess around so much to get attention and would concentrate better on their work.

Others argue that the new exam system should be changed, because it quite obviously
30   favours girls. It has many small tests over a long period of time. This fits in well with the systematic way of learning which girls have. But this new exam does not encourage the "risktaking" attitude of boys. The old exam was definitely a boys' exam: You just had to learn for one big final test and take a high risk.

However, as the discussion about boys' poor marks in British schools goes on, one thing
35   makes many women angry. Why is it that everyone is so worried now that the girls are doing so well at school in the UK? Shouldn't we Britons simply be pleased at the progress girls have made?

(Adapted from: Read On, March 2001)

Anmerkungen

*   Abitur
**   entspricht dem Mittleren Bildungsabschluss

Work Sheet

Part A: Understanding the text

1   Use the information in the text to choose the correct sentence. Put a cross in the correct box.

1.1 Girls

☐   a) are more intelligent than boys.

☐   b) are less intelligent than boys.

☐   c) get better marks in school exams than boys.

☐   d) are as successful as boys are in their school subjects.

1.2 Boys

☐   a) avoid competition with girls at school.

☐   b) are surprised at the progress of girls at school.

☐   c) feel they are almost as good as girls.

☐   d) are only interested in girls at school.

1.3 The government

☐   a) wants to help boys to get better marks at school.

☐   b) is very pleased about the progress girls are making at school.

☐   c) wants girls to become housewives and mothers.

☐   d) has a different exam system for boys and girls.   (3)

2   Answer the following questions in complete sentences using your own words as far as possible. (If you copy the text word for word, you will lose points.)

2.1 Mention one consequence of the performance of British boys at school.   (2/2)

2.2 Why do British boys not want to work as hard at school as girls do? (2 items)   (4/4)

2.3 What motivates girls to do well at school? (1 item)   (2/2)

2.4 What suggestions have been made to help boys do better at school? (2 items)   (4/4)

3   Additional question (You will not find the answer in the text.)

3.1 "There are some jobs which men can do better than women." Do you agree? Explain your answer. Write at least 35 words.   (4/4)

Part B: Vocabulary

4   Complete each of these sentences with the opposite of the underlined word. Do not simply add "not".

4.1 <u>heated</u> (line 5)
This question is at the centre of a heated debate rather than a ... discussion.   (1)

4.2 <u>to pass</u> (line 8)
Many youngsters are happy to learn that sometimes their parents used to ... tests at school. They needed a second chance, too.   (1)

4.3 <u>separately</u> (line 26)
In some British schools, boys and girls are taught separately, but later, at work, of course they have to learn how to work ....   (1)

5 **Which words and definitions go together? Make sure your answer fits the context.**

Fill in:

5.1	to show (2)	☐
5.2	on average (3)	☐
5.3	model (24)	☐
5.4	to fit in (30)	☐
5.5	poor (34)	☐

a) bad, miserable

b) normally, usually

c) a woman displaying fashionable clothes

d) to prove/make clear

e) everyone in the class

f) to put on a performance on TV etc.

g) to have a body which is in excellent shape

h) kind of person many people would like to become

i) having little or no money

k) to go with   (5)

6 **Explain each of the following words or expressions in a complete sentence of your own.**

6.1	surprise (line 2)	(1/2)
6.2	to improve (line 11)	(1/2)
6.3	mess around (line 27)	(1/2)

Part C: Grammar in context

7 **Word forms: Fill in the correct form (e. g. adjective, adverb, noun, verb, participle) of the words in brackets.**

This is part of a speech Mr Dubovy, general manager of *INTA Graphics,* gave to the staff of his company:

"Well, ladies and gentlemen, I am extremely ... (pleasure) to be able to tell you   (1)
that the year 2001 was a very ... (succeed) year indeed for INTA graphics.   (1)
Total ... (sell) reached £20 million.   (1)
As you know, we had to ... (competition) against some major firms so this is   (1)
a really wonderful result. Thank you for all the efforts you have made for our firm. What are our plans for next year?
Well, we will again be investing ... (heavy) in the training of our staff.   (1)
We're sure that, as a result, next year we will see a further dramatic ... (increase) in the number of our customers."   (1)

8   **Verb forms: Complete the text using the correct forms (tenses, infinitive/ing-form, active/passive, if-clauses) of the verbs in brackets. Add prepositions where necessary.**

Ms Tye, owner of "Help your children", a shop specialising in educational materials, is phoning ESA (Educational Software Applications).

8.1   Mr Ellis: Educational Software Applications, good morning. Can I help you?

      Ms Tye: Good morning. Ms Tye from "Help your children", War-wick. Last month we ... (order) 10 of your CD-ROMs "German for Beginners". ... (you, get) our order? I'm asking this because unfortunately we ... (not, hear) from you since then. (3)

8.2   Mr Ellis: Oh, I'm sorry to hear that. Our language CD-ROMs seem ... (be) very popular and we're having difficulties ... (replace) stocks. (2)

8.3   Ms Tye: Well, they're certainly very popular in my family! My son told me he would never have got such a good mark in his last German exam if he ... (not, use) your CD-ROM while he was preparing for it! (1)

8.4   Mr Ellis: We're always happy to hear people are satisfied with our products. If you give me your order number again, I ... (see) to it myself first thing this afternoon. (1)

8.5   Ms Tye: Our order number is, hm yes, here it is: R-X-1-5-7-6. By the way, before I forget – I'd like you ... (send) us 20 CD-ROMs "French for Beginners" as well.. (1)

8.6   Mr Ellis: Certainly, Ms Tye. All the CD-ROMs you have ordered ... (post) by the end of the week at the latest. (2)

8.7   Ms Tye: Glad to hear that and thank you ... (give) me some of your precious time. (1)

      Mr Ellis: You're welcome. Good bye, Ms Tye.

(11)

Part D: Text production

9   **Situation:**

Sie arbeiten in der Einkaufsabteilung der Firma Blue Store, einer Ladenkette für Sport- und Badebekleidung mit Sitz in Passau. Die meisten Filialen befinden sich in Bayern. In letzter Zeit wurden auch in verschiedenen anderen Bundes-ländern und in Österreich Blue Store-Läden eröffnet. Die Kunden von Blue Store sind vorwiegend junge Leute sowie junggebliebene Erwachsene, die gerne Kleidung tragen, die der neuesten Mode entspricht, aber zugleich zweckmäßig und preiswert ist.

Ihre Abteilungsleiterin gab Ihnen diese Anzeige von der Firma Delphine Cool, die diesen Monat in *Fashion International,* einer Zeitschrift für Groß- und Ein-zelhändler der Textilbranche, erschienen ist.

Schreiben Sie einen Brief an Frau Collins.

LATEST TREND LATEST TREND LATEST TREND LATEST

Experience the elements...
Buy and dive in now!

Please ask for further information:

Delphine Cool ♦ attn. Sheila Collins ♦ 33 Butterfly Drive ♦

London SW1A 12JD ♦ Tel: 0171 - 466 2287 ♦

Fax: 0171 - 466 9113 ♦ www.markmiles.com

Der Brief soll nach folgenden Vorgaben aufgebaut sein:
– Anrede
– kurze Vorstellung des Unternehmens
– Bezugnahme auf Anzeige
– Bitte um Information über die neue Kollektion (aktueller Katalog, Preisliste für Einzelhändler)
– Erkundigungen nach Lieferungs- und Zahlungsbedingungen sowie Lieferzeiten
– Erkundigungen, ob Nachlässe gewährt werden (z. B. Mengenrabatt, Skonto)
– Anforderung von Mustern
– freundlicher Schlusssatz
– Gruß

(27)

Part E: Translation

10   Translate the following text into German

Career opportunities abroad

Nowadays lots of companies want young people to get some job experience in foreign countries. But if – for example – you wish to find a job in the UK, there are a number of things to remember. First of all, German job titles and apprenticeships often have no direct British equivalent. Here it is important to look carefully at the job description and decide whether you have the skills required.

When applying to a British firm, don't forget that in an English CV you should not mention your parents' profession. Do not send references, either. An employer prepared to grant you the chance of an interview will ask you to give names of people who know you and he will then write to them directly. Finally, a CV in English is hardly ever handed in with your photograph enclosed.

(24)

Total: 120

Lösungen

Teil A: Textverständnis

1 **Benutze die Information(en) im Text, um den richtigen Satz auszuwählen. Setze ein Kreuz in das richtige Kästchen.**

1.1 Mädchen
   c) bekommen in Schulprüfungen bessere Noten als Jungen. (Z. 1–4)

1.2 Jungen
   a) vermeiden an der Schule den (direkten) Wettbewerb mit Mädchen / vermeiden es, sich in der Schule mit Mädchen zu messen. (Z. 12–15)

1.3 Die Regierung
   a) möchte den Jungen helfen, in der Schule bessere Noten zu bekommen. (Z. 11/12)

2 **Beantworte die folgenden Fragen in vollständigen Sätzen, indem du soweit wie möglich deine eigenen Worte/Formulierungen verwendest. (Wenn du wörtlich vom Text abschreibst, wirst du Punkte verlieren.)**
Du solltest vor der Beantwortung der Fragen aufmerksam die Seite 1 der Lernhilfen durchlesen. Zu den einzelnen Fragen werden zum Teil mehrere Antwortmöglichkeiten bzw. -formulierungen angeboten.

2.1 Possible items:
   – A lot of boys fail their final exams/don't pass their final exams/leave school without any (important) qualifications.
   – They have problems getting a job/have difficulty (in) finding work (= an employment). (Z. 8/9)

2.2 You can choose <u>two</u> of the following items:
   – They don't want to compete with girls in subjects/fields where girls are good. (Z. 13–15)
   – A boy who works hard for school has a bad/poor image among other boys. = Boys who are good at school fear that the other boys in their class look down on them, so they don't do much for school. (Z. 16/17)
   – Many boys think/ hope/ feel that it must/ might be possible to get good marks/ to be good at school without working hard. (Z. 19/20)

2.3 Possible items: (Choose one!)
   – They see their mothers working in a job and so they start planning a career as well/ … and this makes them think of career opportunities, too.
   – They see that more and more women are in top jobs/reach top positions (or make a career in politics). (Z. 20–23)

2.4 The following suggestions have been made:
   – There should be separate classes for boys and girls. = There should be classes for boys and classes for girls. = Some people suppose that boys would do better at school if they were taught in single-sex-classes. (Z. 26–28)
   – There should be a different exam system, one which is fair to girls as well as boys. = The British exam system should be changed, because it brings only advantages for girls. (Z. 29–33)

3 **Zusatzfrage (Du wirst die Antwort nicht im Text finden.)**
Du solltest dich hier auf Zustimmung zur oder Ablehnung der Aussage beschränken und deine Entscheidung begründen. Nachfolgend findest du dazu jeweils ein Beispiel (Zum Teil sind die Beiträge länger als gefordert und können entsprechend gekürzt werden.):

I think there are some jobs which men can do better than women. This goes for jobs in which you need a lot of physical power. Bricklayers and carpenters for example have to lift heavy things like stones etc. all day long. This would probably be too hard for most women. (Apart from that jobs where you are away from home during the week wouldn't be so good for women, especially if they have kids at home.)

I think women can do any job as well as a man. Women aren't less intelligent and they are tough. Even jobs in which you need a lot of physical strength aren't a problem for women any longer, as there is a lot of modern equipment for lifting heavy loads etc.

Teil B: Wortschatz

4 **Vervollständige jeden dieser Sätze mit dem Gegenteil des unterstrichenen Worts. Füge nicht einfach "not" hinzu.** Die Lösungen sind unterstrichen. Bei Mehrfachnennungen steht am Anfang jeweils die beste Lösung.

4.1 This question is at the centre of a heated debate rather than a calm/unemotional/cool discussion.

4.2 Many youngsters are happy to learn that sometimes their parents used to fail/be unsuccessful in tests at school.

4.3 In some British schools, boys and girls are taught separately, but later, at work, of course they have to learn how to work together/in a team/in a group/with each other/ with the other sex.

5 **Welche Wörter und Definitionen gehören zusammen? Vergewissere dich, dass deine Lösung in den Textzusammenhang passt.** Setze ein:

5.1 to show (line 2)   d) to prove / make clear

5.2 on average (line 3)   b) normally, usually

5.3 model (line 24)   h) kind of person many people would like to become

5.4 to fit in (line 30)   k) to go with

5.5 poor (line 34)   a) bad, miserable

6 **Erkläre jedes der folgenden Wörter oder jeden der Ausdrücke in einem vollständigen, selbstformulierten Satz.** (Mehrere Alternativen)

6.1 A surprise is something which you didn't expect/which you think won't happen/which you thought wouldn't happen. A surprise is something (absolutely) unexpected/an unexpected event.

6.2 This word/expression means to get better/to become better.

6.3 When boys "mess around" they don't behave the way they should/the correct way. The expression "to mess around" means to act or speak stupidly or to play the fool.

Teil C: Grammatik im Textzusammenhang

7 **Wortarten: Setze die richtige Form (Adjektiv, Adverb, Nomen, Verb, Partizip) der Wörter in Klammern ein.** (Lösungen unterstrichen)

Well, ladies and gentlemen, I am extremely <u>pleased</u> to be able to ... (→ Adjektiv als prädikative Ergänzung zu "am")

... the year 2001 was a very <u>successful</u> year ... (Adjektiv zur näheren Bestimmung des nachfolgenden Nomens)

Total <u>sales</u> reached $20 million. (Nomen als Teil eines zusammengesetzten Nomens, wegen Stellung vor dem Prädikat handelt es sich um einen Teil des Subjekts → also Nomen)

As you know, we had to <u>compete</u> against ... (Verb im Infinitiv nach "had to")

... we will again be investing <u>heavily</u> in ... (Adverb, da Bezug auf das Verb "invest")

... we will see a further dramatic <u>increase</u> ... (Nomen nach unbest. Artikel gefolgt von 2 Adjektiven)

8 **Verbformen: Vervollständige den Text, indem du die richtige Form (Zeiten, Infinitiv/Gerund, Aktiv/Passiv, If-Sätze) der Verben in Klammern benutzt. Füge eine Präposition hinzu, wo es notwendig ist.** (Lösungen unterstrichen)

8.1 Last month we <u>ordered</u> 10 of your CD-ROMs ... (Simple Past wg. des Signalworts "last month") <u>Did</u> you <u>get</u> our order? (Simple Past analog zur Zeit des vorhergehenden Satzes; vom Kontext her auch möglich: <u>Have</u> you <u>got</u> our order?)

... we <u>haven't heard</u> from you since then. (Present Perfect wg. des Signalworts „since then")

8.2 ... Our language CD-ROMs seem <u>to be</u> very popular ... (to-Infinitiv nach dem Verb „to seem")

... we're having difficulties <u>(in) replacing</u> stocks. (Gerund mit u. ohne Präp. nach „difficulty")

8.3 ... if he <u>hadn't used</u>/<u>hadn't been using</u> your CD-ROM ... (Past Perfect bzw. Past Perfect Progressive im If-Satz, da im HS Conditional II steht → would ... have got)

8.4 ... <u>will see</u>/<u>'ll see</u> to it first thing myself this afternoon. (Future I, da Zukunftsbezogenheit der Handlung erkennbar und da im If-Satz Simple Present steht)

8.5 ... I'd like you <u>to send</u> us ... (to-Infinitiv nach would like + Objekt)

8.6 ... <u>will have been posted</u>/<u>will be posted</u>/<u>are going to be posted</u> ... (Passiv aus dem Textzusammenhang erkennbar, Future II wg. „by + Zeitangabe", wg. des Kontexts aber auch Future I möglich)

8.7 ... and thank you <u>for giving</u> me ... (Präp. „for" + Gerund nach dem Verb „to thank")

Teil D: Textproduktion

9 **Der Brief sollte nicht nur aus einer Aneinanderreihung der einzelnen Inhalts-punkte bestehen, sondern er sollte logische Satzverknüpfungen enthalten.** *Weiterhin ist zu achten auf entsprechende Höflichkeitsformen und die Anwendung üblicher „standard phrases". Die Vorgabe „freundlicher Schluss" ist nicht zu verwechseln mit dem Schlussgruß. (siehe *!) Der folgende Musterbrief ist ein Vorschlag, weitere Möglichkeiten sind durchaus denkbar. Zum Teil sind Alternativen in Klammern angegeben:*

Dear Ms Collins,

I work in the buying department of "Blue Store" which is a chain of shops for sportswear and swimwear with its headquarters in Passau. Most of our branches are in Bavaria but recently we also opened some shops in various (= several) other federal states and in Austria. Our customers are mainly youngsters/teenagers as well as young trendy adults who like to wear fashionable clothes which are both suitable and good value (= low-priced).

I read your advertisement in *Fashion International* with great interest and therefore I would like you to send us some information about your new collection, especially your current (= latest) catalogue and your price-list for retailers.

Please let us know your terms of delivery and payment as well as your delivery periods. Are there any discounts (= price reductions) such as quantity or cash discounts?

We would appreciate it if you could send us some specimen of your products and we would be very glad/would be ready to do business with you, if the quality of your products and your terms meet our requirements.*

Yours sincerely,

Teil E: Übersetzung

10 **Übersetze den folgenden Text ins Deutsche.** (Zum Teil sind in Klammern Alternativen angeboten.)

Berufliche (= Arbeits-) Möglichkeiten im Ausland[1]

Heutzutage wollen viele Firmen, dass junge Leute Berufserfahrung(en)[2] im Ausland (= in fremden Ländern)[3] bekommen (= sammeln). Aber wenn man – zum Beispiel – im UK (Vereinigten Königreich) Arbeit (= einen Job) finden möchte, (dann) gibt es eine Reihe von Dingen (= einige Dinge) zu beachten[4]. Zuerst einmal haben deutsche Berufsbezeichnungen[5] und Ausbildungen[6] oft keine direkte britische Entsprechung[7] (kein entsprechendes Gegenstück in Großbritannien). Hier ist es wichtig, die Berufsbeschreibung (Arbeitsbeschreibung) genau (= sorgfältig)[8] anzuschauen und zu entscheiden, ob[9] man die geforderten (= verlangten)[10] Fertigkeiten[11] besitzt.

Wenn du dich bei einer britischen Firma bewirbst[12], vergiss nicht, dass du in einem englischen Lebenslauf[13] den Beruf[14] deiner Eltern nicht erwähnen[15] solltest. Schicke auch keine[16] Referenzen. Ein Arbeitgeber[17], der bereit[18] ist, dir die Möglichkeit (= Chance) zu einem Vorstellungsgespräch[19] zu geben[20], wird dich bitten[21], (die) Namen von Leuten anzugeben, die dich kennen, und er wird dann direkt an sie schreiben. Zuletzt* (= Schließlich)[22] wird ein Lebenslauf in Englisch kaum einmal (= kaum jemals)[23] mit deinem beigefügten[24] Foto eingereicht (= eingeschickt)[25].

(*= Zuletzt/Zum Schluss ist zu beachten, dass ein Lebenslauf in Englisch ...)

Anmerkungen

1 abroad   (im/ins) Ausland
2 job experience   Berufserfahrung
3 in foreign countries   im Ausland, in fremden Ländern
4 to remember   *hier:* denken an, beachten
5 job title   Berufsbezeichnung
6 apprenticeship   Lehre, Ausbildung(szeit)
7 equivalent   Entsprechung, Gegenstück
8 carefully   sorgfältig, genau
9 whether   ob
10 required   verlangt, gefordert, notwendig
11 skills   Fähigkeiten, Fertigkeiten, Können, Kenntnisse
12 to apply   (sich) bewerben
13 CV   (= curriculum vitae) Lebenslauf
14 profession   Beruf(sbezeichnung)
15 to mention   erwähnen
16 not ... either   (auch nicht), auch keine
17 employer   Arbeitgeber
18 prepared   bereit, gewillt
19 interview   *hier:* Vorstellungsgespräch
20 to grant   geben, gewähren
21 to ask   *hier:* bitten
22 finally   schließlich, endlich, zuletzt
23 hardly ever   kaum einmal, kaum jemals
24 to enclose   beifügen, beilegen
25 to hand in   einreichen

Tapescript zu Worksheet 1

Jobs: Girls want to work with animals, boys want to work with computers

If you had asked a 16-year-old-boy fifty years ago what he wanted to do when he left school, he would probably have said, "Join the army" or "Be a farmer". A girl of the same age would maybe have answered, "Train to be a hairdresser" or "Study to be a scientist". Those were the most popular jobs at that time.

5 Today, according to a recent article, most boys want a job in information technology or engineering, while the most popular career for girls is vet or fashion designer. Interestingly enough, today's young women put the army in third place. A military career, however, doesn't even get into the top ten for boys.

The third choice for boys is lawyer, followed by pop singer and scientist. For girls,
10 traditional female jobs – like secretary and hairdresser – take fourth and fifth place.

The authors also looked at the ambitions of 11-year-olds. The most popular career in this group was footballer for boys and vet for girls. The second places went to policeman for boys and pop singer for girls. In the 1950s, the most popular job among 11-year-olds was the army for boys and nursing for girls, with the second places taken by footballer and air
15 stewardess.

Fifty years ago, girls included nun, ballerina and being a mother on their lists of the top ten jobs. Racing driver, train driver, plumber and farmer – careers popular with boys in the 1950s – have totally disappeared from today's top ten list.

Tapescript zu Worksheet 2

REPORTER: Hello, it's 5 : 15 and this is your local station: *Radio Liverpool*. I'm Bob Turner with your daily programme 'News for Youngsters'. Here's the latest local news: A new boutique will open in our town on Thursday July 17. And that's why I've invited Barbara Sand to our studio today. Barbara is an American living in Liverpool
5 and she is the owner of this great, new shop. Hello Barbara, I'm so pleased that you're able to join us.
BARBARA: Hello Bob. It's fantastic to be with you in this programme for young people.
REPORTER: Well, Barbara, to start with, could you tell our young listeners something about yourself.
10 BARBARA: Certainly. Well, I'm 48 years old, married with two children and was employed as a secretary in a large firm. But now I'm going to open my very own shop. That's quite a big step forward for me, as you can imagine!
REPORTER: Could you tell our listeners exactly what kind of shop you're going to open.
BARBARA: Sure. Well, in my shop I'll be selling trendy clothes for both girls and boys.
15 It's called 'TF', which is short for 'Teenage Fashion'.
REPORTER: Teenage Fashion? Why did you decide to open a shop of this kind?
BARBARA: There's a simple answer to that question: My children are 13 and 16, and as I'm sure you know teenagers need a lot of clothes. But all these clothes are rather expensive. That's why I had the idea of opening a new shop to sell fashionable clothes
20 for the youngsters at really reasonable prices.
REPORTER: That sounds great. I'm sure our young listeners will welcome your idea. Tell me, will you have any special offers when you open your shop next Thursday?

BARBARA: We certainly will – there'll be a 15 % discount on all articles which are sold in the first week.

25 REPORTER: Well, that's a very generous offer, Barbara! But now I think you'd better tell our listeners where they can find you and your shop on the big day, next Thursday.

BARBARA: Well, nobody will have any difficulty finding us. We're just opposite the 'Youth Centre' in Penny Lane.

REPORTER: Thank you Barbara. I'm sure your shop will be a great success. We'll be keep-
30 ing our fingers crossed for you on Thursday. The next song is especially for you, Barbara. Best of luck for your new project.

Worksheets

1   **The following report was recorded by a secretary at a radio station.**

She couldn't really concentrate on her work so there are **12 words** in the text which are not correct. **Mark** these words during the **first listening** by underlining them, and **write** the correct words into the right column during the **second listening**.   (12)

Jobs: Girls want to work with animals, boys want to work with computers	
1 If you had asked a 15-year-old-boy fifty years ago what he wanted to do when he left school, he would certainly have said, "Join the army" or "Be a farmer". A girl of the same age would	
5 maybe have answered, "Train to be a hair-dresser" or "Study to be a scientist". Those were the most popular jobs at that time.	
Today, according to a recent survey, most boys want a job in information technology or en-	
10 gineering, while the most popular job for girls is vet or fashion designer. Interestingly enough, today's young women put the army in second place. A military career, however, doesn't even get into the top ten for boys.	
15 The third choice for boys is lawyer, followed by pop singer and scientist. For girls, typical female jobs – like secretary and hairdresser – take fourth and fifth place.	
The authors also looked at the ideas of 11-year-	
20 olds. The most popular career in this group was footballer for boys and vet for girls. The second places went to policeman for boys and pop singer for girls. In the 1960s, the most popular job for 11-year-olds was the army for boys and	
25 nursing for girls, with the second places taken by footballer and air stewardess.	
Fifty years ago, girls had nun, ballerina and being a mother on their lists of the top ten jobs. Racing driver, taxi driver, plumber and farmer –	
30 careers popular with boys in the 1950s – have almost disappeared from today's top ten list.	

2   Opening a new shop

Listen to the radio interview and take notes in English. You need not write complete sentences, but **one word is not enough.** You will hear the recording twice and after the second listening you will have two minutes to check your answers.

1	Opening date?		(1)
2	Owner's first and last name?		(1)
3	Owner's last job?		(1)
4	Product they sell?		(1)
5	Full name of the shop?		(1)
6	Reason for setting up the new business?		(1)
7	Reduction?		(1)
8	Where is the shop?		(1)

Lösungen

1   *Hinweis: Der abgedruckte Text unterscheidet sich in <u>12 Ausdrücken</u> vom Original auf der CD. Deine Aufgabe ist es nun, die betreffenden Wörter/Begriffe zu finden und die richtigen Lösungen auf die entsprechenden Zeilen rechts neben dem Text einzutragen. Dabei ist gegebenenfalls darauf zu achten, ob die Wörter im Plural, als Adverb oder in einer bestimmten Zeit stehen (Beispiele dafür sind in den Lösungen unterstrichen). Du solltest nicht mehr als die geforderte Anzahl an Wörtern korrigieren, da bei einer größeren Zahl <u>nur die ersten 12</u> gewertet werden.*

line 1:	15	→	16
line 3:	certainly	→	probab<u>ly</u>
line 8:	survey	→	article
line 9:	job	→	career
line 12:	second	→	third
line 16:	typical	→	traditional
line 19:	ideas	→	ambition<u>s</u>
line 23:	1960s	→	1950s
line 24:	for	→	among
line 27:	had	→	include<u>d</u>
line 29:	taxi	→	train
line 31:	almost	→	total<u>ly</u>

2   **Hinweis:** *Im zweiten Teil des Hörverstehenstests geht es um ein Rundfunkinterview mit Barbara, der Inhaberin einer neuen Boutique, die in Kürze eröffnen wird. Du wirst den Text zweimal hören und sollst dabei auf dem Arbeitsblatt die verlangten Informationen ergänzen. Dazu brauchst du aber <u>keine ganzen Sätze</u> zu schreiben, es genügen Stichpunkte (aber jeweils <u>mehr als ein Wort</u>). Nach dem zweiten Textdurchlauf hast du zwei Minuten Zeit, um die Antworten zu ergänzen bzw. zu überprüfen.*

1   Thursday July 17
2   Barbara Sand
3   Secretary in a large firm
4   Trendy clothes for boys and girls/for teenagers
5   Teenage Fashion
6   High costs of the clothes for her own children / Her children's clothes rather expensive – wants to sell trendy clothes at reasonable prices
7   15 % discount on all articles in / during the first week
8   Opposite the youth centre in Penny Lane

Part A
1   Comparing offers   (23)

Sie arbeiten in der Einkaufsabteilung der Firma Sport & Spiel GmbH in Landshut. Es ist geplant, Hockeyschläger neu in das Sortiment aufzunehmen. Es sollen zunächst 200 Stück eingekauft werden. Ihnen liegen zwei Angebote aus England zum Vergleich vor:

Angebot A

The Hockey Master

Makers of fine hockey equipment
22 Lawn Drive Manchester 5MA 2 4HQ
Tel. +44 (161) 47809-411 Fax +44 (161) 47809-422
E-Mail: h.m@firmnet.co.uk

Sport & Spiel GmbH   18 June 2003
Passauer Strasse 121
84034 Landshut
Germany

Dear Sir or Madam

We are pleased to learn from your letter of June 12 that you have seen our advertisement in the *Fitness Journal* and that you are interested in our products.

By separate mail, we are sending you a copy of the new season's catalogue showing a wide range of hockey equipment as well as our export price list quoting prices ex works.

As you are interested in ice hockey sticks, we can offer you the following at very favourable terms:

HOCKEY STICK POWER BLOW
£ 58.50 each

We grant a quantity discount of 20 % for orders of 50 items or more. Delivery can be effected from stock immediately. As this would be your first order we would request payment in advance, but we would also be prepared to offer you a cash discount of 2 %. This offer is valid for one month only.

We are sure you will agree that this offer is very attractive, especially when you consider that the materials we use are of the best quality.

Our sales representative in Bavaria, Mr Michael Butler, would be pleased to show you the outstanding quality of our hockey sticks. We are enclosing his business card. If you should require further information, Mr Butler would be delighted to help you.

We hope our offer meets your expectations and look forward to doing business with you in the near future.

Yours faithfully
H. McKinley
H. McKinley (Mr)
Sales Manager
Enc

Anderson & Palmer Ltd
Wholesalers Games & Sports

- -

101 Island Road, London SW 4 3 BD

Sport & Spiel GmbH   17 June 2003
Passauer Strasse 121
84034 Landshut
Germany

Dear Sir or Madam

Many thanks for your enquiry of June 12 about our ice hockey sticks. As a major British manufacturer of sports equipment with excellent worldwide business contacts, we have been producing first-class hockey sticks for the past 25 years. For your information we are enclosing our current catalogue, which contains many new articles.

We can offer you the SWEEPIE 3000 STICK which has been our best-selling article on the hockey stick market for the last two years. The price of this product is £ 42.50 per item. If your order is received by the end of this month, we can grant you a special seasonal discount of 5 %. Our prices are to be understood CIF Munich.

For orders from abroad please allow 30 days for delivery. Our terms of payment for initial orders would be cash on delivery.

As our prices are expected to rise in autumn 2003, we would advise you to take advantage of these favourable terms.

If you have any further questions, please feel free top contact Ms Joanna White on +44(181)225-9711, who will be able to give you any additional information necessary.
We look forward to receiving your order.

Yours faithfully

Tony Hallamore

Tony Hallamore
Export Sales
Enclosure

Tel. +44(0)207-3301-48 *** Fax +44(0)207-3305-22 ***
E-Mail: AnPa@firmnet.co.uk

Um diese Angebote besser vergleichen zu können, füllen Sie bitte nachstehende Tabelle **in deutscher Sprache** aus, damit Sie die Annahme eines der beiden Angebote empfehlen können. Ist im Angebot ein Punkt nicht angeführt (z. B. wird kein Skonto gewährt), so ist das betreffende Kästchen mit einem Strich zu entwerten. (20)

Angebotsvergleich	Angebot A	Angebot B
Preis pro Stück		
Mengenrabatt		
Skonto		
sonstige Nachlässe		
Lieferbedingung		
Lieferzeit		
Zahlungsbedingung		
Gültigkeit des Angebots		
Art der Anlagen		
Ansprechpartner		

Geben Sie Ihrem Abteilungsleiter eine Empfehlung, welches Angebot akzeptiert werden sollte. Begründen Sie Ihre Entscheidung mit 2 Argumenten, die nicht in der Tabelle aufgeführt sind, aber aus den Angebotsschreiben hervorgehen **(in deutscher Sprache)!** (3)

2 Reading for detail

In-line skating

In-line skating might seem the latest trend in outdoor activities at the moment – but it dates back nearly 300 years. A Dutchman made the first in-line skate in about 1700, to simulate ice-
5 skating out of season, but this idea never really became popular. The roller skate – with wheels arranged side by side instead of "in-line" (that means in one straight line) – was developed in 1863, and the roller skate remained the norm,
10 although a few models based on the "in-line" skate were still produced until 1980.

In that year two ice-hockey-playing brothers from Minnesota, USA, discovered an old in-line skate in a sports shop and decided it would be ideal for out-of-season training. They improved the skate, began manufacturing the first Roller-
15 blades® in the cellar of their parents' house and, during the Eighties, turned them into a multimillion-dollar business. Their company is now owned by Benetton.

In-line skating arrived in Britain in 1984, and it's now the country's fastest-growing sport, with around 400,000 enthusiasts. They are divided into various
20 groups: There are the street-hockey players and, of course, those skaters, who do amazing stunts and dangerous jumps. Then we have the speed skaters who wear cycling helmets and have five wheels instead of four, allowing them to reach up to 40 miles an hour. But the majority of in-line skaters are much less ambitious – they do it at the weekends simply to keep fit and look cool.

Use the information in the text to say whether these sentences are true or false. Tick the correct box ☑!

true false

1. Somebody from northern Germany produced the first in-line skate. ☐ ☐

2. Roller skates have the wheels in two lines. ☐ ☐

3. In-line skating took over from roller-skating immediately after the invention of the first in-line skate. ☐ ☐

4. In 1980 two brothers from Minnesota found an old in-line skate in the basement of their parents' house. ☐ ☐

5. Benetton financed the development of the in-line skates. ☐ ☐

6. Some in-line skaters use skates with four wheels to go faster. ☐ ☐

7. Most skaters regard skating as a way to stay healthy and to impress friends. ☐ ☐ (7)

Part B: Overall Language Proficiency

1   **Fill each gap in the text with one appropriate word from the word bank below. (There are more words in the bank than you need.)**   (13)

Marathon Woman

On Sunday, October 14, Paula Radcliffe_____[1] the finishing line of the Chicago Marathon in the women's world record time of two hours 17 minutes 18 seconds – 89 seconds _____[2] than the previous record.

The 28-year-old runner had already had a very _____[3] year. She had already won _____[4] races, including the London marathon and the European 10,000 metres in Munich.

Paula Radcliffe is _____[5] but very slightly built. She is 1.73 metres _____[6], but weighs only 54 kg. Long-distance runners need plenty of muscle, but as little fat _____[7] possible, so she has a strict diet that builds strength without adding weight.

Her training programme is very _____[8]. When she is _____[9] for a race, she runs 100 miles (160 kilometres) a week – two or three hours every day. Her physical therapist gives her a two-hour treatment session every day to _____[10] her avoid injuries to her muscles and joints that can easily be caused _____[11] such intensive training.

The _____[12] for Paula Radcliffe's hard work have been good. Reports say she was _____[13] $250,000 just to take part in the Chicago Marathon.

> **Word bank:** help – big – crossed – hardly – strong – faster – as – preparing – tall – hard – rewards – paid – much – by – succeeded – than – successful – from – many – fastest

2   **Give synonyms or paraphrase the underlined words or expressions.**

… After that she got another $250,000 for winning the Marathon, plus a Volkswagen car worth $30,000 and $200,000 from her <u>sponsors</u> Nike. Then the world-record breaker took a well-earned rest after Chicago. Her ambitions for the future? She says she would like to <u>win</u> an Olympic <u>title</u>. Her chance to do that will come in 2004, at the Athens Olympics.

(Adapted from an article in Read On December 2002)

1. What are <u>sponsors</u>? _____ (2)

_____

_____

2. Paula Radcliffe says she would like to <u>win</u> an Olympic <u>title</u>. What does that mean? _____ (2)

_____

_____

Auf der Suche nach weiteren Informationen über Paula Radcliffe sind Sie im Internet auf die Seite von www.london-marathon.co.uk gestoßen. Mit den Ergebnissen der online-Übersetzungshilfe Ihrer bevorzugten Suchmaschine waren Sie nicht zufrieden. Nutzen Sie die abgedruckten Wörterbucheinträge, um die unterstrichenen Wörter passend zu übertragen.

cov-er [ˈkʌvə] **I.** *s.* **1.** Decke *f*; Dek-kel *m*; **2.** (Buch)Decke *f*, Einband *m*: from ~ to ~ von Anfang bis Ende; **3.** ˈBriefˌumschlag *m*: *under (the)same* ~ beiliegend; *under separate* ~ mit getrennter Post; *under* ~ *of* unter der (Deck)Adresse von; **4.** ˈSchutzˌumschlag *m*, Hülle *f*, Futteˌral *n*; ˈOber-, Bezug *m*: *loose* ~ loser Bezug *(Stuhl etc.)*; **5.** Gedeck *n (bei Tisch)*; ~ *charge* Kosten für das Gedeck *(ohne Essen)*; **6.** ✗ Deckung *f*: *to take* ~ Deckung nehmen; *air* ~ Luftsicherung; **7.** *hunt.* Dickicht *n*, Lager *n*: *to break* ~ ins Freie treten; **8.** Ob-, Schutzdach *n*: *to get under* ~ sich unterstellen; **9.** *fig.* Schutz *m*: *under* ~ *of night* im Schutz der Nacht; **10.** *fig.* Deckmantel *m*, Vorwand *m*: *under* ~ *of friendship*; ~ *name* Deckname; **11.** ✝ Deckung *f*, Sicherheit *f*; **12.** ⊕ Decke *f*, Mantel *m (Bereifung)*; **13.** Einbeziehung *f*, Einschließung *f*, **II.** *v/t.* **14.** be-, zudecken: *to remain ~ed* den Hut aufbehalten; **15.** *mst pass. ~ed with* voll von; **16.** einhüllen, -wickeln *(with in acc.)*; **17.** be-, überziehen: *~ed button* bezogener Knopf; *~ed wire* umsponnener Draht; **18.** ✗, *a. spart* decken; **19.** *fig.* decken, schützen, sichern *(from vor dat., gegen)*: *to* ~ *o.s.* sich absichern *(against gegen)*; **20.** be-, verdecken, verhüllen, verbergen; **21.** ✝ decken: *to* ~ *the cost*; **22.** ✝ decken, (ver-) sichern; **23.** decken, genügen für; **24.** enthalten, einschließen, umfassen; erfassen; **25.** *Gebiet* bearbeiten, bereisen; **26.** sich erstrecken über *(acc.)*; *Strecke* zurücklegen; **27.** *mit e-r Waffe* zielen auf *(acc.)*, *j-n* in Schach halten; ✗ beherrschen;

dis-a-ble [dɪsˈeɪbl] *v/t.* **1.** unfähig machen, außerˈstand setzen *(from doing s.th. et. zu tun)*; **2.** unbrauchbar *od.* untauglich machen *(for* für, zu*)*; **3.** ✗ a) dienstuntauglich machen, b) kampfunfähig machen; **4.** verkrüppeln; **5.** 🏛 geschäfts- *od.* rechtsunfähig machen; **dis'a-bled** [-ld] *adj.* **1.** 🏛 geschäftsod. rechtsunfähig; **2.** arbeits-, erwerbsunfähig, invaˈlide; **3.** ✗ a) dienstuntauglich, b) kriegsversehrt: *a* ~ *ex-soldier* ein Kriegsversehrter, c) kampfunfähig; **4.** ✗ manövrierunfähig, seeuntüchtig; **5.** *mot.* fahruntüchtig: ~ *car*, **6.** unbrauchbar; **7.** (körperlich *od.* geistig) behindert; **dis'a-ble-ment** [-mənt] *s.* **1.** → *disability* 2, 3; **2.** ✗ a) (Dienst-)Untauglichkeit *f*, b) Kampfunfähigkeit *f*.

en-try [ˈentri] *s.* **1.** Zugang *m*, Zutritt *m*, Einreise *f*; *fig.* Beitritt *m*: ~ *permit* Einreisegenehmigung; ~ *visa* Einreisevisum; *no* ~ Zutritt verboten!; **2.** Eintritt *m*, -gang *m*, -fahrt *f*, -zug *m*, -rücken *n*; **3.** *thea.* Auftritt *m*; **4.** 🏛 Besitzantritt *m*, -ergreifung *f* (upon *gen.*); **5.** ✝, ⚓ Einklarierung *f*: ~ *inwards* Einfuhrdeklaration; **6.** Eintragung *f*, Vermerk *m*; **7.** ✝ Buchung *f*; *credit* ~ Gutschrift; *debit* ~ Lastschrift; *to make an* ~ *(of)*, *(et)* buchen, b) Posten *m*; **8.** *bsd. sport* a) (An)Meldung *f*, Nennung *f*, Teilnahme *f*: ~ *form* (An)Meldeformular, b) → *entrant* 3.

slice [slaɪs] **I.** *s.* **1.** Scheibe *f*, Schnitte *f*, Stück *n*: *a* ~ *of bread*; **2.** *fig.* Stück *n Land etc.*; (An)Teil *m*: *a* ~ *of the profits* ein anteiliger Gewinn; *a* ~ *of luck fig.* e-e Portion Glück; **3.** *(bds.* Fisch)Kelle *f*; **4.** ⊕ Spa(ch)tel *m*; **5.** *Golf:* Schlag *m* mit Rechtsdrall; **II.** *v/t.* **6.** in Scheiben schneiden, aufschneiden: *to* ~ *off Stück* abschneiden; **7.** *a. Luft, Wellen* durchˈschneiden; **8.** *fig.* aufteilen; **9.** *Golf: dem Ball* e-n Rechtsdrall geben; **III.** *v/i.* **10.** Scheiben schneiden; **11.** *Golf:* dem Ball e-n Rechtsdrall geben; ˈslic·er [-sə] *s. (Brot-, Gemüse- etc.)* ˈSchneidemaˌschine *f; (Gurken-, Kraut- etc.)* Hobel *m*.

pace¹ [peɪs] **I.** *s.* **1.** Schritt *m (a. als Maß);* **2.** Gang(art *f) m: to put a horse through its ~s* ein Pferd alle Gangarten machen lassen; *to put s.o. through hist ~s fig.* j-n auf Herz u. Nieren prüfen; **3.** Paßgang *m (Pferd);* **4.** a) ✗ Marschschritt *m,* b) (Marsch)Geschwindigkeit *f,* Tempo *n (a. sport; a. fig. e-r Handlung etc.),* Fahrt *f,* Schwung *m: to go the ~* a) ein scharfes Tempo anschlagen, b) *fig.* flott leben; *to keep ~ with* Schritt halten *od.* mitkommen mit *(a. fig.); to set the ~ sport u. fig.* Schrittmacher sein, das Tempo angeben; *at a great ~* in schnellem Tempo; **II.** *v/t.* **5.** *a. ~out (od. off)* abschreiten; **6.** *Zimmer etc.* durchschreiten, -'messen; **7.** *sport* Schrittmacher sein für; **8.** *Pferd* im Paßgang gehen lassen; **III.** *v/i.* **9.** (ein'her)schreiten; **10.** im Paßgang gehen *(Pferd)*

pace² [peɪsi] *(Lat.) prp.* ohne *(dat.)* nahetreten zu wollen.

pacel-mak-er *s. sport* Schrittmacher *m;* **~mak·ing** *s. sport* Schrittmacherdienste *pl.*

---

1 Last month Paula <u>sliced</u> eight seconds <u>off</u> the World 10 km road record in Puerto Rico.

Im Vormonat _____ Paula in Puerto Rico den Weltrekord über 10 km auf der Straße. (1)

2 The Men's and Women's race will remain separate, but there will be male <u>pacemakers</u> for the Women.

Es bleibt bei getrennten Wettkämpfen für Frauen und Männer, aber bei den Frauen werden Männer als _____ eingesetzt. (1)

3 The Marathon Directors will now be seeking a selection of men who will <u>cover</u> the distance in a time between 2:15 and 2:24.

Die Marathon-Veranstalter suchen nun eine Reihe von Männern, die die Strecke in einer Zeit zwischen 2:15 und 2:24 _____. (1)

4 <u>Entry forms</u> and further information can be obtained here.

_____ und weitere Informationen sind hier erhältlich. (1)

5 <u>Disabled people</u> may contact our special help desk on 020 7902 0189.

Für _____ haben wir unter der 020 7902 0189 einen eigenen Anschluss geschaltet. (1)

Part C: Productive Skills

Vorschlag I

1   Writing a formal letter (18)

Sie sind in der Übungsfirma Ihrer Schule eingesetzt. Die Firma plant eine Modernisierung der Büroausstattung. Sie finden folgende schriftliche Arbeitsanweisung Ihrer Geschäftsführerin, Frau M. Riene vor:

Internes Memo

Datum:	24. Juni 2003	☑ mit der Bitte um Erledigung
an:	Schreib-Pool	☑ zurück an mich
von:	Marga Riene	☑ Anlage: BOS-Online-Werbung

Entwerfen Sie bitte noch heute eine unterschriftsreife Anfrage an Bradford Office Solutions (BOS) in englischer Sprache. Auf dem Ausdruck habe ich einige handschriftliche Anmerkungen angebracht, die Sie bitte in den Entwurf einfließen lassen. Erwähnen Sie dabei auch, dass wir die Anzeige der Internet-Präsenz von BOS entnommen haben und dass wir ein führender Importeur von Büromöbeln mit ausgezeichneten Geschäftsbeziehungen in Bayern sind.

Anlage: Online-Werbung von BOS

www.BOS.co.uk
Bradford Office Solutions

Finding the right office furniture can be a very time consuming job. However, help is at hand! We at Bradford Office Solutions have the answer. We are specialized in all types of office furniture. In particular, among our new wide range of desks you are sure to find the one that fits your needs. We supply our desks in a variety of woods – oak, pine and mahogany at very attractive prices and on highly favourable terms.

As we cannot possibly display all the many styles and makes we have available, we suggest that you get in touch with us as soon as possible so that we can find solutions to your individual needs.

When we have heard from you, we will then send you the details of all our desks so that you and your computer can work in comfort!

aktuellen Farb-Katalog mit der gesamten Produktpalette und neueste Preisliste anfordern!

Infos über Liefer- und Zahlungsbedingungen anfordern!

Nachlässe?

bedeutende Aufträge möglich bei konkurrenzfähigen Konditionen

höflichen Schlusssatz nicht vergessen!

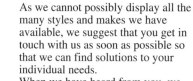

Write your letter on the extra sheet of paper provided by your school!

2 Drawing up a programme (12)

Mit dem italienischen Büromöbel-Produzenten „*Ufficii Fiorentini*" aus Florenz steht die Übungsfirma Ihrer Schule bereits in Geschäftsbeziehungen. Die Korrespondenz zwischen Ihrer Firma und *Ufficii Fiorentini* läuft in englischer Sprache.

Ihre Geschäftsführerin M. Riene empfängt am Dienstag, dem 1. Juli 2003, zwei Vertreter von *Ufficii Fiorentini* zu Unterredungen in Ihrer Übungsfirma. Erst am Freitag, dem 4. Juli, nehmen die italienischen Gäste die Abendmaschine von München zurück nach Florenz.

Die Florentiner besuchen noch weitere Unternehmen in Ihrer näheren Umgebung. An zwei Nachmittagen und einem Abend haben die italienischen Besucher keine geschäftlichen Verpflichtungen.

Das Büro von *Ufficii Fiorentino* ließ deshalb per E-Mail anfragen, welche Aktivitäten Sie als Freizeit-Programm den italienischen Besuchern in Ihrer näheren Umgebung vorschlagen könnten.

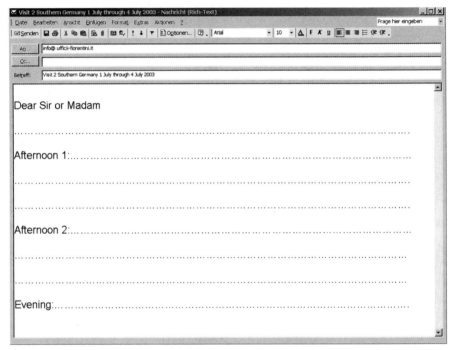

Write your email on the extra sheet of paper provided by your school!

Vorschlag II

1   Writing a report   (18)

Your school has organized a project day on what can be done against violence.
There are eight different groups, each dealing with one aspect of the problem.

Write a report for the English part of your school homepage.
Use <u>three</u> of the following prompts. Write about 80 words.

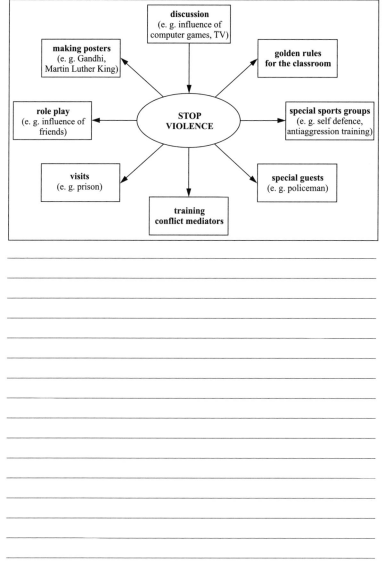

_____

_____

_____

_____

_____

_____

_____

_____

_____

_____

_____

_____

_____

_____

_____

_____

_____

_____

2   Filling in a form   (12)

Ihre Klasse nimmt an einem von der EU geförderten COMENIUS 1 Fremdsprachenprojekt teil. Ihre Partnerschule ist in Bilbao, Spanien. Zu diesem Projekt gehört ein 14-tägiger gegenseitiger Aufenthalt in einer Gastfamilie im Partnerland. Um die passenden Schülerinnen und Schüler und ihre Gasteltern herauszufinden, haben die zuständigen Lehrkräfte ein Formular entworfen, in dem die Jugendlichen ihre persönlichen Daten eintragen und per E-Mail an die Partnerschule schicken. Als gemeinsame Kommunikationssprache wurde Englisch festgelegt, da die Kenntnisse in der jeweils anderen Sprache noch begrenzt sind. Sie sind Teilnehmer dieses Schüleraustausches. Füllen Sie folgendes Formular mit Ihren persönlichen Daten aus.

Personal Details

Photo

Last name: _____

First name: _____

Date of birth: _____

Brothers and sisters: _____

Address: _____

Telephone: _____

Mobile phone (if you have one): _____

E-mail (if you have one): _____

Give information about yourself and your parents *(interests and free time activities – what you like and dislike: food, people, school subjects, ... – place where you live – pets – holidays – your parents' job – ...).* Write about 80 words in complete sentences.

_____

_____

_____

_____

_____

_____

_____

_____

Lösungen

1   *Hinweis: Um die beiden Angebote der englischen Firmen besser vergleichen zu können, sollst du in die vorgegebene Tabelle die entsprechenden Informationen aus Angebot A und B eintragen. Ist im Angebot ein Punkt nicht erwähnt, so ist die Position in der Tabelle durch einen Strich zu entwerten. Als Vorgehensweise empfiehlt es sich, ein Angebot **nach dem anderen** durchzulesen und dabei die entsprechenden Punkte in die Tabelle einzufügen. Du erschwerst dir die Arbeit, wenn du zeilenweise vorgehst und in beiden Briefen gleichzeitig nach der verlangten Information suchst.*
In Klammern findest du, wo nötig, Hinweise auf die entsprechenden Textstellen in den Angeboten.

Angebotsvergleich	Angebot A	Angebot B
Preis pro Stück	58,50 £	45,20 £
Mengenrabatt	20 % *(quantity discount)*	---
Skonto	2 % *(cash discount)*	---
sonstige Nachlässe	---	5 % *(special seasonal discount)*
Lieferbedingung	ab Fabrik/ab Werk *(prices ex works)*	CIF München *(CIF Munich)*
Lieferzeit	sofort *(delivery ... from stock immediately)*	30 Tage *(allow 30 days for delivery)*
Zahlungsbedingung	im Voraus *(payment in advance)*	per Nachnahme *(cash on delivery)*
Gültigkeit des Angebots	einen Monat *(valid for one month only)*	bis Herbst *(prices rise in autumn)*
Art der Anlagen	Visitenkarte *(... business card)*	Katalog *(enclosing current catalogue)*
Ansprechpartner	Michael Butler	Joanna White

Mögliche Empfehlungen für den Abteilungsleiter (mit Begründung/2 Argumente):
Für Angebot A: – Es wird Material von bester Qualität zugesichert.
                     (→ ... the materials we use are of the best quality.)
                – M. Butler, ein Vertreter der Firma, könnte vor Ort informieren und
                     Muster zeigen. (→ Our sales representative ... to help you. / siehe
                     vorletzter Absatz!)

Für Angebot B: – Die Firma besitzt langjährige Erfahrung in der Produktion von Hockey-Schlägern. (→ ... have been producing hockey sticks for the past 25 years.)
– Der angebotene Artikel ist seit zwei Jahren ein Verkaufsschlager. (→ ... has been our best-selling article on the hockey stick market for the last two years.)

2 *Hinweis: Du findest als Lösungshilfe die entsprechenden Textstellen in Kursivdruck in Klammern.*

1. falsch
Hinweis: "A Dutchman made the first in-line skate in about 1700, ..." (Z. 3/4)

2. richtig
Hinweis: „The roller skate – with wheels arranged side by side ..." (Z. 6/7)

3. falsch
Hinweis: „The roller skate - ... – was developed in 1863, ..." (Z. 6–9)

4. falsch
Hinweis: „... discovered an old in-line skate in a sports shop ..." (Z. 12/13)

5. falsch
Hinweis: "They (= The brothers) improved the skates, began manufacturing the first ..." (Z. 14–16)

6. falsch
Hinweis: "... speed skaters ... and have five wheels instead of four, allowing them to reach up ..." (Z. 21–23)

7. richtig
Hinweis: "But the majority of in-line-skaters ... do it ... simply to keep fit and look cool." (Z. 23/24)

Part B: Overall Language Proficiency

1 *Hinweis: Hierbei geht es um allgemeines Textverständnis, d. h. man muss den Sinn des Textes erfassen, um die Sätze mit geeigneten Wörtern vervollständigen zu können. Dazu empfiehlt es sich, den Text erst einmal gründlich durchzulesen. Selbstverständlich muss auch die Bedeutung der in der „word bank" vorkommenden Vokabeln klar sein. Genau überlegen heißt es, wenn in der „word bank" mehrere Wörter aus derselben Wortfamilie auftauchen (z. B. hardly/hard, faster/fastest, succeeded/successful). In so einem Fall muss aus dem Textzusammenhang erschlossen werden, welche Wortart davon geeignet ist.*

1 crossed

2 faster
Hinweis: Da es heißt „world record", muss sie schneller gewesen sein; ein weiterer Hinweis auf den Komparativ „faster" ist „than".

3 successful
Hinweis: Geht aus dem nachfolgenden Textzusammenhang hervor. Da Bezug auf das Nomen „year", muss es sich um ein Adjektiv handeln und nicht um das Verb „succeeded". Eine weitere, noch denkbare Lösung wäre „big".

4 many
Hinweis: Hier ist nur „many" möglich, da Bezug auf das zählbare Nomen „race" im Plural; auf keinen Fall „much"

5 strong

6 tall
Hinweis: nicht möglich: „big" → *bedeutet* „dick"

7 as
Hinweis: „as" *als Teil der Vergleichskonstruktion* „as ... as".

8 hard
Hinweis: Vermeide hier „hardly" → *1. Adjektiv nach* „to be", *2. Andere Bedeutung*

9 preparing
Hinweis: Hier kommt nur das „present participle" *als Teil der* „progressive form" *in Frage.*

10 help

11 by
Hinweis: „by-agent" *vor Objekt im Passivsatz*

12 rewards

13 paid

2   *Hinweis: Eine Hilfe kann bei dieser Aufgabenstellung auch der Textzusammenhang sein.*

1. Sponsors are people who support an athlete / a sportsman / a sports club with money (or/and equipment).
Sponsors are firms or people who give money or/and equipment to an athlete ...
Sponsors support sports clubs in return for advertising on sports shirts etc.

2. This (expression) means (that) Paula Radcliffe would like to get a (gold) medal in a race in the Olympic Games.
It means she wants/would like to get Olympic gold in a race at the Athens Olympics (in 2004).

3   *Hinweis: In den fünf Sätzen dieser Aufgabe ist jeweils ein englischer Begriff unterstrichen, der in der nachfolgenden übersetzten Version fehlt. Mithilfe der abgedruckten Wörterbucheinträge sollst du die betreffenden Wörter gut ins Deutsche übertragen. Du musst also diejenigen Begriffe verwenden, die am besten in den Satzzusammenhang passen.*
Manchmal ist es allerdings notwendig – besonders beim ersten Beispiel „sliced off" – *den geeignetsten Eintrag zusätzlich zu interpretieren bzw. umzudeuten.*

1 Im Vormonat **unterbot / verbesserte** Paula in P. R. den Weltrekord über 10 km auf der Straße.
Hinweis: Der geeignetste Eintrag für **sliced** *eight seconds* **off** *" wäre* „Stück abschneiden", *was aber so nicht im Satzzusammenhang passt. Man überlegt also: Was hat sie abgeschnitten?* → *acht Sekunden vom Weltrekord* → *d. h. sie hat ihn um acht Sekunden* unterboten *oder* verbessert.

2 Es bleibt bei getrennten Wettkämpfen für Männer und Frauen, aber bei den Frauen werden Männer als **Schrittmacher** eingesetzt.

3 Die Marathon-Veranstalter suchen nun eine Reihe von Männern, die die Strecke in einer Zeit zwischen 2:15 und 2:24 **zurücklegen** (können).

4 **Anmeldeformulare** und weitere Informationen sind hier erhältlich.

5 Für **Behinderte/behinderte Menschen** haben wir unter 020 7902 0189 einen eigenen Anschluss geschaltet.

Part C: Productive Skills

Hinweis: Aufgabenteil C besteht aus zwei Vorschlägen, die sich wiederum aus jeweils zwei Aufgaben zusammensetzen. Von den Vorschlägen muss nur einer bearbeitet werden, dieser jedoch komplett. Es ist keine Mischung aus Aufgaben von Vorschlag I und II erlaubt.

Vorschlag I

1 *Hinweis: Markiere sowohl im Memo als auch in der Werbung von BOS alle Fakten, die du in die Anfrage einfließen lassen sollst, damit du nachher nichts davon vergisst. Achte beim Entwurf auf eine sinnvolle Anordnung der einzelnen Punkte. Es lohnt sich, die Werbung aufmerksam durchzulesen, da man die eine oder andere Vokabel im Brief verwenden kann.*

Im folgenden Lösungsvorschlag finden sich in Klammern z. T. Alternativen oder Ergänzungen.

June 24, 2003

Dear Sirs, (Dear Sir or Madam)

We discovered (saw) your advertisement on your website and were very impressed by it. (Your internet presence gave us the opportunity to read your advertisement, which seems very interesting to us.)

As we are a leading importer of office furniture with excellent business relations in Bavaria, we always look for good manufacturers on this market. Therefore we would like you to send us (We would appreciate very much if you sent us) your latest coloured catalogue with your complete range of products as well as your current price-list. Please let us also know your terms of delivery and payment (and if there are any discounts). Do you grant any discounts such as cash or quantity discount etc.?

Due to our good business relations we would place regular major (= large) orders (... we can guarantee regular ...) if you can offer competitive (= favourable) terms (if your terms are competitive).

We are looking forward to hearing from you soon (and starting new business relations).

Yours sincerely,

2 *Hinweis: Du wählst am besten Ziele in deiner oder um deine Schulstadt (bzw. Heimatstadt), die für die italienischen Gäste von touristischem Interesse sein könnten (Sehenswürdigkeiten). Gib dazu evtl. kurze Anmerkungen. Weniger geeignet sind Firmenbesuche (Freizeitprogramm, keine geschäftl. Verpflichtungen!).*

Für den Abend empfiehlt sich der Besuch einer Party für die Gäste oder eines Volksfestes (am besten Typisches, Traditionelles). Theaterbesuche eignen sich wegen der vermutlich geringen Deutschkenntnisse (Korrespondenz in englischer Sprache!) kaum, eher schon ein Konzertbesuch.

Dear Sir or Madam

For the time in which you are not involved in business we suggest the following activities:

Afternoon 1: Trip to Landshut, the capital of Lower Bavaria, about 60 kilometres from Eggenfelden: Tour of the old city district and visit to the famous Landshut castle, Italian-speaking guide

Afternoon 2: Trip to Salzburg, one of Austria's most beautiful cities, about 70 km from Eggenfelden: birthplace and home of the famous composer W. A. Mozart; guided tour of the city, time for shopping

Evening: Visit to a "Volksfest", something like the smaller copy of the Munich Oktoberfest, or to a "Wirtshaus", the Bavarian version of a pub. Enjoy typical Bavarian food and music as well as Bavarian beer.

Alternative: Summernight party at our school with music, theatre (in English), food and drinks

Vorschlag II

1 *Hinweis: Hier sollst du einen Bericht für den Englischteil der Schul-Homepage schreiben und dazu <u>drei beliebige</u> der sprachlichen Vorgaben verwenden. Selbstverständlich musst du Letztere genauer ausführen, um auf die geforderte Wortzahl zu kommen. Überlege dir also gut, zu welchen drei der Vorgaben dir genügend Brauchbares einfällt.*
Der folgende Lösungsvorschlag enthält <u>mehr als drei Punkte</u>, was dir eine größere Auswahl an Formulierungsmöglichkeiten bietet. (Es handelt sich dabei um Auszüge aus Berichten von Schülern, die entsprechend verbessert wurden, es kommen also keine „abgehobenen" bzw. besonders schwierige Formulierungen vor.)

Our school has organized a project day on what can be done against violence. This is a report which points out different ways which can help to stop violence, so that people can live together in peace.

One thing that can be done by a class is to invite a special guest such as a policeman, who can give examples for violent actions from his experience and explain to the students that there is severe punishment for violence against others. You can also act out scenes of violence in a role play showing the bad influence of false friends in difficult situations or the influence of good friends who try to solve a problem without fighting other people. Having the right friends who don't look for trouble can help you to avoid turning a quarrel into a violent action. Visiting a jail can help in two ways. If you talk to prisoners, you will sometimes hear that they got involved in fights and hurt somebody without really having the intention to do so. This will show you that almost everybody can get into severe trouble. Besides seeing the conditions in a prison by yourself may frighten you and cause you to keep away from violence.

A good thing to start with would be to develop/write golden rules for the classrooms. This means you fix rules which every student in class has to follow/accept. One rule could be not to interrupt a classmate while talking when you are not of the same opinion or not to call somebody names or insult him when you are angry with him.

Of course you should discuss about the bad influence of quite a lot of computer games or violent films on TV, because too many people play these games or watch these films and often get influenced by all the violence they meet. Quite often they get the idea that using violence in a conflict is quite normal.

A good thing would be to make researches about the lives of famous people like Martin Luther King or Mahatma Gandhi who managed to make non-violent revolutions. You could make posters with pictures and the ideas of these people and fix them to a wall in your classroom.

2   *Hinweis: Du sollst hier die geforderten Angaben zu deiner Person eintragen und an-schließend in ganzen Sätzen bestimmte Informationen über dich und deine Familie er-gänzen. Versuche dabei nichts Kompliziertes zu formulieren und beschränke dich auf Dinge, die deinen Wortschatz nicht übersteigen.*
Wenn man nur ca. 80 Wörter schreibt, reduzieren sich die persönlichen Informationen fast auf Stichpunkte bzw. sehr knappe einfache Sätze, doch dürfte dies nicht zu einem Punktabzug führen. Bei „holidays" könnte man natürlich auch nur schreiben, wann die nächsten Ferien sind.

Personal Details

Photo	Last name: Mustermann
	First name: Kathrin
	Date of birth: May 7, 1987
	Brothers and sisters: 2; Sabine (18), Sebastian (14)

Address: Mustergasse 11, 00009 Musterbach

Telephone: → *your phone number*

Mobile phone (if you have one): → *your number*

E-mail (if you have one): ---

Give information about yourself and your parents:

I am especially interested in music and sports. In my free time I play the guitar, read novels, go swimming or skating and play tennis.

I like Greek and Italian food, but I hate fish. I like people you can talk to and who listen to you, but I hate people who don't tell the truth.

At school I like geography, history, sports and English, but I hate German.

The place where I live is a small town in Lower Bavaria with about 5,000 inhabitants. There is a good sports club, but we have no disco or youth centre.

We have two pets in our home, two cats, who usually sleep on the sofa in my room.

In my next holidays I will work in an office for three weeks and then I will travel to France with my family.

My father is a police officer in a bigger town about 8 km from here and my mother works as a secretary in a big company. We are a happy family and I can talk to my parents whenever I have a problem.

Tapescript zu Worksheet 1

ANITA F: Good morning; Rocky Valley Holiday Camp. Anita Feldman here. How can I help you?

DAVID: Oh, er, good morning. My friend and I are thinking of spending two weeks at the Rocky Valley Holiday Camp in August and …

5 ANITA F: I'm sure you'll have the time of your life. A day at our camp is definitely action packed with fun, friends and new experiences at every turn.

DAVID: Well, can I ask …

ANITA F: Between 9 and 5 o'clock there are five activity periods. The type of activities varies according to the age group. All campers have three instructional classes, one
10 elective and one period of free time.

DAVID: And what about the evenings?

ANITA F: Oh, you'll just love our evening activities. There's never a boring moment at the Rocky Valley Holiday Camp – and that goes for the evenings, too. After dinner comes the exciting evening programme, which varies from night to night. Camp fires, talent
15 shows – you name it, we've got it. And a snack is served midway through the evening activities. You'll just love it.

DAVID: What exactly are the instructional classes?

ANITA F: Well, in our instructional classes – with qualified sports instructors – you can do water skiing, horseback riding, sailing, climbing, basketball, jazz dance or wrestling
20 and lots of other elective periods each day, and electives are chosen upon arrival at the camp.

DAVID: I see, and what are the electives?

ANITA F: Well, each camper attends a different elective each day and this makes it possible for everyone to get to know the wide range of activities our holiday camp has to
25 offer. They vary slightly from week to week, but our offers always include canoe trips, sailing on our 39-foot sailboat, speedboat tours, the climbing tower, a movie and special crafts like pottery and painting.

DAVID: And what can I do when I'm not doing an elective or I'm not in an instructional class?

30 ANITA F: Basically – whatever you want. Swim, sunbathe at the pool, eat a snack at the Rocky Valley snack bar, shop for a souvenir at the camp store, go on a mountain bike trail ride – the options are endless. And what's more, all these activities at our holiday camp are centrally located – within a ten minute walk of the central administration building.

35 DAVID: There are still a few things I'd like to know about the instructional classes.

ANITA F: Well, why not contact us at our web site: RockyValley – that's one word – dot holiday dash camp dot ca.

Tapescript zu Worksheet 2

FLIGHT CAPTAIN:

- Good morning ladies and gentlemen. I'm Captain Larry Smith and my First Officer is Marcos Williams. Stephanie, James, Margaret, Stacey, Bob and Jane are your flight attendants today. We would like to welcome you on board Ontario Air flight 901 to
5   Toronto and are happy that you are flying with us today. The weather is ideal. No heavy winds, no clouds, it's sunny. On behalf of Ontario Air we would like to apologize for the short delay. We are still waiting for a passenger to board the aircraft, so we'll be taking off in about 10 minutes.
- I'll be back with you to tell you more about our flight route as soon as we've reached
10   our cruising altitude of 30,000 feet. Now, here's Stephanie with some more information.

FIRST FLIGHT ATTENDANT STEPHANIE:

- Good morning ladies and gentlemen. My name is Stephanie and I'm the First Flight Attendant on board today. Shortly after we are in the air, we will be serving a soft
15   drink and a light snack. Later, we will be offering you lunch. Please do not hesitate to ask for any non-alcoholic drinks at any time.
- The small screen in the seat in front of you can be programmed by the controls in your armrest. We offer seven different movies to choose from, each one is in English or in French and in a few minutes you can lie back and watch the film of your choice.
20 - Soon we will be offering you a number of duty-free items. This week's special offer is an mp3-player.
- In just a few minutes we will be showing you our safety instruction video which will give you important information, including information about the oxygen-masks and life-jackets under your seats. In case of emergency, please remember that for safety
25   reasons you will be asked to leave all of your belongings behind and exit as quickly as possible. My colleagues will now show the emergency exits on our plane. Please note the one nearest to your seat.
- So that we can get ready for take-off, please make sure that you have placed all hand luggage under the seat in front of you or in the luggage compartment above your seat.
30   And now please fasten your seat belts and keep them fastened until the seat belt sign is switched off. Put your seats in an upright position and make sure all tray tables are folded up and locked. We would like to remind you that there is no smoking on Ontario Air flights.
- Thank you for flying with Ontario Air.

Worksheets

1   **A typical day at Rocky Valley Holiday Camp**

You and your friend David are interested in summer camps for a group of youngsters. While David is phoning someone from The Rocky Valley holiday camp, you are listening over the loudspeaker of the phone. Afterwards you check the notes David has taken.

Read the notes carefully first. Then listen to the text twice and check if the statements are right or wrong. Tick the correct box. Finally write down the website address.

You will hear the recording twice and after the second listening you will have one minute to check your answers.   (8)

		true	false	
1.	The morning at the camp is divided into five activity periods.	☐	☐	(1)
2.	The evening programme is the same every night.	☐	☐	(1)
3.	It is possible to get something to eat during the evening programme.	☐	☐	(1)
4.	In the instructional classes you can only do outdoor activities.	☐	☐	(1)
5.	Sailing and canoe trips are only offered from time to time.	☐	☐	(1)
6.	For activities like shopping or swimming you don't have to leave the camp.	☐	☐	(1)

David has forgotten to take down the website of the camp.

7. Write down the website address giving more details about the instructional classes:
http://www._____   (2)

2   Airline flight to Canada

You are a German scout group leader. Together with a party of twelve other
scouts you are on your way to a holiday camp in Toronto, Canada. You had to
stop over at Heathrow Airport, London. At this moment you're listening to the
announcements by the Flight Captain and First Flight Attendant before take-off.
Laura, a young member of the scout group, is sitting next to you. Laura's knowledge of English is not very good, so she asks you for help.
Answer Laura's questions **in German** by taking notes while listening. You
needn't write down complete sentences, but one word is not enough. You will
hear the announcements twice and after the second listening you will have
two minutes to check your answers.

L.: *Mir wird so leicht schlecht. Wie wird das Wetter während des Fluges?*	G.:	(2)
L.: *Wir sollten doch schon lange in der Luft sein. Wieso geht's denn nicht los?*	G.:	(1)
L.: *Wie hoch, hat der Kapitän gesagt, werden wir fliegen?*	G.:	(1)
L.: *Was gibt's zu essen und zu trinken?*	G.:	(3)
L.: *In welchen Sprachen werden die Filme gezeigt?*	G.:	(2)
L.: *Was gibt es Besonderes im Duty-Free Verkauf?*	G.:	(1)
L.: *Was zeigen die zwei Stewardessen da vorne jetzt?*	G.:	(1)
L.: *Wie lange, hat sie gesagt, müssen wir angeschnallt bleiben?*	G.:	(1)

Lösungen

1   *Hinweis: Der abgedruckte Text gibt den Inhalt eines Telefongesprächs wieder, wobei du mehrere Aussagen dazu auf ihre Richtigkeit beurteilen und schließlich die vollständige und korrekte Internetadresse des Holiday Camps angeben sollst. Wichtig ist konzentriertes Zuhören bzw. Lesen, damit man nicht auf kleine Fallen in der Formulierung hereinfällt.*

	true	false
1. The morning at the camp is divided into five activity periods.	☐	☒

    Hinweis: Zu beachten ist hier, dass zwar im Text „five activity periods" genannt sind, aber nicht „in the morning", sondern „between 9 and 5 o'clock".

	true	false
2. The evening programme is the same every night.	☐	☒
3. It is possible to get something to eat during the evening programme.	☒	☐
4. In the instructional classes you can only do outdoor activities.	☐	☒
5. Sailing and canoe trips are only offered from time to time.	☐	☒
6. For activities like shopping or swimming you don't have to leave the camp.	☒	☐

7. Website address: http://www.**rockyvalley.holiday-camp.ca**
    Hinweis: Um die Internetadresse richtig schreiben zu können, muss man zwei wichtige Begriffe kennen, nämlich „dot" für „Punkt" und „dash" für „(Binde)Strich".

2   *Hinweis: Im zweiten Teil des Hörverstehenstests geht es um zwei Lautsprecherdurchsagen im Flugzeug. Dazu soll man auf Deutsch die Fragen eines Gruppenmitglieds, das nicht gut Englisch spricht, beantworten. Es müssen keine vollständigen Sätze formuliert werden, doch ein einzelnes Wort pro Frage genügt auch nicht.*

G.:   ideal, kein starker Wind, keine Wolken, sonnig
G.:   ein Passagier noch nicht an Bord/fehlt noch
G.:   30.000 Fuß
G.:   – alkoholfreie Getränke/Limonaden
       – kleine Mahlzeit/kleiner Imbiss
       – Mittagessen
G.:   in englischer und französischer Sprache
G.:   einen mp-3 Spieler/Player
G.:   die Notausgänge
G.:   bis die Sicherheitsgurtanzeige nicht mehr aufleuchtet

Part A

1   **Reading for specific information**   (13)

Im Unterricht sollen Kurzreferate über verschiedene Internetunternehmen ge-
halten werden. Um die Konkurrenten besser vergleichen zu können, haben Sie
sich mit Ihren Mitschülern vorab auf nachstehendes Inforaster geeinigt.
Füllen Sie dieses Raster mit Informationen über die Firma EZBuy (siehe
nächste Seite) **in deutscher Sprache** aus.

Gesuchte Informationen	Auswertung
Mit welchem Produkt begann die Erfolgsgeschichte des Unternehmens? Zu welchem Preis wurde es verkauft?	• .... • ....
Ergänze die folgenden Kennzahlen des Unternehmens: a) Marktanteil: b) Gewinn: c) Anzahl der Gegenstände, die durchschnittlich jährlich zum Verkauf angeboten werden:	 a) .... b) .... c) ....
Durch welche Einnahmen finanziert sich die Firma?	....
Wo wurde normalerweise die Ware angeboten, bevor es den Online-Anbieter gab?	• .... • ....
Aus welchen Gründen verkaufen Menschen ihre Gegenstände bei dieser Firma?	• .... • .... • ....
Welche Probleme können beim Online-Handel auftreten?	• .... • ....

EZBuy – the flea market on the internet

The world's biggest internet auction house has come a long way since it started with the sale of a second hand camera in 1998.

Do you want to buy a cheap computer? Or a designer dress? Or a train set for your little brother? Or maybe you would like to get rid of an old stamp collec-
5 tion, you think might be worth something, some clothes that are as good as new but don't fit you any more, or a DVD player you don't need any more?

Anyone with a computer and a link to the internet knows the best place to buy or sell any of the above items – EZBuy, one of the most interesting online auc-tion houses. While many internet companies have disappeared after making big
10 losses, EZBuy has been a huge success.

The company plays a major role in the online auction market. EZBuy makes its money by taking a share of every deal on the site.

ONLINE AUCTION MARKET SHARE

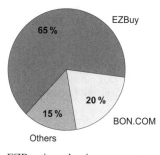

EZBuy in numbers worldwide in 2002

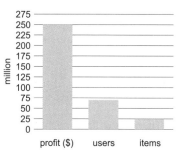

EZBuy is a classic success story of the computer age. The company was set up in 1998 by a student in Silicon Valley, California. The first thing he offered was
15 a second hand camera. Someone agreed to pay $30 for it, and the business took off.

For most users it is the ideal place to buy and sell stuff that you would normally find at flea markets or in the newspaper small ads. But now you can buy really expensive things like houses and cars on EZBuy.

20 Some people have even found that they can make a living by selling things on EZBuy. Around 10,000 earn their money to pay their bills in this way. Many more use EZBuy as a way to boost their incomes.

The system is built on trust. You trust the person you buy from to send you good quality items. The seller relies on the buyer to pay him or her. The risks
25 are not as great as you might think. Customers report on the quality of the sellers' goods and there is a secure credit card payment system which customers can use.

There are, of course, people who try to sell stolen goods and they are difficult to trace because they use false identity cards. EZBuy says that although a number
30 of people do this it is not however, a major problem.

You are doing a period of work experience at the firm *Outdoor Sports & More*. It is part of your job to help Ms Elaine Waters by filling in standardized forms that deal with complaints. Elaine has given you the following letter of complaint.
Fill in the form on page on the next page, adding comments where necessary.

Outdoor Sports & More
attn. Ms Elaine Waters
74 Summer Lane
Birmingham BH3 8GR
England

St Albans Scouts
16 Hythe Road
St Albans
Herfortshire
AL3 6DU
email: info@albanscouts.org

14 June, 2004

Our order no. 0351 of 10 May, 2004

Dear Ms Waters

Today we have finally received your consignment of various outdoor items – 3 days after the date you had promised us. The items delivered are, unfortunately, not at all to our satisfaction.

- The 6 kits of light-weight cooking equipment are all incomplete (the knives are missing).
- Some of the tents delivered are of a very poor quality.
- You sent us only 8 rain-proof windbreakers in size L, although we had offered 12 (8 in size L, 4 in size M).
- The colour of the sleeping-bags is completely different from the colours shown in the catalogue (light blue instead of the dark blue we wanted).
- The fleece jumpers have got the wrong logo (we wanted "Albans Scouts" but you printed "Albanian Scouts").

We are prepared to keep the sleeping-bags if you grant us a reasonable price reduction, but the tents and the fleece jumpers are unfortunately of no use to us at all. We are therefore sending them back at your expense, together with the incomplete cooking equipment. Please replace the jumpers and the cooking equipment as soon as possible. We would also be grateful if you could send us the jumpers and the cooking equipment as well as the missing windbreakers by express freight. Please inform us immediately by email if you agree to our suggestions. We do hope this unpleasant matter can be settled soon.

Yours sincerely

Emma Thompson

---

date of the complaint ....

order number ....

customer's name ....

delay in delivery ☐ no

☐ yes   details ....

reason(s) of complaint	products	details
damaged goods	....	
wrong articles	....	
bad quality	....	
wrong quality / missing goods	....	
wrong prices	....	
others	....	

customer's suggestion(s)	products
price reduction	....
replacement	....
additional supply	....
cancellation	....

next step(s) to take

☐ telephone call   ☐ email

☐ fax   ☐ visit

Part B: Overall Language Proficiency

1   **Multiple Choice**   (14)

A girl from your scouts group wants to send a letter in English to Louise from Ontario. Louise spent a lot of time with you and your group. Your friend's English is not really good, so she asks you to help her to **choose the right expressions. Underline them for her.**

To
Louise DeFabre
55 Mersham Road
Muirkirk
NOL 1XO
Canada

Dear Louise,

I've been back in Germany (**since / for / from**) two weeks now. But I've been so busy that I couldn't write to you before.

First of all I'd like to thank you very much for (**make / to make / making**) our stay in Toronto so enjoyable. It was very (**nicely / nice / beautiful**) of you to spend so much time showing us the sights of this wonderful city. What a shame that we didn't have time to go up the (**interested / interest / interesting**) CNN tower in Toronto. Never mind! Perhaps we will visit your great city again one day.

Do you (**remind / remember / forget**) Michael Keller? He's the boy (**whom / who / which**) was sitting at the next table in the restaurant we went to on our last day – the boy (**who / who's / whose**) grandparents live in Canada. You know, he told us that he was visiting (**they / them / their**). Well, a few days ago I (**received / have received / was receiving**) a letter from him and yesterday I (**get / got / became**) a phone call from him, too. He says that he and his brother Andreas would like to come to Munich in September. They want us (**go / to go / going**) shopping with them: Michael says they have to buy a *Dirndl* for their grandmother in Canada. And, of course, they are planning to visit the *Oktoberfest*. They will be travelling from Hamburg to Munich with the *ICE* train. We will pick them up at the station. As you know, we have (**lent / rented / borrowed**) a flat (**nearby / near / nearly**) Neuhauser Straße – one of Munich's biggest shopping areas. So (**much / many / money**) people go there to buy all sorts of things. That's why we've decided to do some shopping with Michael and Andreas there.

Well, that's all for now.

Very best wishes to you and your family,
Susanne Kaufmann

2 Giving explanations (6)

Two weeks later Susanne gets a postcard from Canada:

> Dear Susanne
>
> Thank you for your letter. It was lovely hearing from you. There were, however, a few words I didn't understand: *Oktoberfest*, *ICE* and *Dirndl*. Could you explain them to me?
>
> Yours
>
> Louise

Please help Susanne and **give explanations for these three words**:

Oktoberfest _____

_____

ICE _____

_____

Dirndl _____

_____

Part C: Productive Skills

Vorschlag I

1 Getting your opinion across (12)

Josée Taffet aus Montréal, Kanada, war mit Ihnen im kanadischen Ferienlager. Leider haben Sie Josées Adresse verlegt. Über den Online-Jahresbericht von Josées kanadischer Schule finden Sie die Anschrift wieder.
Auf der Homepage der Schule sehen Sie nebenstehendes Bild.

Verfassen Sie ein **kurzes persönliches** Schreiben an Josée **in englischer Sprache**, in dem Sie

– sich erkundigen, ob Uniformen an kanadischen Schulen Pflicht sind;
– berichten, dass neuerdings auch in einigen deutschen Schulen Uniformen auf freiwilliger Basis getragen werden;
– Ihre persönliche Haltung zu Schuluniformen zum Ausdruck bringen. (Begründen Sie Ihre Meinung).

Please write the body of your message on an extra sheet of paper provided by your school.

2   Writing a formal letter (18)

Ihre Gruppe möchte erneut nach Nordamerika reisen, dieses Mal weiter in den Westen. Josée empfahl Ihnen dazu folgende Internet-Adresse:

"See wildlife in Canada's Yukon Territory. This month, parks are just opening up for the summer, making it a perfect time to see things before the crowds arrive. You can see moose, caribou, bears, sheep, coyotes, wolves and more here. The Yukon Territory is also a good place for courses in climbing mountains and canoeing.
www.canadanow.ca or mail to: yukon@canadanow.ca"

Verfassen Sie eine **Anfrage** per E-Mail in **englischer Sprache**, in der Sie

- auf die obige Quelle Bezug nehmen;
- sich als Leiter/in einer Pfadfinder-Gruppe von 15 Jugendlichen vorstellen, die im Frühjahr 2005 eine Reise in das Yukon-Gebiet planen;
- sich nach den dortigen Wetterverhältnissen im Frühjahr erkundigen;
- um ein Angebot für eine 10tägige Wandertour mit Führer ab/bis Vancouver bitten;
- ausführliches Begleitmaterial zur Information der Reisegruppe anfordern, besonders mit Empfehlungen für angemessene Bekleidung;
- die Anfrage höflich beenden.

Please write <u>the body</u> of your message on an extra sheet of paper provided by your school.

Vorschlag II

1 Filling in a form (12)

Aufgrund des verspäteten Rückflugs aus Kanada musste Ihre Gruppe am 17. August letzten Jahres einmal im „Queen's & Knight's" in London Heathrow übernachten, bevor es weiter nach München gehen konnte. Bei der Gepäckausgabe am Münchner Flughafen warten Sie vergeblich auf Ihre hellblaue Reisetasche. Darin befanden sich neben Reisemitbringseln auch Ihr Tagebuch, Ihr Fotoapparat und Medikamente. In der Hektik des Aufbruchs hatten Sie Ihr Gepäckstück in Ihrem Zimmer 4714 des Flughafenhotels in London vergessen.

Auf Ihre telefonische Rückfrage hat Ihr Hotel Ihnen ein Formular zugefaxt. Füllen Sie dieses Formular auf nachstehender Seite sorgfältig aus.

→

2 Reporting/Telling a story (18)

Zwei Wochen nach Ihrer Kanada-Reise finden Sie zu Hause einen Brief von Josée aus Montréal, Kanada vor. Josée, mit Ihnen Gast im kanadischen Ferienlager, möchte wissen, wie Sie den tagelangen Stromausfall zum Zeitpunkt des Rückflugs Ihrer Gruppe gemeistert hatten.

The Toronto Star:

Two nights in the dark

Verfassen Sie ein **persönliches Schreiben** an Josée **in englischer Sprache**, in welchem Sie in **mindestens 80 Wörtern** über Ihren Rückflug berichten.

Ihr Schreiben sollte auf folgende Punkte eingehen:

– Auf welche Schwierigkeiten stießen Sie und Ihre Gruppe am Flughafen Toronto während des Stromausfalls?
– Welche Sorgen machten Sie sich persönlich als Gruppenleiter/in in Toronto? Welche Ängste trugen Mitglieder Ihrer Gruppe an Sie heran?
– Wie wurden Sie mit Ihrer Gruppe nach der erheblich verspäteten Landung am Flughafen München von Ihren Angehörigen empfangen?

Please write your message on an extra sheet of paper provided by your school.

Queen's & Knight's
Lost and Found Desk

If you're not satisfied, we're not satisfied.

Thank you for choosing the Heathrow **Queen's & Knight's** for your recent trip.
We will do our best to find and forward your precious items to your home address.

To help us, we would be grateful if you could fill in this form.

1	**Items have been**	☐ **lost**	**or**	☐ **found**	

2.1 Room No. was: **QK-LHR-**_____

2.2 Check-in was on _____ (yy-mm-dd)

2.3 Check-out was on _____ (yy-mm-dd)

3 No. of items: ☐ **1 only** ☐ **please specify** _____

3.1 Kind of item(s)?

☐ Passport/ID ☐ Ticket/Voucher ☐ Credit/Debit Card

☐ Luggage ☐ Clothing ☐ None of the above

3.2 Please <u>describe</u> the item(s) as precisely as you can.

....

....

3.3 Please state the <u>contents</u> of the item(s).

....

....

....

4 Personal Details

4.1 Surname_____ ☐ Mr ☐ Ms

4.2 Given name(s) _____

4.3 Address _____

4.4 City _____ Post code _____

4.5 Email _____@_____

4.6 Day Time Phone No. _____

Please return ASAP by fax to +44 (022) 555 7989

Lösungen

1 *Hinweis:* Um die die verlangten Informationen zu erhalten, sollte man bereits **vor** dem Durchlesen des Textes die Fragen genau studieren, sodass man anschließend im Text gleich entsprechende Stellen markieren kann. Dies ist vor allem deshalb wichtig, weil die Informationen nicht in chronologischer Reihenfolge und – wie bei der zweiten und der vorletzten Frage – nicht zusammengefasst an einer Stelle im Text zu finden sind. Beachten ist zudem, dass sowohl der Text wie auch die Diagramme ausgewertet werden müssen.

Gesuchte Informationen	Auswertung
Mit welchem Produkt begann die Erfolgsgeschichte des Unternehmens?	• **Verkauf einer gebrauchten Kamera**
Zu welchem Preis wurde es verkauft?	• **$ 30**
Ergänze die folgenden Kennzahlen des Unternehmens:	
a) Marktanteil:	a) **65 %**
b) Gewinn:	b)**$ 250 Millionen** (= *profit*)
c) Anzahl der Gegenstände, die durchschnittlich jährlich zum Verkauf angeboten werden:	c)**$ 25 Millionen** (= *items*)
Durch welche Einnahmen finanziert sich die Firma?	**Das Auktionshaus bekommt bei jeder Auktion einen Anteil an der Verkaufssumme.** (… *by taking a share of every deal on the site*)
Wo wurde normalerweise die Ware angeboten, bevor es den Online-Anbieter gab?	• **auf Flohmärkten** • **über Kleinanzeigen (in Zeitungen)** (… *in the newspaper small ads*)
Aus welchen Gründen verkaufen Menschen ihre Gegenstände bei dieser Firma?	• **um sich ihren Lebensunterhalt zu verdienen** (→ *can make a living by selling things on EZBuy*) • **um ihr Einkommen aufzubessern** (→ *use … a way to boost their incomes*) • **um Dinge loszuwerden, die sie nicht mehr gebrauchen können** (→ *Or maybe you would like to get rid of …*)
Welche Probleme können beim Online-Handel auftreten?	• **Es werden gestohlene Waren angeboten.** • **Es wird eine falsche Identität benutzt.**

2 *Hinweis:* Bei dieser Aufgabe geht es um das Ausfüllen eines Standardformulars zum Erfassen der wesentlichen Mängel und Ausführungsvorschläge, die ein Kunde in seiner

Mängelrüge aufgeführt hat. Zudem sollen, wenn notwendig, Anmerkungen (hier: „details") ergänzt werden.

date of the complaint ....*14 June, 2004*...............................

order number ....*0351*...............................

customer's name ......*Emma Thompson*...............................

delay in delivery   ☐ no

            ☒ yes   details ...*three days*.........................

reason(s) of complaint	**products**	**details**
damaged goods		
wrong articles	*sleeping bags*	*wrong colour*
	fleece jumpers	*wrong logo*
bad quality	*tents*	
wrong quality / missing goods	*windbreakers*	*4 in size M are missing*
	cooking equipment	*knives are missing*
wrong prices		
others		

customer's suggestion(s)	**products**
price reduction	*sleeping bags*
replacement	*jumpers, cooking equipment*
additional supply	*4 windbreakers in size M*
cancellation	*tents*

next step(s) to take

☐ telephone call   ☒ email

☐ fax   ☐ visit

Part B: Overall Language Proficiency

1   *Hinweis: Im vorliegenden Brief findest du an verschiedenen Stellen jeweils drei Wör-*
ter/Ausdrücke zur Auswahl, wobei es immer nur eine richtige Lösung gibt. Manchmal
geht es dabei darum, die richtige Vokabel auszuwählen, dann wiederum ist die richtige
Verbform (Zeit, Infinitiv, Gerund) zu finden oder zwischen Adjektiv und Adverb zu ent-
scheiden, also eine Mischung aus Wortschatz- und Grammatikarbeit. Hinweise auf die
richtige Lösung findet man immer im Textzusammenhang, also in der Regel in der un-
mittelbaren Umgebung der Klammerausdrücke.

Im Folgenden findest du die betroffenen Sätze aus dem Brief mit den richtigen Lösun-
gen in Fettdruck. Die unterstrichenen Stellen liefern Hinweise für die jeweilige Ent-
scheidung und in Klammern stehen z. T. zusätzliche Erläuterungen.

Dear Louise,

I've been back in Germany **for** two weeks now *(„for" in Zusammenhang mit Present*
Perfect).

First of all I'd like to <u>thank</u> you very much <u>for</u> **making** *(Gerund nach Verb + Präp.)*
our stay in Toronto so enjoyable.

It <u>was</u> very **nice** *(Der Kontext verbietet „beautiful" als Lösung/Entscheidung für Adj.,*
da prädikative Ergänzung zum Hilfsverb „to be" → *was)* of you to spend ...

What a shame that we didn't have time to go up the **interesting** *(einzige Möglichkeit*
von der Wortbedeutung her) CNN tower ...

Do you remember *(einzig richtige Wortbedeutung/„remind" wäre „jem. erinnern")*
Michael Keller?

He's the boy **who** was sitting ... *(Relativpronomen SUBJEKT des Rel.Satzes/ "which"*
nur für Dinge)

... the boy **whose** <u>grandparents</u> *(Relativpronomen in Possessivform/Bezug zu „grand-*
parents") live in Canada.

... that he was visiting **them** *(Personalpronomen in Objektstellung)*

Well, a few days <u>ago</u> I **received** *(Simple Past wg. „ago") ...* and <u>yesterday</u> I **got** a
phone call *(Simple Past wg. des Signalworts „yesterday"/became = false friend* →
andere Bedeutung)

They <u>want us</u> **to go** *(to-Infinitiv nach best. Verben + Objekt)* shopping with them.

As you know, we <u>have</u> **rented** a <u>flat</u> *(vom Textzusammenhang her nur „rent a flat"*
möglich) **near** Neuhauser Straße ... *(Textzusammenhang!).*

So **many** <u>people</u> go there ... *(vom Kontext her „money" unmöglich/„many", da Bezug*
auf zählbares Nomen „people")

2   1. Oktoberfest: The Oktoberfest is a big traditional Bavarian festival with lots of rides
                    and beer halls in Munich that begins at the end of September and goes
                    on for two weeks.
                    It is a big fair/festival with rides/rollercoasters and beer halls in (Ba-
                    varia's capital) Munich lasting for two weeks at the end of September.

     2. ICE: An ICE is a very fast train/a high-speed train which connects big
                    cities in Germany.

     3. Dirndl: This is a traditional Bavarian dress for girls and women which varies
                    in colour and design from region to region.

Part C: Productive Skills

Hinweis: Dieser Aufgabenteil besteht aus zwei Vorschlägen, die sich wiederum aus jeweils zwei Aufgaben zusammensetzen. Von den Vorschlägen muss nur einer bearbeitet werden, dieser allerdings vollständig. Eine Mischung der Aufgaben aus den beiden Vorschlägen ist nicht erlaubt.

Vorschlag I

1   *Hinweis: Es geht hierbei nur um ein kurzes persönliches Schreiben in englischer Sprache und gerade deswegen ist unbedingt auf inhaltliche Vollständigkeit zu achten.*

Dear Josee/Hi Josee,

When I had a look at the homepage of your school, I saw/discovered a picture of students wearing school uniforms and I wondered/would like to know if uniforms are compulsory at Canadian schools (if you have to wear uniforms at schools all over Canada).

Recently, some German schools also introduced school uniforms, but on a voluntary basis (but you don't have to wear them if you don't want to).

I hate school uniforms because they are not as comfortable as jeans and a T-shirt or a sweater. Besides, they are pretty expensive.

What do you think about them?

I hope to hear from you soon.

See you

Stefan

2   *Hinweis: Auch hier ist letztlich ein „Brief" zu schreiben, allerdings von eher formeller Natur, sodass man insbesondere auf Höflichkeit und Sachlichkeit achten muss. Vollständigkeit des Inhalts versteht sich von selbst. Wenn du dich an die zweite Aufgabe des Hörverstehenstests erinnerst, so kann das bei der einen oder anderen Formulierung* hilfreich sein.*

Dear Sirs, (Dear Sir or Madam)

Your website address *www.canadanow.ca* was recommended to me by a Canadian friend and after looking at it I was sure that the Yukon Territory would be perfect for my plans.

My name is Stefan Mustermann and I'm a scout group leader* of 15 teenagers/young people who intend to take a trip to the Yukon Territory in spring 2005.

Can you tell me/let me know what the weather there is like in spring (Can you give me information about the weather conditions in the Yukon in spring)?

I would like you to send me/Please send me an offer for a ten day walking tour/hiking tour with a guide (guided hiking tour) from/to Vancouver, and brochures with useful information for my group. I'm especially interested in advice/recommendations concerning suitable clothing/equipment.

Thank you very much for your help.

I'm looking forward to hearing from you.

Yours sincerely

Stefan Mustermann

1

Queen's & Knight's
Lost and Found Desk

If you're not satisfied, we're not satisfied.

Thank you for choosing the Heathrow **Queen's & Knight's** for your recent trip. We will do our best to find and forward your precious items to your home address.

To help us, we would be grateful if you could fill in this form.

1 **Items have been** ☒ **lost** **or** ☐ **found**

2.1 **Room No. was:** **QK-LHR-** _4717_

2.2 Check-in was on _03-08-17_ (yy-mm-dd)

2.3 Check-out was on _03-08-18_ (yy-mm-dd)

3 **No. of items:** ☒ **1 only** ☐ **please specify** _____

3.1 Kind of item(s)?

☐ Passport/ID ☐ Ticket/Voucher ☐ Credit/Debit Card

☒ Luggage ☐ Clothing ☐ None of the above

3.2 Please <u>describe</u> the item(s) as precisely as you can.

a light blue bag (with a sticker "Living Blues")

3.3 Please state the <u>contents</u> of the item(s).

a diary, a (digital) camera, aspirin, gifts, two books, a Yukon travel guide

4 **Personal Details**

4.1 Surname _Mustermann_ ☒ Mr ☐ Ms

4.2 Given name(s) _Stefan_

4.3 Address _Musterstraße 3_

4.4 City _Musterstadt_ Post code _85432_

4.5 Email _mustermanns_ @ _gmx.de_

4.6 Day Time Phone No. _08761/92244_

Please return ASAP by fax to +44 (022) 555 7989

2   *Hinweis: Da es sich bei Josée um einen Freund aus dem Ferienlager handelt, kann der Brief etwas lockerer abgefasst werden. Zu beachten ist allerdings, dass die geforderte Wortzahl erreicht werden muss.*
Das folgende Lösungsbeispiel umfasst zwar erheblich mehr Wörter, kann aber entsprechend gekürzt werden.

Hi Josée,

Thanks for your letter and for worrying about us. That power failure/blackout was a real adventure.

When we arrived at Toronto Airport, we couldn't enter the building because the automatic doors didn't work. But some security staff helped us to get in through a side entrance. Inside it was pretty dark because there was only emergency lighting. (Apart from that) The electronic display boards, the escalators and the lifts weren't working either, so we had to carry our luggage all the way to the Lufthansa check-in desk. There we were told that there would be no flights for the next ten hours.

I was worried because I thought that some of the teenagers might break down because they couldn't get home and had to stay at the airport. But they were pretty cool/calm. They were only worried that they wouldn't get anything to eat or drink and would have to sleep at the airport.

After three hours of waiting, a Lufthansa employee told us that there was a bus outside that would take us to a hotel where they had organized rooms/accommodation for us. They would inform us about our flight the next day. Now everything was fine again.

When we finally arrived at Munich Airport with a delay of almost three days, the teenagers' families were waiting for them and were happy that everybody was OK. And my "cool" scouts were glad to be home again.

You see, everything was fine in the end.

Hope to hear from you soon

Stefan

Tapescript zu Worksheet 1

SPEAKER: Ladies and Gentlemen, this is an announcement from WESSEX TRAINS for services to Exeter. Due to technical problems there will be a delay of about one hour. We ask our passengers to go by coach to Exeter station. The coach is operated by National Express. It leaves from outside the station at 09:10. WESSEX TRAINS
5 apologizes for any inconvenience this may cause you.
(Sounds of footsteps, creaking swing doors, people)
ANDREAS: Excuse me, my friend and I need to go to Exeter. But we didn't quite understand the announcement over the loudspeakers on the platform. We're afraid we won't catch the train in Exeter for Carlisle and Edinburgh at 09:15. Could you help us,
10 please?
BOOKING CLERK: Exeter? Problems on the Exeter line? Uhm, yes, there are technical problems along the Exeter line, no trains for the next hour, I'm afraid. But you've got two possibilities to get to Exeter. One possibility is to go there by coach. The second one is to wait and take the next train. The train leaves at a quarter to ten.
15 ANDRES: When will we arrive in Edinburgh if we take that train?
BOOKING CLERK: Just a second, please … at six o'clock in the evening …
ANDREAS: Oh no. That's much too late.
BOOKING CLERK: … and you have to change trains three times. The best thing might be to take the coach to Exeter and try to get an earlier connection there.
20 ANDREAS: Great, that sounds better. We'll do that. Could you give us details about times of departure and arrival?
BOOKING CLERK: Err, let me see … If you take the coach to Exeter station at 09:10, you'll arrive there half an hour later. … Then there is VIRGIN TRAINS to Birmingham … at 09:58. You won't have to change trains in Carlisle, but you will in Birmingham. And
25 you'll be there at 11:26. … Then you can take the connection by VIRGIN TRAINS from Birmingham to Edinburgh. Should I write that down for you?
ANDREAS: No, thanks. My friend will take some notes on our timetable. So, we'll have to change trains in Birmingham. We'll be there at 11:26. How much time have we got to change trains?
30 BOOKING CLERK: You've got more than half an hour. The train to Edinburgh leaves at 12 o'clock and arrives at 4:25 in the afternoon.
ANDREAS: OK, we've got that. One last question. We have to return to London in two weeks' time to get our flight to Munich. Where can we find out if there are any specials?
35 BOOKING CLERK: Well, we've got a brochure. Hang on, let me see –Yes, I've got it here. Here you are.
ANDREAS: Oh, thanks.
BOOKING CLERK: By the way, do you have Internet access?
ANDREAS: Yes, I do.
40 BOOKING CLERK: Well, you might be interested in looking up our very latest special offers on our web site. These offers change from week to week, so the information given in the brochure might not be up to date, I'm afraid. But here's the web-site address: www.nationalrail.co.uk/specrate … That's <u>www.nationalrail.co.uk/S-P-E-C-R-A-T-E</u>"
ANDREAS: Thank you, you've been most helpful. Bye.
45 BOOKING CLERK: You are welcome. Goodbye.

Tapescript zu Worksheet 2

Undrinkable water has led to an unexpected global sales boom. Brian Ball, a manager at a store in Dundee, Aberdeenshire, is taking water out of the Loch, home to the famous monster, and selling it at a startling price of £ 3.99 for a half-litre plus £ 2.83 packaging. Mr Ball's advert on an internet auction site says: "I go to the Loch every month or so and
5 get fresh water and this makes an absolutely super talking point having a bottle of real, I repeat real, Loch Ness water sitting on the cupboard of your house."

The manager admitted: "It's totally mad, I know. But there are clearly a lot of people out there, particularly in America, who are keen on the whole Loch Ness thing and getting this is clearly the highlight of their day."

10 He added that the water is sold legally under the condition of the health officials, that it is for display only and not fit for human consumers. The bottle carries a label with the warning, a picture of the monster and a guarantee of its origin.

He and his elder brother got the idea of selling the water after an American friend – and Nessie fan – asked them to bring some water from the famous Loch as a souvenir when
15 they went to visit her in New Hampshire, USA.

"I went out to the visitors' centre at the Loch thinking I should be able to buy some – but no such thing was available. So I emptied this mineral water bottle I had and filled it with water from the Loch. I took it to New Hampshire and she and all her friends went mad over it and I came back with orders for 20 more. So then I started selling it on the Internet
20 and it started going like hot cakes."

Armed with empty mineral water bottles, Mr Ball now makes the 100-mile round trip to the Loch from his home about once a month. So far he has sold almost 200 bottles to buyers in America, Australia, New Zealand, Kenya and Canada, with some biddings as high as £ 5.50. This is a business plan that has worked effectively. So why not try
25 unconventional ideas for running your business?

1   A train journey to Edinburgh   (12)

After attending a language course in the South of England you and your friend
Andreas want to take the train from Torquay to Edinburgh to visit your friend
Chris. At the station you hear an announcement about the delay of your train
and you decide to contact the information desk to find out another way to get to
Edinburgh.

Listen to the text twice and complete your personal timetable. Finally write
down the website address.

You will hear the recording twice and after the second listening you will have
one minute to check your answers.

National Rail Enquiries

Your personal timetable

Station	Arrival	Departure	Travel by	Operator
Torquay	–			
Exeter			Train	Virgin Trains
			Train	
Edinburgh		–	–	–

Website for special offers:

http://www. _____

2   Monster profit: Loch Ness water is top seller on Internet auctions   (8)

You recorded a report on the radio to present it as a new business idea in your project lessons at commercial school. Unfortunately in your print-out of the text there are **8 mistakes.**

Mark these words during the **first listening** by underlining them, and **write** the correct words into the right column during the **second listening.** You will hear the report twice and after the second listening you will have one minute to check your answers.

Undrinkable water has led to an unexpected total sales boom. Brian Ball, a manager at a store in Dundee, Aberdeenshire, is taking water out of the Loch, home to the popular monster, and selling it at a startling price of £ 3.99 for a half-litre plus £ 2.83 packaging. Mr Ball's advert on an internet auction site says: "I go to the Loch every month or so and get fresh water and this makes an actually super talking point having a bottle of real, I repeat real, Loch Ness water sitting on the cupboard of your house."	_____ _____ _____ _____ _____ _____ _____ _____ _____ _____
The manager admitted: "It's totally mad, I know. But there are clearly a lot of people out there, especially in America, who are keen on the whole Loch Ness thing and getting this is clearly the highlight of their day."	_____ _____ _____ _____
He added that the water is sold legally under the condition of the health experts, that it is for display only and not fit for human consumers. The bottle carries a label with the warning, a picture of the monster and a guarantee of its origin.	_____ _____ _____ _____ _____
He and his elder brother got the idea of selling the water after an American friend – and Nessie fan – asked them to bring some water from the famous Loch as a souvenir when they went to visit her in New Hampshire, USA.	_____ _____ _____ _____ _____
"I went out to the visitors' centre at the Loch thinking I should be able to buy some – but no such thing was affordable. So I emptied this mineral water bottle I had and filled it with water from the Loch. I took it to New Hampshire and she and all her friends went mad over it and I came back with orders for 20 more. So then I started selling it on the Internet and it started going like hot cakes."	_____ _____ _____ _____ _____ _____ _____ _____
Armed with empty mineral water bottles, Mr Ball now makes the 100-mile round trip to the Loch from his	_____ _____

home about once a month. So far he has sent almost 200 bottles to buyers in America, Australia, New Zealand, Kenya and Canada, with some biddings as high as £ 5.50. This is a business plan that has worked successfully. So why not try unconventional ideas for running your business?

1 Worksheet 1: A train journey to Edinburgh

Hinweis: *Der abgedruckte Text gibt einen persönlichen Fahrplan wieder. Die Tabelle enthält Lücken, die du ergänzen musst. Das Problem dabei ist, dass mehrere Fahrmöglichkeiten vom Bahnangestellten vorgeschlagen werden. Deine Aufgabe ist es, die Verbindungen aufzuschreiben, für die sich die Reisenden entscheiden. Zum Schluss musst du eine Webadresse vervollständigen.*
Wichtig ist es, dass du dir die Situation vorstellst und dich hinein versetzt. Mache dich so schnell wie möglich mit den in der Tabelle stehenden Überschriften vertraut, damit du weißt, welche Informationen du brauchst. Versuche beim ersten Zuhören einen Überblick zu gewinnen. Bekomme keine Panik, wenn du nicht gleich alle Antworten weißt. In der Regel ist es beim zweiten Zuhören viel leichter die relevanten Informationen mitzubekommen. Weil Webadressen sehr oft vorkommen, ist es empfehlenswert, folgende Begriffe zu lernen: „dot" für „Punkt", „dash" für „Bindestrich", „slash" für „Schrägstrich".

National Rail Enquiries

Your personal timetable

Station	Arrival	Departure	Travel by	Operator
Torquay	–	9:10	coach	National Express
Exeter	9:40	9:58	Train	Virgin Trains
Birmingham	11:26	12:00	Train	Virgin Trains
Edinburgh	4:25 p.m. 16:25	–	–	–

Website for special offers:
http://www. _nationalrail.co.uk/specrate_

2   **Worksheet 2: Monster profit: Loch Ness water is top seller on Internet auctions**

Hinweis: Der vorgegebene Text enthält Fehler, die du beim Zuhören finden und korrigieren musst.
Bei dieser Art von Aufgabe ist es sehr wichtig, die Anweisungen genau zu beachten. Wenn du das erste Mal zuhörst, versuche nicht, die Fehler zu finden und gleichzeitig zu verbessern. Es gibt zwei Gründe dafür: Erstens ist es wahrscheinlich, dass du den nächsten Fehler verpassen wirst. Zweitens bekommst du schon einen halben Punk, wenn du ein falsches Wort nur unterstreichst.

Undrinkable water has led to an unexpected <u>total</u> sales boom. Brian Ball, a manager at a store in Dundee, Aberdeenshire, is taking water out of the Loch, home to the <u>popular</u> monster, and selling it at a startling price of £ 3.99 for a half-litre plus £ 2.83 packaging. Mr Ball's advert on an internet auction site says: "I go to the Loch every month or so and get fresh water and this makes an <u>actually</u> super talking point having a bottle of real, I repeat real, Loch Ness water sitting on the cupboard of your house."	*global*
	famous
	absolutely
The manager admitted: "It's totally mad, I know. But there are clearly a lot of people out there, <u>especially</u> in America, who are keen on the whole Loch Ness thing and getting this is clearly the highlight of their day."	*particularly*
He added that the water is sold legally under the condition of the health <u>experts</u>, that it is for display only and not fit for human consumers. The bottle carries a label with the warning, a picture of the monster and a guarantee of its origin.	*officials*
He and his elder brother got the idea of selling the water after an American friend – and Nessie fan – asked them to bring some water from the famous Loch as a souvenir when they went to visit her in New Hampshire, USA.	
"I went out to the visitors' centre at the Loch thinking I should be able to buy some – but no such thing was <u>affordable</u>. So I emptied this mineral water bottle I had and filled it with water from the Loch. I took it to New Hampshire and she and all her friends went mad over it and I came back with orders for 20 more. So then I started selling it on the Internet and it started going like hot cakes."	*available*

Armed with empty mineral water bottles, Mr Ball now makes the 100-mile round trip to the Loch from his home about once a month. So far he has <u>sent</u> almost 200 bottles to buyers in America, Australia, New Zealand, Kenya and Canada, with some biddings as high as £ 5.50. This is a business plan that has worked <u>successfully</u>. So why not try unconventional ideas for running your business?

_____
_____
sold _____
_____
_____
_____
effectively _____
_____

Part A

1   Reading for details   (16)

Einer Ihrer Freunde hat in einer Zeitschrift ein Preisausschreiben entdeckt, bei
dem man einen Sprachkurs in England gewinnen kann (siehe S. 2005-9). Da die
entsprechende Seite in englischer Sprache veröffentlicht wurde, seine Englisch-
kenntnisse aber sehr schlecht sind, bittet er Sie, ihm einige Fragen zu beantworten.

Tragen Sie Ihre Antworten **in deutscher Sprache** in nachfolgender Tabelle ein.
Stichpunkte genügen.

1	Wie komme ich nach Torquay	(2)
2	Wie werde ich untergebracht?	(2)
3	Was erfährt man im Text über die Verpflegung?	(1)
4	Wann kann man an dem Kurs teilnehmen?	(3)
5	Welche Freizeitangebote gibt es außerhalb der Unterrichtsstunden?	(3)
6	Welche Kosten muss man selbst übernehmen?	(3)
7	Wie erfahre ich, ob ich gewonnen habe?	(1)
8	Wie kann ich mehr über den Sprachkurs erfahren?	(1)

WIN

a two-week language course on the English Riviera!

Our two week intensive course will give you the perfect opportunity to improve your English.

You will also be able to explore one of the most beautiful parts of south-west England.

The prize includes:

- a two-week intensive general English course in Torquay
- 15 hours of English instruction per week
- accommodation and full board with a host family
- return economy-class flight
- coach transfers between London and Torquay
- an interesting and varied programme of leisure activities and tours
- a test of your language level and a certificate of attendance

NOTE: SEE INFORMATION ON THE RIGHT FOR FULL DETAILS!!!

Fill in the entry form and answer the following question on the back of this page:

In which county is the town of St Ives?

Competition rules

1. The language holiday is nontransferable, and no cash alternative can be given.
2. The holiday is for one person for two weeks. The course includes 15 lessons of English per week, private accommodation in a single room, full board, use of course materials, a diagnostic English test on arrival and a certificate of course attendance.
3. A leisure programme is part of the prize, including two half-day tours, a round town quiz and a wide range of various sports programmes.
4. The prize also includes an economy-class return flight from Munich, Nuremberg or Frankfurt to London Heathrow, and transfers between London and Torquay.
   A two-week bus pass for the Torbay region is also included.
5. Insurance, spending money and transfers to and from the airports in Germany are not included in the prize.
6. The course may be taken during the autumn of 2005, at Easter 2006 or in the summer of 2006.
   The exact dates are at the discretion of EuroLangs Ltd.
7. EuroLangs Ltd's standard terms and conditions applay.
8. Closing date for entries is 30 July 2005.
9. The winner will be announced in the September 2005 issue of this magazine.
10. No correspondence will be entered into.

For further information:
www.eurolangs.com

2005-10

2   **Translation**   (14)

Sie haben sich auf der Website der EuroLangs School nach weiteren Informationen über diese Sprachenschule und ihr Kursangebot umgesehen. Ihre Eltern haben Sie gebeten, das Wichtigste daraus für sie zu übersetzen.

Übersetzen Sie die Abschnitte **Teachers**, **Classes** und **Accommodation** ins Deutsche. Benutzen Sie dafür ein Extrablatt, das Ihnen von Ihrer Schule bereitgestellt wird.

EuroLangs School

26 Years of Experience

We offer language experience and language instruction in the country where it is spoken – in an environment which is helpful to learning, like in the town of Torquay, the beautiful seaside resort in the South West of England. We have taken care of our students for more than 20 years.

Teachers

- We only employ highly qualified native English speaking teachers.

Classes

- The maximum number of students in a class is 15.
- Our courses are designed to improve your ability in speaking, listening, reading and writing in the English language. You will increase your knowledge and understanding of English grammar, learn new vocabulary and get help with your pronunciation.
- You will be given a test at the start of the course to check your level of English.
- Based on this test, students are sent to different classes: from beginners to advanced.
- Course material is provided.

Accommodation

- Living with a carefully selected English host family also gives you a real opportunity to practise your English outside the classroom and to understand more about the country and its people.

Part B: Overall Language Proficiency

1   **Fill in each gap in the text with one appropriate word**   (12)

From Torquay you've arrived in Scotland one hour late, but unlike people on another train you're safe and sound. Your delay was not due to a "technical failure", there had been a terrible train disaster earlier that day. The Edinburgh Evening Post published a short report on the disaster. A few days later it also published the letter below.

Your friend Sabine shows you the copy of the Edinburgh Evening Post. The paper got wet in the Scottish rain and, as a consequence, Sabine can't read all the words. She asks you for help. Write one word in each gap.

Letter to the Editor:
Unsafe At Any Speed?

Sir,

I feel I _____ add a few words to your report about the train which got derailed on its _____ from Exeter to Birmingham two days ago.

My husband and I _____ travelling on board the train which crashed into a lorry on a level crossing _____ Birmingham, leaving 65 passengers injured. The two of us were extremely lucky to escape from the disaster with just a _____ scratches. No serious injuries – it could have been much _____. There must have been a guardian angel _____ us on the train.

We hope that this letter will be _____ by all those helpful people at the site of the crash. Thanks to the brave train staff for giving first aid to the injured, thanks to fire-fighters, nurses and doctors for their courageous work saving many passengers' _____, and – last but not least – thanks to Transport Police officers for protecting us from the cameras and microphones of the _____. They all did a _____ job.

Our feelings are with the families whose beloved parents, children or friends were injured in the _____.

Yours truly

2   Error spotting   (8)

When she was in Edinburgh, Sabine wrote a letter to her Polish friend Jan. Unfortunately she made eight mistakes. Please underline these mistakes and write the corrections in the right hand column.

Dear Jan,

I've been in Sheffield now since three days. As I told you in my last letter, a train got derailed somewhere between Exeter and Birmingham. So we all had to go by coach to Birmingham.

On the coach I suddenly remembered Mr Feldman. He was our English teacher in class 8b and he stood at our school for a year as an exchange teacher. Well, I was in Birmingham, so I decided to visit him – he lives in Aston Villa who is near Birmingham. He was very surprising to see me. However he and his family were very friendly. Mr and Mrs Feldman and their son Marshall take me out for a nice meal.

I must say that I had great difficulty in understanding Marshall while he speaks English in the Birmingham dialect. That's a strange dialect. However, Marshall tried hardly to speak clearly and so I managed to understand almost everything that he said.

Anyway, I must say we had a fantastic day together and I was sorry to have to go on to Edinburgh.

Well, dear Jan, it's time to post this letter to you. I hope we can meet in Warsaw next year. I'm looking forward to hear from you soon.

Very best wishes,

Sabine

Part C: Productive Skills

Vorschlag I

1   **Reporting/Telling a story**   (12)

You have spent ten days in Edinburgh, Scotland, doing lots of things in and
around the city. Before returning home from Scotland, you are about to send
two pictures you took to a pen pal of yours.

First make up your mind on **two** pictures from below to get some ideas. **Then**
write about 60–80 words **in English** explaining to your pen pal why you **have
or haven't fully enjoyed** your stay in Scotland.

Please write the body of your letter on an extra sheet of paper provided by your
school.

2   Writing a formal letter   (18)

Nach Ihrer Rückkehr aus Großbritannien absolvieren Sie an Ihrem Schulort ein Praktikum bei *Wanderlust*. Dieses Unternehmen steht bereits in Geschäftskontakt mit Firmen in Frankreich. Frau König, Ihre Betreuerin bei *Wanderlust*, hat Sie mit folgendem Memo gebeten ein Schreiben für sie zu entwerfen.

Verfassen Sie den Hauptteil des Briefes **in englischer Sprache** und benutzen Sie dafür ein Extrablatt, dass Ihnen von Ihrer Schule bereitgestellt wird.

Memo

Datum:	29. Juni 2005	☑ eilig
Von:	Fr. König	☑ mit der Bitte um Erledigung
An:	Praktikant(in)	☑ zurück an mich

Bitte ein Schreiben an Besucher aus Frankreich mit folgendem Inhalt entwerfen:
- Leider Änderungen zum vereinbarten Besuchsprogramm
- Besuch bei der IHK <u>nicht</u> am Vormittag, sondern erst ab 14.30 Uhr, deswegen ab 9 Uhr Rundgang bei der Firma „Cherry", einem weltweit führenden Hersteller für Tastaturen; dort vor allem die Abteilungen „Einkauf" und „Verkauf"
- Bitte um Bestätigung der Ankunftszeit der Besuchergruppe aus Frankreich am Bahnhof um 8.15 Uhr
- Erwarten Besuchergruppe am Bahnhof mit Schild „Cherry"
- Höflicher Schlusssatz

Vorschlag II

1 Writing a formal letter (18)

Nach Ihrer Rückkehr aus Großbritannien absolvieren Sie an Ihrem Schulort ein Praktikum bei *Wanderlust*, einer Firma, die international erfolgreich als Ausrüster von Expeditionen tätig ist. Die Firma steht bereits in Geschäftskontakten mit Mr Hutchinson in England. Frau König, Ihre Betreuerin bei *Wanderlust*, hat Sie mit folgendem Memo gebeten ein Schreiben für sie zu entwerfen.

Verfassen Sie den Hauptteil des Briefes **in englischer Sprache** und benutzen Sie dafür ein Extrablatt, dass Ihnen von Ihrer Schule bereitgestellt wird.

Memo

Datum:	29. Juni 2005	☑ eilig
Von:	Fr. König	☑ mit der Bitte um Erledigung
An:	Praktikant(in)	☑ zurück an mich

Bitte ein Schreiben an Mr Hutchinson mit folgendem Inhalt entwerfen:
- Freude, dass unsere letzte Lieferung von Zelten Mr Hutchinsons Erwartungen entsprochen hat
- Angebot für neue Wanderrucksäcke unterbreiten: jetzt aus noch leichterem und völlig wasserdichtem Material
- vorrätig in verschiedenen Farben und Größen, Einzelheiten dazu auf www.wanderlust-outdoor.de
- Mengenrabatt bei Abnahme von mehr als 50 Stück
- Lieferung innerhalb von zwei Wochen nach Eingang der Bestellung möglich
- baldige Rückmeldung erbeten

---

2 Getting your opinion across (12)

Die Sprachenschule in Torquay hat sich bei Ihnen zu Hause in Bayern gemeldet. Man bittet Sie um einen kurzen, ehrlichen Erfahrungsbericht über Ihren Aufenthalt in Torquay. Ihr Beitrag könnte im Werbeprospekt der Sprachenschule für 2006 aufgenommen werden. Für die beste Rückmeldung vergibt die Sprachenschule einen kostenlosen einwöchigen Sprachkurs.

Verfassen Sie einen Beitrag in englischer Sprache anhand folgender Notizen:

Prima war …	Nicht so toll war …
• Schwerpunkt im Kurs aufs Sprechen, weniger aufs Schreiben	• jeden Tag Eier mit Speck zum Frühstück
• Lage der Schule: Strandnähe und viele Verbindungen mit öffentlichen Verkehrsmitteln in die Innenstadt	
• Teilnehmer aus der ganzen Welt, wenige Deutsche	

Schreiben Sie in vollständigen Sätzen und benutzen Sie dafür ein Extrablatt, das Ihnen von Ihrer Schule bereitgestellt wird.

Lösungen

Part A

1 Reading for details

Hinweis: Ein englischer Text wird vorgegeben, jedoch werden die Fragen zum Text in deutscher Sprache gestellt und müssen ebenso auf deutsch beantwortet werden.
Es ist ratsam, die Fragen zu lesen, bevor du den Text liest. So kannst du die entsprechenden Stellen im Text während des Lesens markieren. Du solltest aber unbedingt den ganzen Text gründlich lesen und nicht nur gewisse Informationen suchen. Beim Überfliegen eines Textes gehst du das Risiko ein, dass du wichtige Informationen verpasst und den allgemeinen Zusammenhang nicht wirklich verstehst.

1	Wie komme ich nach Torquay	(2)
	Flugzeug — *Bus*	
2	Wie werde ich untergebracht?	(2)
	Gastfamilie — *Einzelzimmer*	
3	Was erfährt man im Text über die Verpflegung?	(1)
	Volle Verpflegung / 3 Mahlzeiten täglich	
4	Wann kann man an dem Kurs teilnehmen?	(3)
	Herbst 2005 — *Ostern 2006* — *Sommer 2006*	
5	Welche Freizeitangebote gibt es außerhalb der Unterrichtsstunden?	(3)
	2 Halbtagsausflüge — *Stadtrallye* — *Verschiedene Sportangebote*	
6	Welche Kosten muss man selbst übernehmen?	(3)
	Versicherung — *Transfer zum/vom Flughafen in Deutschland* — *Taschengeld*	
7	Wie erfahre ich, ob ich gewonnen habe?	(1)
	Bekanntgabe in der Septemberausgabe 2005 dieser Zeitschrift	
8	Wie kann ich mehr über den Sprachkurs erfahren?	(1)
	Unter angegebener Internet-Adresse: www.eurolangs.com	

2 Translation

Hinweis: Hier sind gewisse Teile einer Website ins Deutsche zu übersetzen. Durch die Übersetzung musst du zeigen, dass du den Sinn des Textes verstanden hast. Versuche nicht, Wort für Wort zu übersetzen. Lies einen ganzen Satz, bevor du den deutschen Satz formulierst. Wenn du ein Wort im englischen Text nicht verstehst, versuche die mögliche Bedeutung durch den Zusammenhang herauszufinden.

Lehrkräfte
– Wir stellen nur hoch qualifizierte muttersprachliche Englischlehrer ein.

Klassen
– Die höchste Zahl der Schüler in einer Klasse ist 15.
– Unsere Kurse sind so gestaltet, um Ihre Fähigkeiten im Sprechen, Zuhören, Lesen und Schreiben in der englischen Sprache zu verbessern. Sie werden Ihr Wissen und Verständnis der englischen Grammatik erweitern, neue Vokabeln lernen und Hilfe bei Ihrer Aussprache bekommen.
– Am Anfang des Kurses werden Sie einen Test schreiben, der Ihr Niveau in der englischen Sprache überprüfen wird.
– Auf diesem Test basierend werden Schüler von Anfängern bis zu Fortgeschrittenen verschiedenen Klassen zugeteilt.
– Das Kursmaterial wird gestellt.

Unterkunft
– Das Leben in einer sorgfältig ausgesuchten englischen Gastfamilie gibt Ihnen auch eine echte Gelegenheit, Ihr Englisch außerhalb des Klassenzimmers zu üben und mehr über das Land und seine Leute zu erfahren.

Aufgabenteil B – Overall Language Proficiency

1   Fill in each gap in the text with one appropriate word.

Hinweis: Aus diesem Text sind Wörter entfernt, die wieder eingesetzt werden müssen. Du musst Wörter einsetzen, die den Text sinnvoll und grammatikalisch korrekt ergänzen.
Obwohl der vorgegebene Text nicht komplett ist, solltest du trotzdem den Text durchlesen, um einen Überblick zu bekommen. Diese Strategie hat den Vorteil, dass du dir besser vorstellen kannst, worum es sich handelt und hilft dir passende Wörter zu finden.

Sir,

I feel I **should/must** *(Modalverb vor einem Vollverb)* add a few words to your report about the derailed train on its **journey/way** *(von Exeter nach Birmingham)* from Exeter to Birmingham two days ago.
My husband and I **were** *(Verlaufsform in der Vergangenheit)* travelling on board the train which crashed into a lorry on a level crossing **in/near** Birmingham *(in oder in der Nähe von Birmingham)* leaving 65 passengers injured. The two of us were extremely lucky to escape from the disaster with just a **few** *(„few" und nicht „little", da Bezug auf zahlbares Nomen „scratches")* scratch<u>es</u>. No serious injuries – it could have been <u>much</u> **worse** *(Steigerung eines unregelmäßigen Adjektives: bad, worse, worst)*. There must have been a guardian angel **with** *(Hinweis: bei uns = „with us", nicht „by us")* <u>us</u> on the train.
We hope that this letter will be **read** *(Partizip im Passivsatz)* <u>by</u> all those helpful people at the site of the crash. Thanks to the brave train staff for giving first aid to the injured, thanks to firefighters, nurses and doctors for their courageous work saving many <u>passengers</u>' **lives** *(Plural von „life", da Bezug auf Nomen im Plural)* and – last but not least – thanks to Transport Police officers for protecting us from the <u>cameras and</u>

microphones of the **media/reporters/press/journalists** *(Textzusammenhang)*. They all did a **tremendous/fantastic/good/wonderful/excellent/great** *(Adjektiv, da Bezug auf ein Nomen)* job.
Our feelings are with the families whose beloved parents, children or friends were injured in the **crash/accident/disaster** *(Textzusammenhang. Nicht „train", da man in Englisch „on the train" sagt)*.
Yours truly

2 Error spotting

Dear Jan,	
I've been in Sheffield now <u>since</u> three days. As I told you in my last letter, a train got derailed somewhere between Exeter and Birmingham. So we all had to go by coach to Birmingham.	*for*[1]
On the coach I suddenly remembered Mr Feldman. He was our English teacher in class 8b and he <u>stood</u> at our school for a year as an exchange teacher.	*taught/stayed/was*[2]
Well, I was in Birmingham, so I decided to visit him – he lives in Aston Villa <u>who</u> is near Birmingham. He was very <u>surprising</u> to see me. However he and his family were very friendly. Mr and Mrs Feldman and their son Marshall <u>take</u> me out for a nice meal.	*which*[3] *surprised*[4] *took*[5]
I must say that I had great difficulty in understanding Marshall <u>while</u> he speaks English in the Birmingham dialect. That's a strange dialect. However, Marshall tried <u>hardly</u> to speak clearly and so I managed to understand almost everything that he said.	*because*[6] *hard*[7]
Anyway, I must say we had a fantastic day together and I was sorry to have to go on to Edinburgh.	
Well, dear Jan, it's time to post this letter to you. I hope we can meet in Warsaw next year. I'm looking forward to <u>hear</u> from you soon.	*hearing*[8]
Very best wishes,	
Sabine	

Hinweise:
1 Bei einem Zeitraum „for", bei einem Zeitpunkt „since".
2 „stood" (2. Form von „to stand") macht keinen Sinn in diesem Satz.
3 Relativpronomen bezieht sich auf den Ort „Aston Villa", „which" bei Dingen und Orten, „who" bei Personen.
4 Bezieht sich auf „he" und drückt ein Gefühl aus.
5 Vergangenheit
6 False friends („while" = während)
7 Unregelmäßiges Adverb
8 „to look forward to" + Gerundium

Aufgabenteil C – Productive skills

Hinweis: Hier sind zwei Vorschläge, die aus jeweils zwei Aufgaben bestehen. In der Prüfung wählt dein Lehrer einen der Vorschläge aus.

Vorschlag I

1   Reporting / Telling a story

Hinweis: In dieser Aufgabe musst du den Hauptteil eines informellen Briefes an einen Brieffreund schreiben. Hier ist es besonderes wichtig, auf die Zeiten zu achten.

Pictures 1 and 3

I've been in Scotland for 10 days and have enjoyed it so far. Last week we went horse riding on a beach near Edinburgh. It was great but the weather was terrible – it rained all day!

I've met lots of nice people in Edinburgh. At the youth hostel there are young people from all over the world. The only thing that I don't really like about Scotland is the food. I'm looking forward to getting some Bavarian food again soon.

Hope that you like the pictures. Please write back soon!   *90 words*

2   Writing a formal letter

Hinweis: Bei formellen Briefen ist es wichtig, auf Sachlichkeit und Höflichkeit zu achten. Denke an die üblichen Redewendungen, die du im Laufe der Jahre gelernt hast. Hier ist es sehr wichtig, festzustellen, wer den Brief schreibt und wer den Brief empfängt.

Dear Sir or Madam

We are writing to inform you that the arranged programme of visits has unfortunately been changed. The visit to the IHK will not take place in the morning but in the afternoon at 2 p.m.

Therefore, at 9 a.m. there will be a tour of the company "Cherry", a world-leading manufacturer of keyboards. We are especially interested in seeing the purchasing and sales departments.

Could you please confirm that your group is arriving from France at the railway station at 8:15 a.m. There will be someone waiting for you at the railway station holding a sign with "Cherry" on it.

We look forward to hearing from you soon.

Yours faithfully   *114 words*

Vorschlag II

1   Writing a formal letter

Hinweis: Auch hier ist ein formeller Brief zu schreiben.

Dear Mr Hutchinson

We are so pleased that our last shipment of tents met your expectations.

We would now like to submit an offer for new hiking rucksacks made of an even lighter and completely waterproof material. They are in stock in a variety of colours and sizes. For further information, please visit our website: www.wanderlust-outdoor.de

A quantity discount will be granted on all orders exceeding 50 items. Delivery can be made within two weeks after receipt of order.

We hope you will make use of this advantageous offer and we look forward to hearing from you soon.

Yours sincerely   *100 words*

2   Getting your point across

Hinweis: Achte darauf, dass du alle vorgegebenen Stichpunkte in deinem Beitrag erwähnst. Die Zeiten sind auch hier zu beachten.

I thought it was great that the course's emphasis was on speaking and not on writing. The language school was ideally located near the beach with lots of public transport connections to the city centre. It was super that there were participants from all over the world but not many from Germany. The only thing that I didn't like was getting bacon and eggs for breakfast every day.

68 words

Tapescript zu Worksheet 1

Message # 1

Thank you for calling the Cork Language Experts.
Staff will be available to take your enquiry at the following times:
From Mondays to Fridays our head office is open from 9 am to 4.15 pm.
5 From Tuesdays to Thursdays our teachers will be pleased to answer your questions from
5 pm to 9 pm.
The school is also open on certain Saturdays with a limited information service. Should
you call outside these times, please leave a clear message after the beep.

Message # 2

10 Enjoy County Mayo's beautiful countryside from its waterways. Be your own captain and
explore lakes, rivers and canals at a relaxed speed of 5 miles an hour. Why not rent one of
our comfortable riverboats? They sleep up to eight people, come with a fully equipped
kitchenette, air-conditioned rooms below and a large sun deck. Should you wish to
receive an illustrated free brochure on County Mayo's waterways, please leave your name
15 and address after the beep.

Message # 3

Thank you for calling Grey's City Tours. Unfortunately all our lines are engaged at the
moment. Please hold the line until one of our staff is available.
[Jingle]
20 From the upper platform of Grey's double-deckers you'll have a fantastic view of
Dublin's sights and attractions. Our three-hour and six-hour tickets allow you to hop off
and on again at any stop along the route.
[Jingle]
At the moment all our lines are engaged. Please hold the line until one of our staff is
25 available.

Message # 4

This is the Limerick YMCA.
We are sorry but you are calling outside office hours. If you wish to speak to our
receptionist, please call this number between 8 am and 5.30 pm. The switchboard is not
30 open on Sundays and bank holidays. If you wish to listen to recorded information on the
types of accommodation, group booking, and leisure facilities we offer for under 18-year
olds, please press 1. You can also visit us on the Internet at YMCA-Limerick.ei. I repeat
YMCA-Limerick.ei. Thank you for calling.

Message # 5

35 Thank you for calling Sealink, the fastest connection on the Irish Sea. Please choose one
of the five options.
- To listen to our talking timetable, press 1.
- To make a booking for a trip from Dublin to the UK, press 2.
- To make a reservation for heavy goods vehicles, camper vans or caravans, press 3.
40 - If you are calling about an existing booking, press 4.
- For other enquiries, press 5.

Message # 6

Ths is the Odeon box office.

Unfortunately all our lines are busy at the moment, but your call will be answered as soon
45   as possible.

We are taking bookings by phone and in person for our live music shows to 17 July.

If you have a touch-tone phone and you'd like to hear a sound bite of this week's special
artists and ticket availability, press 1.

Tapescript zu Worksheet 2

(**T** = travel agent; **P** = Paul)

    T.: Good morning. Delta Travel, Barbara Flynn speaking. Can I help you?

    P.: Oh, good morning. This is Paul Huber from Amberg. My friends and I have booked a
        trip with your agency, but we have a few more questions we'd like to ask you.

    T.: Ah yes, Mr. Huber from Germany, I remember. Well, let me see – it's here in the
5   computer – you've booked a one-week stay in one of our holiday homes in Cork from
        the 14th to the 21st of September.

    P.: Yes, that's right. Could you tell me a bit more about the rooms, please?

    T.: Yes, of course. Well, we've made a reservation for a standard apartment with three
        bedrooms, a small kitchen with a cooker and fridge, a widescreen TV, free DVDs and
10   tea and coffee facilities are also available in each bedroom.

    P.: I see. That sounds great. And what about the bathroom? There's only one, isn't there?

    T.: Well, in each of our apartments there's a bathroom and a shower. Towels are provid-
        ed.

    P.: Fine. We'll be spending most of our time travelling around the South of Ireland or just
15   lying on the beach, so we probably won't always have time for cooking …

    T.: Oh, don't worry about that! We have a special arrangement with Greene's restaurant
        just next door. You can get a full Irish or Continental breakfast there and a good three-
        course evening meal for quite a reasonable price.

    P.: Ah, that sounds OK. There's only one small problem. Sarah, one of our group, is a
20   vegetarian. She just refuses to eat any meat at all.

    T.: Oh, that's really no problem. Vegetarian meals are also available in the evening.

    P.. And what about lunches?

    T.: Well, the restaurant has a nice range of salads and other light snacks.

    P.: Ah, wonderful. In your brochure you say that there are a number of day trips that your
25   agency arranges …

    T.: Yes, there's a hiking tour with a qualified guide along the river from Cork. Now, let
        me see … Um, yes, that's on Thursday starting at 6:30 am. The second tour we offer
        is a boat trip around the coast starting at 9.00 am on Tuesday.

    P.: That sounds very interesting. I'm sure we'll find time to go on at least one of those. –
30   Oh, by the way, can you give me the flight information again?

    T.: Certainly, sir. You'll be flying with Aer Lingus and the flight departure from Munich
        is at half past two in the afternoon on the 14th of September, economy class. Your
        return flight from Cork is on the 21st … Let me just look at the computer … yes, … at
        11:45 am. The flights both ways take about two and three quarter hours.

35   P.: Many thanks for your help. Oh, one last thing. Where do we pick the keys up when
        we arrive?

    T.: Oh, Mr. Sean Connally, the manager of the Castle Ross Holiday Homes, will be
        waiting for you with keys on your arrival on the 14th. By the way, if you need any
        further information, he's the man to contact. Once again, that's Mr. Scan Connally –
40   I'd better spell that for you, hadn't I? That's S-E-A-N C-O-DOUBLE-N-A-DOUBLE

-L-Y. And he can be contacted at the following telephone number: 00353 21425 2215. That's the number from Germany. I hope you enjoy your stay in our country! The weather should be fine when you come.

P.: Thank you very much, you've been most helpful. I think that's everything, isn't it? ... Oh, gosh, I nearly forgot. How do we get from the airport to the hotel? There's a bus connection I suppose.

T.: Well, there is a train connection but the trains don't run very often, I'm afraid. I think they're about once every two hours. But I tell you what – if you phone us on your mobile as soon as you arrive, we'll send a shuttle to pick you up.

P.: Wonderful! I suppose we could come by taxi but I'm sure we'd all prefer to be picked up by your shuttle bus after such a long flight. Once again, many thanks for your help. Goodbye.

T.: You're more than welcome. Goodbye, sir.

Worksheets

1   Telephone messages (6)

You are collecting information over the phone to prepare for a journey to Ireland.

You will hear <u>six</u> different telephone messages. Match the messages to the organisations below. Write the correct numbers of the messages into the boxes.

You'll hear each message twice and afterwards you'll have 30 seconds to check your answers.

Example: Message 0 comes from a computer shop.

|0| *a computer shop*

☐	an art school	☐	a ferry company
☐	a language school	☐	a company that hires out camper vans
☐	a youth hostel	☐	a tourist bus operator
☐	a concert hall	☐	a company that hires out boats
☐	an airline ticket office	☐	a telephone service provider

2   A trip to Ireland (14)

You and your friends have booked a trip to Ireland with an Irish travel agency in Dublin. This morning one of your party, Paul, is calling the agency again to make sure that there will be no changes to the arrangements you have made.

Listen to the conversation and take down some notes <u>in German</u> so that you can inform the rest of your party.

You will hear the recording twice and after the second listening you will have two minutes to check your answers.

1. Dauer der Reise?	_____	(1)
2. **Apartment:**		
Anzahl der Schlafzimmer?	_____	(0,5)
Ausstattung der Küche?	_____	(1)
Handtücher?	_____	(0,5)
3. **Verpflegung:**		
Wo?	_____	(1)
Frühstück?	_____	(1)
Mittagessen?	_____	(1)
Abendessen?	_____	(1)

4. Tagesausflüge:	
Art und Wochentag?	_____ (1)
	_____ (1)
5. Abflugzeiten:	
München (Tag und Uhrzeit)?	_____ (1)
Cork (Tag und Uhrzeit)?	_____ (1)
6. Name der Kontaktperson?	_____ (1)
7. Telefonnummer der Kontaktperson?	_____ (1)
8. Bevorzugtes Transportmittel vom Flughafen zum Hotel?	_____ (1)

Lösungen

1 Worksheet 1: Telephone messages

Hinweis: Du hörst sechs verschiedene Anrufbeantworternachrichten. Die Aufgabe besteht darin, herauszufinden, auf welches der vorgegebenen Unternehmen die Nachrichten jeweils bezogen sind. Die Reihenfolge der Nachrichten muss stimmen. Wichtig ist, dass du dich mit den möglichen Antworten vertraut machst, da sie sich teilweise sehr ähneln.

☐	an art school	5	a ferry company
1	a language school	☐	a company that hires out camper vans
4	a youth hostel	3	a tourist bus operator
6	a concert hall	2	a company that hires out boats
☐	an airline ticket office	☐	a telephone service provider

2 Worksheet 2: A trip to Ireland

Hinweis: Hier geht es um ein Telefongespräch auf Englisch. Deine Aufgabe ist es, Notizen auf Deutsch zu machen. Die „Fragen" sind zum Teil etwas knapp und es ist nicht immer klar, wie viele Informationen nötig sind. Um die ganze Punktzahl zu bekommen, solltest du daher so viele Details wie möglich aufschreiben. Zum Beispiel Frage 3: Frühstück? Hier muss man angeben, was zum Frühstück angeboten wird, anstatt einfach nur „ja" hinzuschreiben.

1. Dauer der Reise?	*1 Woche / 14. – 21. Sept.*
2. Apartment:	
Anzahl der Schlafzimmer?	*3.*
Ausstattung der Küche?	*Herd / Ofen, Kühlschrank*
Handtücher?	*ja / werden gestellt*
3. Verpflegung:	
Wo?	*Restaurant nebenan*
Frühstück?	*irisches oder kontinentales Frühstück*
Mittagessen?	*Salate und andere leichte Snacks*
Abendessen?	*3-Gänge-Menü (auch vegetarisch)*
4. Tagesausflüge:	
Art und Wochentag?	*- Fahrradtour am Donnerstag*
	- Bootsausflug am Dienstag
5. Abflugzeiten:	
München (Tag und Uhrzeit)?	*14. September um 14:30 Uhr*
Cork (Tag und Uhrzeit)?	*21. September um 11:45 Uhr*
6. Name der Kontaktperson?	*Sean Connally*

7. Telefonnummer der Kontaktperson?	_0035321-4252215_
8. Bevorzugtes Transportmittel vom Flughafen zum Hotel?	_Minibus_

Part A

1   Translation   (8)

Ihre Nachbarin beschäftigt sich in ihrer Freizeit mit zwei Lieblingsthemen: Irland und irischer Küche. Sie möchte einen Aufenthalt auf der grünen Insel mit einer Arbeitsaufnahme dort verbinden und bittet Sie beim Lesen einer Stellenanzeige um Hilfe:

„Hilf mir bitte und übersetze die von mir eingekreisten Sätze ins Deutsche! Ich möchte ganz genau wissen, welche Aufgaben ich übernehmen müsste und welche Chancen mir diese Arbeitsstelle bei Happy Deals bietet."

Lesen Sie die Stellenausschreibung der irischen Firma *Happy Deals* (siehe Text nächste Seite) und übersetzen Sie den eingekreisten Teil der Stellenausschreibung ins Deutsche!

Benutzen Sie dafür ein Extrablatt, das Ihnen von Ihrer Schule bereitgestellt wird!

2   Reading for detail   (7)

Lesen Sie nun auch den Rest der Stellenausschreibung sorgfältig und beantworten Sie die folgenden Fragen Ihrer Nachbarin. Kreuzen Sie Zutreffendes an!

„Hilf mir bitte! Habe ich dem <u>übrigen</u> Text richtig entnommen, dass die irische Firma Happy Deals ..."   ja   nein

1. ihr erstes Restaurant bereits vor 1978 eröffnete?   ☐ ☐

2. eine Kette von Restaurants betreibt?   ☐ ☐

3. auch Bewerbungen aus dem Ausland berücksichtigt?   ☐ ☐

4. Bewerbungen ohne vorherige Erfahrung aus dem Hotel- und Gaststättenbereich unberücksichtigt lässt?   ☐ ☐

5. mir zunächst eine Unterkunft bereitstellt?   ☐ ☐

6. Fortbildungen an meinem künftigen Arbeitsort durchführt?   ☐ ☐

7. einen Einstieg in die Selbstständigkeit garantiert?   ☐ ☐

Assistant Restaurant Manager – Dublin
Location: Dublin
Salary: To Be Discussed

About Us:
Happy Deals is Ireland's largest and fastest growing food group. *Happy Deals'* first restaurant opened its doors back in 1978 in Main Street, Cork. Our company's success is built on a menu ideally designed for Irish tastes. We only use real, fresh vegetables and fruit from organic farming in Ireland. Last year we were given the Irish Award for Food Excellence. The quality of service is guaranteed by management and staff of *Happy Deals,* who give our restaurants a friendly, warm atmosphere. Currently we operate 65 branches in various counties of the republic and employ more than 2,500 members of staff from all over the world.

We want to employ an Assistant Manager who will work with the General Manageress and support her in the day to day running of our new restaurant in Dublin.

About You:
The successful candidate will be responsible for all cash transfers, for arranging shifts and for hiring new employees. You will work as part of the management team. You will receive training in all aspects of the management of a restaurant, which will offer you the chance to apply for a position in General Management later on.

You should have some experience in the service industry, be organised and able to motivate staff on a daily basis.

Our Benefits:
- highly-competitive starting salary
- short-term accommodation for new members of staff in the capital's boom town area
- regular in-house training sessions at our headquarters in Cork
- opportunity to start up your own *Happy Deals* restaurant

3 Note taking (15)

Ihre Klasse arbeitet an einem Projekt zum Thema „Gesunde Ernährung". Sie wollen wesentliche Informationen aus einem Artikel einer britischen Zeitung einbringen.

Lesen Sie diesen Artikel und vervollständigen Sie stichpunktartig folgendes Inforaster in <u>deutscher Sprache</u>!

Schools ban on soft drinks and sweets

1.	Maßnahmen zur Bekämpfung von Übergewicht bei Schulkindern in Connecticut:	– _____ – _____	(2) (2)
2.	Jamie Olivers Anregung für britische Schulen:	– _____ _____	(2)
3.	Grund, warum andere US-Staaten nicht so entschieden vorgehen:	– _____ _____	(2)
4.	Maßnahmen der Schulbehörde in Connecticut:	– _____ – _____	(1) (1)
5.	Gegner der neuen Regelung:	– _____ – _____	(0,5) (0,5)
6.	Gründe für die Ablehnung dieser Regelung:	– _____ – _____	(1) (2)
7.	Ausnahmeregelung:	– _____ _____	(1)

Text zu Task 3 Schools ban on soft drinks and sweets

Americans realized how serious the problem was when former president Bill Clinton and the Governor of Arkansas, Mike Huckabee, came together 45 **to fight against America's epidemic of overweight. The two men started a ten-year campaign to get the fast-food industry to serve smaller and healthier portions, and to improve school din-** 50 **ners. Now the federal state of Connecticut has begun with the most radical campaign ever to fight childhood overweight in America.**

Schools in Connecticut were forbidden 55 yesterday from selling high-calorie fizzy drinks and junk food.

Children under 11 will also have to take an extra 20 minutes of exercise a day in addi- 60 tion to their normal physical education classes. The rules are the result of the Senate passing America's strictest anti-over- 65 weight law. This means that all sugary drinks, chocolate and crisps will be banned from all schools.

The state will not, however, follow Jamie Oliver's campaign for healthy eating and 70 ban burgers and chips from school canteens as the famous chef has tried to do in Britain. Seventeen other US states have passed laws in an effort to fight against 75 overweight in children, but none has gone so far as to introduce a total ban on sugared soft drinks. These are products 80 of an industry that carries a huge financial

power and political influence across America.

Connecticut's Education Department will not allow schools to sell anything considered to cause overweight or to be generally harmful to the students' health. Moreover, a list of unhealthy items will be published in the near future to inform schools what they can or cannot offer their students.

The decision was one of the most hotly debated in Connecticut's Senate – with a debate lasting far longer than debates on many other matters.

Over 70 per cent of Connecticut parents supported a ban of soft drinks in schools.

However, there have been strong protests by the soft-drink industry and by some people running school canteens who fear a loss in income if the drinks are banned:

About $ 700 million of soft drinks were sold last year – and many of them to students nationwide.

Soft drink companies want to reach consumers when they are young and still easy to influence. In this way they establish brand loyalties: 11-year-olds who have developed a taste for a particular soft drink are likely to remain loyal to this drink when they are grown-ups.

So the critics of the ban will be pleased to hear that politicians have finally agreed on a compromise: Sales of sugared drinks at sports games and other school events will be allowed.

(Adapted from The Times, 27 May 2005)

Part B: Overall Language Proficiency

1 **Fill in each gap in the text with one appropriate word** (14)

Im lokalen Fernsehprogramm tritt Ihr Freund Andreas erfolgreich als Fernseh-Koch auf. Im Rahmen einer Bewerbung für eine Koch-Sendung bei „*Young Adults' Cooking TV*" muss er sich in englischer Sprache schriftlich vorstellen. Andreas ist sich bei einigen Formulierungen seiner Bewerbung unsicher.

Er bittet Sie, die korrekte Lösung aus seinen vier Vorschlägen (A, B, C, D) auszuwählen. Schreiben Sie den richtigen Buchstaben in die entsprechende Lücke, z. B. (0) A̲!

I have always been a bit of an entertainer and played the funny man. As a youngster, I was a carnival comedian (1) _____ years, so I learned how to stand in front of (2) _____. It made me sure of myself. I like being liked and I love making (3) _____ smile and laugh.

I (4) _____ in Bavaria all my life. We have just moved to a larger house in the countryside. That's where you can find about the best traditional meals. I (5) _____ up in a family where cooking is important because my dad was a chef himself.

My working day is divided (6) _____ my local TV programme and writing cookbooks, (7) _____ writing the books takes up most of my time: I spend about four evenings a week working on new recipes.

At home we eat all sorts of things but I insist on (8) _____ quality food that we buy only from local farmers. When I am cooking, I experiment with (9) _____ is in the fridge – it is good practice for my TV series!

I am very much interested (10) _____ vegetarian diets. I really enjoy mixing Asian food with Bavarian sauces, but my brothers and sisters (11) _____. We do go out about twice a month but there is nothing better (12) _____ a night at home having a delicious dinner with the family. I hardly ever go to bed before midnight. Late (13) _____ the evening is when fresh thoughts on cooking usually come to my mind, so I often write or plan my TV programmes then. But I never miss a good night's sleep and, (14) _____ I finally get to bed, I have no trouble sleeping.

	A	B	C	D
1	since	for	ago	in
2	stages	crowded	public	audiences
3	each	all	everyone	someone
4	have been living	live	was living	lived
5	grew	has grown	am growing	am grown
6	among	on	between	by
7	although	because	while	even
8	to buy	bought	buying	buy
9	whichever	whatever	whoever	wherever

10	on	for	of	in
11	haven't	aren't	don't	weren't
12	than	how	like	as
13	at	in	on	from
14	when	while	if	who

2 Explanations (6)

Your Italian friend Francesca has asked you out for dinner to *CHOPPERS* in Dublin. After you have entered the restaurant, Francesca points at three signs on the walls.

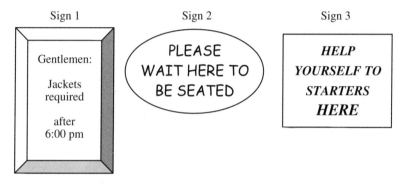

Sign 1   Sign 2   Sign 3

Gentlemen:

Jackets
required

after
6:00 pm

PLEASE
WAIT HERE TO
BE SEATED

*HELP
YOURSELF TO
STARTERS
HERE*

Francesca would like **you** to explain to her in **your own words** what the three sings mean. **Please write at least one sentence each.**

1. Sign 1 means: _____
   _____ (2)
   _____

2. Sign 2 means: _____
   _____ (2)
   _____

3. Sign 3 means: _____
   _____ (2)
   _____

Part C: Productive Skills

Vorschlag I

1 Writing a formal letter (18)

Sie planen nach Abschluss der Wirtschaftsschule eine längere Reise nach Irland. Im Internet sind Sie auf folgende Anzeige aufmerksam geworden:

Working Holidays for Backpackers in Ireland!

If you are backpacking in Ireland there is a service designed to find you a job.

Live-in-jobs is run by Dee Cooper, who can find you a hotel job including free food and accommodation. The jobs are in waiting, bar, housekeeping and kitchen and make the ideal summer job for 1 to 4 months. So if you are looking for a job in Ireland, hotel employment may be the answer. Please send your application to Mr. Dee Cooper.

For more details, please have a look at our website: www.live-in-jobs.ei

---

Verfassen Sie eine Bewerbung an Mr. Cooper in englischer Sprache.
Benutzen Sie dafür ein Extrablatt, das Ihnen von Ihrer Schule bereitgestellt wird. Ihr Schreiben sollte folgende Punkte beinhalten:
- Anrede
- Bezugnahme auf Internet-Anzeige
- Interesse an Ferienarbeit in einem Hotel, gewünschter Zeitraum: September 2006
- Wunsch äußern, wenn möglich an der Westküste Irlands zu arbeiten
- bisher schon regelmäßige Tätigkeit als Kellner/in an Wochenenden in einem Café
- Gründe für Bewerbung: Aufbesserung der Urlaubskasse und Vertiefung der Sprachkenntnisse
- Lebenslauf als Anlage beigefügt
- höflicher Schlusssatz
- Grußformel

2 Writing an informal letter (12)

Seit Ihrem Backpacking-Urlaub in Irland stehen Sie mit Francesca aus Italien in Kontakt. In ihrer letzten E-Mail erkundigte sich Francesca nach dem „Rock im Park"-Festival.

Schreiben Sie eine Antwort an Francesca **in englischer Sprache** und gehen Sie dabei auf die folgenden Punkte ein:
- Rock im Park: größtes und bekanntestes Musik-Festival in Bayern
- alljährliche Veranstaltung im Juni in Nürnberg
- Auftritte vieler berühmter Bands aus der ganzen Welt über drei Tage auf mehreren Bühnen
- Einladung an Francesca zum nächsten Festival
- Übernachtungsmöglichkeit bei Ihnen zu Hause
- Freude auf ein Wiedersehen

Benutzen Sie dafür ein Extrablatt, das Ihnen von Ihrer Schule bereitgestellt wird.

Vorschlag II

1 Telling a story (12)

Während Ihres Aufenthaltes in Irland möchten Sie an einem Schreibwettbewerb der *Irish Times* teilnehmen. Als Preis für die besten Einsendungen winken zwei Eintrittskarten für ein Konzert der irischen Band U2.

Schreiben Sie die folgende Geschichte weiter! Ihr Beitrag in englischer Sprache sollte etwa 80 Wörter umfassen.

Benutzen Sie dafür ein **Extrablatt**, das Ihnen von Ihrer Schule bereitgestellt wird.

It was already midnight. Sam was walking along a narrow street. He had left the disco only a few minutes before because he hadn't been able to stand the music any longer. Meeting his girlfriend wasn't a great success either – why was she always so jealous when he talked to other girls? Sam passed the church and turned left. It was only a five minutes' walk now.

Lost in his thoughts he put his hand into the pocket of the jacket he was wearing and was surprised to feel a small package there. Before he could check what it was, he suddenly heard footsteps behind him ...

---

2 Writing a formal letter (18)

Nach Ihrer Rückkehr aus Irland arbeiten Sie in einem Reisebüro in Ihrer Nähe. Ihre Chefin bittet Sie, eine Anfrage für eine Reisegruppe mit Ziel Irland zu verfassen. Die Gruppe möchte unter anderem die Keksfabrik *Mother's Pride* bei Dublin besichtigen.

Entwerfen Sie diese Anfrage **in englischer Sprache** nach den folgenden Anweisungen Ihrer Chefin!

- Anrede
- Kurze Vorstellung unseres Reisebüros, führender Anbieter in Süddeutschland von Gruppenreisen nach Irland
- Interesse einer Reisegruppe an einer Werksbesichtigung von *Mother's Pride*
- Kekse dieser Marke aus der Fernsehwerbung bekannt und in Deutschland sehr beliebt
- Termin am 20. oder 21. Juli?
- Kostproben und Werksverkauf im Anschluss an die Führung?
- Teilnahme auch für drei behinderte Gruppenmitglieder möglich?
- Höflicher Schlusssatz
- Grußformel

Benutzen Sie dafür ein **Extrablatt**, das Ihnen von Ihrer Schule bereitgestellt wird.

Lösungen

Part A

1 Translation (Happy Deals)

Hinweis: Hier musst du den eingekreisten Teil der Stellenanzeige ins Deutsche überset-zen. Durch die Übersetzung musst du zeigen, dass du den Sinn des Textes verstanden hast. Versuche nicht, Wort für Wort zu übersetzen. Lies einen ganzen Satz, bevor du den deutschen Satz formulierst. Wenn du ein Wort im englischen Text nicht verstehst, dann versuche, die mögliche Bedeutung aus dem Zusammenhang zu erschließen.

Der erfolgreiche Kandidat wird für alle Geldüberweisungen, das Arrangieren von Arbeitsschichten und das Einstellen von neuen Arbeitnehmern verantwortlich sein. Sie werden als Teil des Managementteams arbeiten. Sie werden eine Schulung zu allen Aspekten der Verwaltung eines Restaurants bekommen, die Ihnen später die Chance bieten wird, sich um eine Stelle in der Hauptverwaltung zu bewerben.

2 Reading for detail (Happy Deals)

Hinweis: Ein englischer Text wird vorgegeben, jedoch werden die Fragen, die als rich-tig oder falsch markiert werden müssen, in deutscher Sprache gestellt.
Es ist ratsam, die Fragen zu lesen, bevor du den Text liest. So kannst du die entspre-chenden Stellen im Text während des Lesens finden. Du solltest aber unbedingt den ganzen Text gründlich lesen und nicht nur einzelne Informationen suchen. Beim Über-fliegen eines Textes gehst du das Risiko ein, dass du wichtige Informationen verpasst und den allgemeinen Zusammenhang nicht wirklich verstehst.

	ja	nein
1. ihr erstes Restaurant bereits vor 1978 eröffnete?		X
2. eine Kette von Restaurants betreibt?	X	
3. auch Bewerbungen aus dem Ausland berücksichtigt?	X	
4. Bewerbungen ohne vorherige Erfahrung aus dem Hotel- und Gaststättenbereich unberücksichtigt lässt?		X
5. mir zunächst eine Unterkunft bereitstellt?	X	
6. Fortbildungen an meinem künftigen Arbeitsort durchführt?		X
7. einen Einstieg in die Selbstständigkeit garantiert?		X

3 Note taking

Hinweis: Hier ist ein englischer Text gründlich zu lesen. Das Inforaster muss stich-punktartig in deutscher Sprache vervollständigt werden. Es ist empfehlenswert, zuerst das Raster genau anzusehen und dann den ganzen Text zu lesen. Es ist vielleicht hilf-reich, mit einem Bleistift zutreffende Stellen des Textes zu kennzeichnen. So kannst du gezielter die richtigen Lösungen finden. Achte darauf, dass deine Antworten immer auf die Informationen des Textes bezogen sind.

1.	Maßnahmen zur Bekämpfung von Übergewicht bei Schulkindern in Connecticut:	– Gesetz gegen Verkauf von kalorienreichen/zuckerhaltigen Sprudelgetränken und Junkfood an Schulen	(2)
		– täglich 20-minütiges Extratraining für unter 11-Jährige (zusätzlich zum Sportunterricht)	(2)
2.	Jamie Olivers Anregung für britische Schulen:	– Verbot von Burgern und Pommes in brit Schulkantinen	(2)
3.	Grund, warum andere US Staaten nicht so entschieden vorgehen:	– finanzielle Möglichkeiten und politischer Einfluss der Getränkeindustrie	(2)
4.	Maßnahmen der Schulbehörde in Connecticut:	– Verbot des Verkaufs von ungesunden Snacks	
		– Veröffentlichung einer entsprechenden Liste	(2)
5.	Gegner der neuen Regelung:	– Getränkeindustrie – Kantinenbetreiber	(1)
6.	Gründe für die Ablehnung dieser Regelung:	– Einkommensverluste	(1)
		– fehlende Bindung junger Konsumenten an die Produkte	(2)
7.	Ausnahmeregelung:	– Verkauf von zuckerhaltigen Getränken bei Schulveranstaltungen zulässig	(1)

Aufgabenteil B – Overall Language Proficiency

1   Multiple choice
Fill in each gap in the text with one appropriate word.

Hinweis:
1. *„for" bezeichnet einen Zeitraum in der Vergangenheit.*
2. *false friends („audience" = Publikum, „public"= öffentlich)*
3. *„everyone" ist ein Pronomen im Plural – „all" passt hier nicht, weil kein Nomen dabeisteht.*
4. *Present perfect continuous, weil die Handlung noch nicht abgeschlossen ist.*
5. *Simple past, weil die Handlung abgeschlossen ist.*
6. *„between" = zwischen (zwei Sachen) – „among" = unter (ab drei Sachen)*
7. *„although" = obwohl – Textzusammenhang*
8. *„insist on" + Gerundium*
9. *„whatever" ist ein Pronomen, das sich auf Gegenstände bezieht. Man verwendet es, wenn die Auswahlmöglichkeit größer ist.*
10. *feste Verbindung „interested in"*
11. *Verneinung vom Verb „to enjoy"*
12. *Vergleich von zwei Sachen*
13. *feste Verbindung „in the evening" = am Abend*
14. *wenn = „when" in diesem Zusammenhang, weil es sich um die Zeit handelt und nicht um einen Bedingungssatz.*

Lücke No.	Lösung	Lücke No.	Lösung
1	B	8	C
2	D	9	B
3	C	10	D
4	A	11	C
5	A	12	A
6	C	13	B
7	A	14	A

2   Explanations

Hinweis: Hier müssen die Bedeutungen der Schilder im Kontext eines Restaurants auf Englisch beschrieben werden. Wichtig ist, dass du so weit wie möglich deine eigenen Worte verwendest.

1. Sign 1 means: Men must/have to/need to wear a jacket after 6:00 p.m.
2. Sign 2 means: Customers should stand there and a waiter/waitress will come and take them to their table.
3. Sign 3 means: Customers can choose/ take appetizers from the buffet themselves.

Aufgabenteil C – Productive skills

Hinweis: Hier findest du zwei Vorschläge, die jeweils aus zwei Aufgaben bestehen. In der Prüfung wählt dein Lehrer einen der Vorschläge aus.

Vorschlag I

1   Writing a formal letter

Hinweis: Bei formellen Briefen ist auf Sachlichkeit und Höflichkeit zu achten. Denke an die üblichen geschäftlichen Redewendungen, die du im Laufe der Jahre gelernt hast. Hier ist es sehr wichtig, festzustellen, wer den Brief schreibt und wer den Brief empfängt.

Dear Mr. Cooper

I saw your advertisement on the Internet. I'm interested in a holiday job in a hotel. The best time for me would be September 2006. If it is possible, I would like to work on the west coast of Ireland. Until now I have been working regularly as a waiter in a café at weekends. The reasons for my application are that I would like to earn money for my holiday and improve my English.
I have enclosed a copy of my CV. I look forward to hearing from you soon.

Yours sincerely
Paul Smith

2   Writing an informal letter

Hinweis: Hier sind die Zeiten besonders zu beachten.

Dear Francesca

Thanks for your e-mail. You wanted to know more about the "Rock im Park" music festival. It is the biggest and most well-known music festival in Bavaria. The festival takes place every year in Nürnberg in June. There are performances from lots of famous bands from all over the world on several stages. The festival lasts for three days. I would like to invite you to the next festival. You could stay at our house. I am looking forward to seeing you soon.

Best wishes
Annie

Vorschlag II

1   Telling a story

Hinweis: Hier darfst du kreativ sein, allerdings muss die Geschichte einen Sinn ergeben. Besonders zu beachten sind Satzbau und Grammatik.

He turned around and saw two men. One of the men showed him an identity card and explained that they were detectives. The two men wanted to see what was in Sam's pockets. Sam suddenly remembered the little package and became nervous. Sam gave it to one of the detectives who opened it. There were drugs inside. Afterwards the police explained that they had been watching the disco trying to catch a drug dealer. Before Sam left the disco they had seen the dealer hide the package in Sam's jacket.

2 Writing a formal letter

Hinweis: Auch hier ist ein formeller Brief zu schreiben.

Dear Sir or Madam

We are a travel agency in southern Germany and are the market leader in offering group travel to Ireland. One of our travel groups is interested in touring your factory. This brand of biscuit is well-known in Germany because of the TV advertisement and is very popular. Could we make an appointment for 20th or 21st of July? Would it be possible to try some biscuits and shop at your factory store at the end of the tour? Would it be possible for three disabled group members to take part in the tour?
We look forward to hearing from you soon.

Yours faithfully
Theresa Braun

Tapescript zu Worksheet 1

(**R** = Receptionist; **S** = Stefan Schneider; **H** = Peter Hutchins)

R.: Good afternoon, Music Xpress Ltd., Monica Trevor speaking. How can I help you?

S.: Good afternoon, Ms Trevor. Well, I'm calling because I have a few questions about my application that I sent to your company a couple of weeks ago.

R.: Oh, one moment please, I'll put you through to the personnel department.

5 [internal dialling tone]

H.: Good afternoon, personnel department, Peter Hutchins speaking. What can I do for you?

S.: Good afternoon. My name is Schneider, Stefan Schneider, and I'm calling to enquire about my application. I was wondering if you got my letter of uhm May the 25th

10 because I haven't received a reply yet.

H.: Oh, well, let me see. Could you repeat your name, please?

S.: Stefan Schneider.

H.: OK. I'll check that in my computer, [keyboard clicking] Ah, yes, here you are. Now then, let's have a look. I can confirm that we got your letter three weeks ago and that

15 our reply was posted to you on June the 9th. So it's a bit of a surprise to me that you haven't received it yet. I'm terribly sorry, but there must have been a mistake in the mailing process somewhere. The reply may have got lost in the post. But actually, from what I can see on my screen that we did in fact invite you to an interview.

S.: Oh, really? That's fantastic!

20 H.: So I guess you're still interested?

S.: Yes, Sir, I certainly am.

H.: Great. So let's fix an appointment, shall we? I'll get my diary. Right, we have a number of interviews next week on Tuesday, Thursday and on Friday. Would Thursday morning, uhm the fourteenth that is, be convenient?

25 S.: One moment, please, let me think now. In the mornings I attend a language course, so could I come in the afternoon?

H.: Well, I'm afraid Thursday afternoon is unfortunately not possible, but Friday at half past three would fit in nicely.

S.: Friday, the fifteenth of June? That's fine with me.

30 H.: OK, Mr Schneider. Oh; just one more thing. You've already mentioned some interesting things in your CV. However, we're also interested in further skills you might have, such as uhm word processing. Could you please send any certificates you've got to me?

S.: Sure, Mr uhm?

35 H.: Hutchins, that is H U T C H I N S.

S.: OK, Mr Hutchins. I'll send that off as soon as possible. Thank you very much and goodbye.

H.: You're welcome. Goodbye, Mr Schneider.

Tapescript zu Worksheet 2

(**S** = Stefan Schneider; **P** = person on a street in Sheffield)

[a bit of traffic background noise]
S.: Excuse me, please. Could you help me?
P.: Hello, young man. What's up?
S.: Well, I'm looking for the quickest way to get to Music Xpress Ltd. I've got a job
5   interview there in three quarters of an hour. So I'm rather in a hurry.
P.: Music Xpress? You're lucky. I just passed that on my way back from work. My first
    advice, young man, would be to take a taxi. Over there, on your right, there are lots of
    taxis waiting for you. They'll take you across the steep hills north of Leith Street in
    next to no time at all.
10 S.: Taxis? Oh, I'm afraid I can't afford one. What about public transport?
P.: No chance! There's been an accident right at the crossroads of George and Dundas
    Street. For you, I'm afraid, it's a walk.
S.: A walk?
P.: Yes, my dear. It's a bit complicated, but don't worry. If you hurry, you can still make
15   it in time. First of all, go down Princes Street past the high building on your left,
    which is the NatWest Bank, until you get to the bus stop. On the corner of Princes
    Street and The Mound, there's no pedestrian crossing, so you have to take the subway.
    Where you come out again, there's the so-called 'One-Pound-Shop'. Go straight on
    and follow Princes Street to the next turning on your right. Turn right there and go
20   along this street. Cross George Street, the next big street, and walk past Wilberforce
    Column with a statue of William Wilberforce, on your right, till you get to Queen
    Street. There, you must turn right. Go a bit further on until you get to Dundas Street.
    Turn left at the crossroads and go along Dundas Street. Stay on that road and go
    straight on. You'll go past Georgie's Gymnasium on your right.
25 S.: A school, you mean?
P.: I'm afraid you're not quite right. It's Sheffield's most recent indoor fitness and games
    club.
S.: Oh, I see. Is it still a long way to go from there?
P.: Don't worry, you've almost made it when you've got there.
30   Go straight on until you reach Victoria Gardens with its beautiful lawns on your left.
    At the next crossroads still go straight on and follow the street that slightly turns to the
    right, and keep going. Then take a sharp turn to the right and right ahead, on your left,
    you'll see the blue building of Music XPress.
S.: That sounds rather complicated, but I am sure I'll make. Thank you very much.
35 P.: You'd better hurry as quickly as you can. Wish you the best of luck for your inter-
    view.
S.: Thank you.
[footsteps fading out]

Tapescript zu Worksheet 3

(**S** = Stefan Schneider; **H** = Peter Hutchins)

H.: Good afternoon, Mr Schneider. Please take a seat.
S.: [breathlessly] Thank you very much, Sir.
H.: I hope it wasn't too difficult for you to find your way here?
S.: [still trying to catch his breath] Oh no, no, it wasn't.
5 H.: Well, thank you for coming at such a short notice and showing such interest in the
    position of an office clerk. My name is Peter Hutchins, junior manager of our Person-

nel Department. We had the pleasure of talking with each other over the phone the other week, didn't we?

S.: Yes, we did, and thank you very much again for inviting me to this interview.

10 H.: It's a pleasure. Let's start with a few questions. First of all, I'd like to know a bit more about you, maybe your school career and so on. Uhm, could you tell me why you changed from a secondary school to a commercial school?

S.: Yes, of course. Well, at the age of eleven, I started attending a secondary school in Munich, Germany. I must say I really liked life at that school in Munich. I think it was

15 in year 7 or 8, when my results in maths and science started to become rather poor. That's why I wanted to change schools anyway. And on top of that the next year our family moved from Munich to Kronach in northern Bavaria.

H.: I see. Let's move on a bit: Why actually did you choose to apply for this particular job with Music Xpress Ltd?

20 S.: Well, working in a music company like yours would really be a dream come true. Day in – day out, the latest releases of the leading artists around the world would be at my fingertips. I could listen to my favourite group, the "Green Eyed Pears," before anyone else can. And there's something else, which I've learned from your website. You'd be prepared to grant a generous staff discount of 50 per cent on all mp3 down-

25 loads. Half the price for employees, which is more than I could have hoped for. And what's most important to me – my friend Cindy lives in Greenwood.

H.: That's near here, isn't it?

S.: Yes, it is: It's a village in Derbyshire, just 12 miles from here.

H.: Aha. I've got just one more question for now, Mr Schneider. What do you see your-

30 self doing in five years' time?

S.: In five years' time, that would be in the year two thousand and twelve, wouldn't it? I hope I will have succeeded in running a studio of my own. Alternatively, I'd like to organize parties in a country with lots of sun and miles of sandy beaches.

H.: Very interesting, because we have some vacancies in our branches in Spain and Italy.

35 Whereabouts would you like ... [fade out]

Worksheets

1   **Arranging an interview**   (5)

Stefan Schneider from Kronach is spending some time in England. He has applied for a job with *Music Xpress Ltd.* in Sheffield. As he hasn't heard anything from the company yet, he is making a phone call.

You will hear a conversation between Stefan Schneider and someone from the personnel department. Take down some notes <u>in English</u> to complete the telephone memo below. You need not write complete sentences. You will hear the recording twice and after the second listening you will have one minute to check your answers.

☎ Telephone Memo ☎

1 **Company:**

   Music Xpress Ltd. Sheffield

2 **Person responsible in personnel department?**

   _____   (1)

3 **No answer to application! Reason?**

   _____   (1)

4 **Interview: When exactly?**

   Date: _____   (1)

   Time: _____   (1)

5 **Anything else required?**

   _____   (1)

---

2   Asking the way   (6)

Stefan Schneider is on his way to *Music XPress Ltd.* for his job interview. You are going to hear a dialogue between Stefan and someone he has met on a street in Sheffield. They are standing in front of the Tourist Information Office. Look at the map and find out which places or facilities Stefan is going to pass on his way to *Music XPress Ltd.*

Match the numbers of the places/facilities in the map with the places/facilities listed below. Write the correct numbers into the boxes. You will hear the dialogue twice and after the second listening you will have one minute to check your answers.

Be careful: there are more numbers and places/facilities listed than you actually need.

Example: Place/facility number 0 in the map is where the taxis are.

☑   taxis

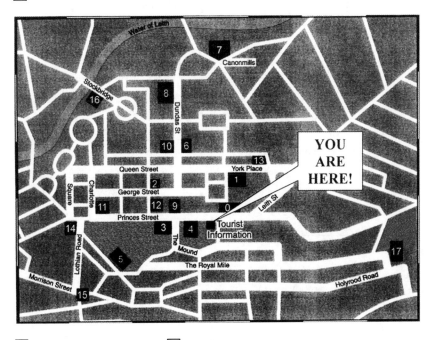

☐	a park	☐	a church
☐	a school	☐	a monument
☐	a restaurant	☐	Music Xpress Ltd.
☐	a bank	☐	a leisure centre
☐	a shopping mall	☐	a football ground
☐	a pedestrian crossing	☐	a shop for cheap things

3   **Job interview**   (9)

Stefan Schneider is having his interview at Music Xpress Ltd.

You will hear a dialogue between Mr Schneider and the human resources manager.

Fill in the missing information <u>in English</u> *into the INTERVIEW FORM below.*
Tick the correct box(es) and take notes. *You need not write complete sentences. You will hear the dialogue twice and after the second listening you will
have one minute to check your answers.*

MUSIC XPRESS LTD INTERVIEW FORM		
Applicant's name:	*Mr Stefan Schneider*	
Applying for current vacancy as:	☐ **office cleaner** ☐ **member of office staff** ☐ **junior personnel manager** ☐ **studio manager**	(1)
Schools attended:	• _____ • _____	(0,5) (0,5)
Reasons for school change:	• _____ _____ • _____ _____	(1) (1)
Reasons for applying:	• _____ • _____ • _____	(1) (1) (1)
Future plans:	• _____ • _____	(1) (1)

Part A 1

1   Worksheet 1: Arranging an interview

Hinweis: Im ersten Teil der Hörverstehensprüfung geht es um ein Telefongespräch. Es ist immer hilfreich, wenn du die Fragen liest, bevor du den Text hörst. Mache dir ruhig Notizen beim ersten Zuhören, dann hast du am Schluss Zeit, um deine Antworten zu vervollständigen.

☎ Telephone Memo ☎

1   Company:

Music Xpress Ltd, Sheffield

2   Person responsible in personnel department?

Peter Hutchins

3   No answer to application! Reason?

mistake in mailing process

4   Interview: When exactly?

Date: (Friday) 15th June

Time: 3:30 pm

5   Anything else required?

certificates

---

2   Worksheet 2: Asking the way

Hinweis: Im zweiten Teil der Hörverstehensprüfung hörst du eine Wegbeschreibung. Während des Zuhörens folge der Strecke mit deinem Finger oder einem Stift und stelle fest, an welchen Gebäuden Stefan vorbeigeht. Trage die Nummern auf dem Stadtplan in die entsprechenden Kästchen ein.

8	a park	☐	a church
☐	a school	2	a monument
☐	a restaurant	7	Music Xpress Ltd.
4	a bank	6	a leisure centre
☐	a shopping mall	☐	a football ground
☐	a pedestrian crossing	3	a shop for cheap things

Worksheet 3: Job interview

Hinweis: Im letzten Teil der Hörverstehensprüfung musst du ein Formular für Vorstellungsgespräche ausfüllen.

MUSIC XPRESS LTD INTERVIEW FORM	
Applicant's name:	*Mr Stefan Schneider*
Applying for current vacancy as:	☐ **office cleaner** ☒ **member of office staff** ☐ **junior personnel manager** ☐ **studio manager**
Schools attended:	• *secondary school* • *commercial school*
Reasons for school change:	• *poor results in maths and science* • *family moved (house) to Kronach*
Reasons for applying:	• *chance to listen to new releases* • *50 percent staff discount* • *friend Cindy lives nearby*
Future plans	• *run a studio* • *organize beach parties (in the south)*

Part A

Text 1: A Shopping Mall in Sheffield, England

Before the early 1980s Sheffield was the heart of a
booming industry. However, life became hard in England's
fourth-largest city when later factory production was auto-
mated and in addition the UK faced a serious recession.

5 In 1984 *Hatfield's Steelworks* went out of business and the
factory site, just three miles outside Sheffield's city centre,
could be used for other purposes. One of the UK's largest
investment companies purchased the area for £1.17 billion
and decided to develop a huge retail and entertainment

10 centre: *Meadowhall*. At that time, the city of Sheffield did
not have as many opportunities for shopping as other towns
in the UK did.

Directly linked to the M1 motorway, *Meadowhall* is within
a 60-minute drive of 8.2 million customers – that is one in

15 eight of the UK population. This is much more than the 3.4
million shoppers that most shopping centres in the nearby
Greater Manchester Area can on average hope to attract.

When *Meadowhall* first opened its doors to customers at
ten a.m. on Tuesday, 4th September 1990, the face of Shef-

20 field had changed forever: What used to be a manufacturing industry had been replaced by an industry which was
based on leisure and retail.

By the end of the first morning over 50,000 people had
visited the Centre and ten days later *Meadowhall's* one

25 millionth visitor walked through the doors to explore 1.4
million square feet of shop floor. From the very beginning
71 percent of the Centre was leased: 270 brand-new stores
opened, including – for the first time – seven major UK
stores together under one roof. Since then another 35 have

30 been added to the list. It was also the first day of work for
over 10,000 employees, whose number has risen to 13,500
so far.

But *Meadowhall* offers more than just shopping. Over the
years, *Meadowhall* has attracted the crowds with some

35 fantastic customer events including celebrity appearances,
fashion shows and – who could forget – the world record
breaking Living Doll Event, when real living people took
the place of 300 store mannequins and posed for six hours
in shop windows around the Centre.

40 *Meadowhall* has always been concerned about the environ-
ment. Back in 1992, the Centre's management established its own 'Green standards'. Today the Centre is taking its environmental responsibilities seriously in a number of areas.
For example, it recycles over 2,000 tons of waste each year. Moreover, *Meadowhall* plays
a leading role in promoting the use of public transport and in improving the quality of air

Meadowhall

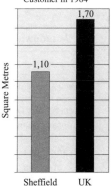

Retail Space per
Customer in 1984

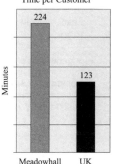

Average Shopping
Time per Customer

45 by replacing oil-fuelled heating by solar panels. *Meadowhall's* excellent record in the area of environmental policies has been recognised even outside Sheffield. In January 2007, the Prince of Wales himself gave the Centre one of the highest awards for its environmental policies in Britain: Five Green Stars.

1   Note taking   (18)

Stefan Schneider möchte sich auch noch über andere Stellen informieren. Er hat Ihnen **Text 1** über die Firma *Meadowhall* zugesandt und Sie gebeten, nachstehendes Info-Raster für ihn in **deutscher** Sprache auszufüllen.

Notizen zum „Einkaufszentrum Meadowhall"		
1. Sheffield		
frühere Bedeutung als:	• _____	(1)
Bedeutungsverlust aufgrund:	• _____	(1)
	• _____	(1)
2. Meadowhall		
geographische Lage in Sheffield:	• _____	(1)
vorherige Nutzung des Geländes:	• _____	(1)
Eignung des Geländes für ein Einkaufszentrum wegen:	• _____	(1)
	• _____	(1)
Anzahl möglicher Kunden im Einzugsgebiet:	• _____	(1)
durchschnittliche Verweildauer der Kunden:	• _____	(1)
Besucherzahl bis zum 14. September 1990:	• _____	(1)
gegenwärtige Anzahl von Geschäften:	• _____	(1)
momentane Anzahl von Angestellten:	• _____	(1)
besondere Werbeaktionen:	• _____	(1)
	• _____	(1)
	• _____	(1)
Auszeichnung mit einem Umwelt-Preis für folgende Leistungen:	• _____	(1)
	• _____	(1)
	• _____	(1)

Text 2: Shops in *Meadowhall*

After collecting some general information about *Meadowhall,* Stefan is especially interested in some of the shops there. These new shops are likely to offer some vacancies:

Pay us a visit in *Meadowhall*	
Grab a Bag ✶✶ An addition to *Meadowhall's* Ground Floor, offering great pancakes and other tasty take-aways. Why not try the *bag of today* at attractive prices? For all orders over £ 20 same-day delivery to your Sheffield front door at no extra cost. New on your next visit in July!	**Pugs & Kisses** – *open* – Stylish products for our four-legged friends. The majority of the products are imported from the USA and have previously not been available in the UK. We offer an extensive range of beds, toys, eating accessories, health and beauty products! Located on the Upper Floor.
Granny's Delight Freshly opened on the Upper Floor, this store stocks a huge range of biscuits, including some of the most wonderful Yorkshire double-creamed ones. Have a try of our selection of cakes made according to recipes from the times when your grandparents were as young as your children are now. The perfect sweets for your sweets.	**Monophone** DJanes and DJs: *Monophone* on the Ground Floor is the place for you with more than 25,000 hits on 33 or 45. Unhappy with the sound of CDs and DVDs? Nothing beats the real thing for your perfect scratching performance. At unbeatable prices, we buy and sell all vinyl records, no matter what their release year was.
Carat – *under new management* – With a workout at *Carat,* it's as easy as ABC for you to get your body into perfect shape before walking along a sunny beach in Barcelona next month. We have now installed 16 of the most modern sun beds all waiting for you on the Upper Floor. If you are prepared to spend the extra pound or two, *Carat* is the name in Sheffield for health, beauty and sun.	*Abacho* – *open soon* – How about taking your family on a delicious journey before your summer holidays have actually begun? Our new chef prepares original appetizers from his mother country – and Barcelona will be on your tongues right here in Sheffield. Hot or cold – all items are to go, too. You can find us on level 2.
	Body Care – *opened recently* – Visit Ground Floor and change your light summer perfume to something more suitable to go with your autumn season's wardrobe. Of course, you will also find a wide selection of lotions and creams for you and your husband or friend.

2   Multiple matching   (7)

Use the information in the text to match the new shops in *Meadowhall* with the information in the right column.

*Write the correct **numbers** into column 2 (one number per shop).*

Grab a Bag	[ ]	1	... sells snacks from abroad.
Granny's Delight	[ ]	2	... is a bag shop.
Carat	[ ]	3	... sells clothes for the autumn season.
Pugs & Kisses	[ ]	4	... is a shop selling products for pets.
Monophone	[ ]	5	... offers beauty articles for men and women.
Abacho	[ ]	6	... sells British items produced in a traditional way.
Body Care	[ ]	7	... buys second-hand CDs and DVDs.
		8	... is a fitness centre.
		9	... brings products to your home.
		10	... purchases and offers albums and singles.

3   Reading for detail   (5)

Stefan has asked you to decide if his statements on **new** shops in *Meadowhall* are right or wrong.

Please tick (✓) the correct boxes.

Stefan, your statement is ...   right   wrong

Two new stores specialize in foreign products.   ☐   ☐

Two new food stores have started their businesses.   ☐   ☐

Two new stores are run by new bosses.   ☐   ☐

Two new stores will open soon on the Ground Floor.   ☐   ☐

Two new stores offer services.   ☐   ☐

Part B: Overall Language Proficiency

1   Multiple Choice   (14)

Stefan has finally got a job at Meadowhall in Sheffield and is writing to his pen friend, Tony, in Vancouver, Canada. Stefan already speaks some English, but he is still not sure of some aspects of grammar and vocabulary, so he asks you to help him to decide on the right expressions. **Underline them for him.**

---

92 Lenham Road

Sheffield
S11 9BX
England

Dear Tony,

Many thanks for your last letter. It's nice to know everything is going well in your life. I don't know if I **(told/said/tell)** you but I have got a great job in Music World, a shop in the *Meadowhall* shopping centre in Sheffield.

I **(am/was/have been)** there since the beginning of the month and the job is great: My boss is a young guy **(whose/who/who's)** only five years older **(as/than/from)** me – I really like him. I am having lots of **(interest/ interesting/interested)** experiences and I really enjoy **(talk/to talk/ talking)** to the customers here – their Yorkshire dialect is lovely to listen to! **(All/Everyone/Everything)** is so friendly to me.

Yesterday something really extraordinary **(happened/has happened/had happened)**. I was standing behind the counter when all of a sudden I saw my old friend Traudi next to the Folk Music section. Just imagine – she's got a job as an au pair in a family in Sheffield. It really is a small world! She had never mentioned to anyone back in Kronach that she **(will/wanted/would)** go to England to improve her English! She seems **(being/be/to be)** quite happy in her 'new' family: The children she looks **(after/with/for)** are very nice. She is usually so busy with the kids that she doesn't have **(some/any/no)** time to go shopping in *Meadowhall*. So we were really lucky to have met! Anyway, she likes the family so much that she is thinking of staying there for another six months. If she **(will stay/ would stay/stays)** so long, her English really will be good! Well I must stop now, and get my beauty sleep! I **(write/wrote/'ll write)** to you again when I have more time next weekend.

Very best wishes,
Stefan

---

1 Gap filling (6)

Stefan wants to see something of Sheffield in his spare time and he has got this brochure from the Tourist Information Agency.

What to do in and around Sheffield

Sheffield is a great place to be! You'll _____ love our parks and woodlands. Don't forget we're only five miles from the wonderful scenery of the Peak National Park! You'll also enjoy our exciting events and great _____. No matter what your _____ is we're sure you'll have a great time – as so _____ people have before you!

To get further information, please call +44 (0) 114 221 1900. The service is available Monday to Saturday between 9.00 am and 5.30 pm. An answering service operates outside of _____ times for ordering brochures.

You can also e-mail us at visitor@sheffield.gov.uk. We aim to reply to email requests and _____ messages by no later than the working day after the one on which they are received.

Fill each gap in the text with one appropriate word from the word bank below. (There are more words in the bank than you need.)

> ## Word bank:
>
> attractions – certainly – choice – many – recorded – these – certain – choose
> – this – recording – attracts – much

Part C: Productive Skills

Vorschlag I

1 Jumble sale notice (18)

Stefan hat schließlich eine Arbeitsstelle im Einkaufszentrum *Meadowhall* gefunden. Aufgrund der ungünstigen Busverbindung will er in der sonntäglichen Radiosendung JUMBLE SALE ein gebrauchtes Fahrrad finden. Er möchte eine E-Mail an den Sender schicken, die in der Sendung vorgelesen werden soll.

Entwerfen Sie für Stefan einen Text in englischer Sprache, der folgende Punkte enthält:
- Kurze Vorstellung
- Suche gebrauchtes Fahrrad, Alter egal, aber guter Zustand
- Farbe bevorzugt silber oder schwarz
- kostengünstig; höchstens 30 Pfund, da Verdienst zurzeit sehr gering
- Reifen, Beleuchtung, Bremsen funktionstüchtig
- Barzahlung bei Übergabe/Abholung; wohne selbst in der Nähe von Sheffield
- Kontakt: 0049178765765 (Handy) oder stefan@t-offline.de (E-Mail)
- Anrufe erst ab 19:00 Uhr, sonst auf Mailbox sprechen, rufe gern zurück
- Hoffnung, dass sich schnellstmöglich jemand meldet

2 Application (12)

An einem schwarzen Brett in *Meadowhall* fand Stefan einen Aushang, den er Ihnen zuschickt.

Actors and actresses wanted!

We are planning to make a film about pupils/students from different schools all over Europe.

Are you interested?

Applications accepted until 20 August.

Please write to:

> Norma Banks
> 16 Mersham Road
> Clapton SW4 10FH
> London

Da Sie sich bewerben möchten, verfassen Sie ein Schreiben in englischer Sprache an Frau Norma Banks, das ca. 80 Wörter umfasst und folgende Punkte enthält:
– Informationen, die Sie über sich selbst geben möchten
– Gründe, aus denen Sie sich bewerben möchten
– Gründe, aus denen Sie sich für die Filmaufnahmen für geeignet halten

Bitten Sie auch um Informationen zu Honorar, Unterkunft und Arbeitszeiten.

Benutzen Sie dafür ein Extrablatt, das Ihnen von Ihrer Schule bereitgestellt wird.

Vorschlag II

1 Personal letter (12)

Stefans Freund Tony aus Kanada kommt im Sommer zu Besuch. Stefan möchte mit ihm eine kleine Rundreise durch England machen.

Verfassen Sie diesen Brief an Tony **in englischer Sprache**! Der Brief soll ca. 80 Wörter umfassen und folgende Punkte beinhalten:
• wie Sie reisen möchten (mit Begründung)
• wo Sie übernachten könnten (mit Begründung)
• welche Städte/Sehenswürdigkeiten Sie einplanen sollten
• was Sie sonst noch zusammen unternehmen könnten

2 Formal letter (18)

Zurück in Deutschland hat Stefan eine Anstellung als Teamassistent bei der Firma AUDIOVISTA gefunden. Dort ist er u. a. für die Korrespondenz mit den ausländischen Zulieferfirmen zuständig. Für seine Chefin muss er ein unterschriftsreifes Fax vorbereiten.

Verfassen Sie dieses Fax in englischer Sprache!

Herr Schneider, bitte geben Sie noch heute eine kurze schriftliche Rückmeldung mit folgenden Inhalten an unseren Zulieferer in Leeds!

– Ansprechpartner dort: Mr Fuller
– Bestätigung unserer telefonischen Bestellung von heute Morgen
– Änderung: statt 50 Plakate der Gruppe The Beauties bitte 100 schicken – die Nachfrage hier ist größer als erwartet!
– Bei einem Mengenrabatt von 10 % auf die Listenpreise weitere bedeutende Aufträge in Aussicht stellen!
– Pünktliche Lieferung dringend erforderlich, da bereits Bestellungen von Kunden vorliegen; spätester Liefertermin: 20. August!
– Zahlungsbedingungen: 30 Tage ab Rechnungsdatum oder abzüglich 2 % innerhalb von 10 Tagen – wie vereinbart
– Hoffnung, dass unser Auftrag wieder zu unserer vollsten Zufriedenheit ausgeführt wird
– Höflicher Schlusssatz

Benutzen Sie dafür ein Extrablatt, das Ihnen von Ihrer Schule bereitgestellt wird.

Part A 2

1 Note taking

Hinweis: Hier wird ein englischer Text vorgegeben, die Fragen, die beantwortet werden müssen, werden jedoch in deutscher Sprache gestellt. Lies die Fragen, bevor du den Text liest. So kannst du die entsprechenden Stellen im Text während des Lesens finden. Du solltest aber unbedingt den ganzen Text gründlich lesen und nicht nur einzelne Informationen suchen. Beim Überfliegen eines Textes gehst du das Risiko ein, dass du wichtige Informationen verpasst und den allgemeinen Zusammenhang nicht wirklich verstehst.

Notizen zum „Einkaufszentrum Meadowhall"

1. Sheffield

frühere Bedeutung als:	• (boomender) Industriestandort
Bedeutungsverlust aufgrund:	• Automatisierung der Fertigung
	• Rezession in GB

2. Meadowhall

geographische Lage in Sheffield:	• in der Nähe des Zentrums (3 Meilen außerhalb)
vorherige Nutzung des Geländes:	• (Standort eines) Stahlwerkes
Eignung des Geländes für ein Einkaufszentrum wegen:	• günstiger Verkehrsanbindungen
	• (vergleichsweise) weniger Einkaufsgelegenheiten in Sheffield
Anzahl möglicher Kunden im Einzugsgebiet:	• 8,2 Millionen
durchschnittliche Verweildauer der Kunden:	• 224 Minuten
Besucherzahl bis zum 14. September 1990:	• 1 Million
gegenwärtige Anzahl von Geschäften:	• 305
momentane Anzahl von Angestellten:	• 13.500

besondere Werbeaktionen:	• Menschen als Schaufensterpuppen
	• Modeschauen
	• Auftritte von Prominenten
Auszeichnung mit einem Umwelt-Preis für folgende Leistungen:	• Solarheizung
	• Werbung für öffentliche Verkehrsmittel
	• (2.000 t) Abfallrecycling

2   Multiple matching

Hinweis: In dieser Aufgabe müssen sieben kurze Texte gelesen werden. Jeder Text beschreibt ein Geschäft in „Meadowhall". Deine Aufgabe ist es herauszufinden, welches Geschäft zu welcher Kurzbeschreibung passt. Hier musst du die Texte sehr genau lesen, weil die Lösungen zum Teil nicht so offensichtlich sind, wie sie erscheinen.

Grab A Bag	[9]
Granny's Delight	[6]
Carat	[8]
Pugs and Kisses	[4]
Monophone	[10]
Abacho	[1]
Body Care	[5]

3   Reading for detail: True or false

Hinweis: Diese Aufgabe bezieht sich auf die gleichen Texte wie in „Task 2". Hier musst du dich entscheiden, ob die vorgegebenen Angaben über „Meadowhall" richtig oder falsch sind. Auch hier musst du sehr vorsichtig sein.

Stefan, your statement is ...

	right	wrong
Two new stores specialize in foreign products	☒	☐
Two new food stores have started their businesses.	☐	☒
Two new stores are run by new bosses.	☐	☒
Two new stores will open soon on the Ground Floor.	☐	☒
Two new stores offer services, but no products.	☒	☐

Part B: Overall Language Proficiency

1 Multiple choice

Hinweis: In diesem Brief werden jeweils drei Wörter zur Wahl gestellt. Deine Aufgabe ist es, das passende Wort zu markieren, damit der Text grammatikalisch richtig ist. Hier ist es wichtig, auf die Zeiten und Signalwörter zu achten.

---

92 Lenham Road
Sheffield
S11 9BX
England

Dear Tony,

Many thanks for your last letter. It's nice to know everything is going well in your life. I don't know if I **told**[1] you but I have got a great job in Music World, a shop in the Meadowhall shopping centre in Sheffield.

I **have been**[2] there since the beginning of the month and the job is great: My boss is a young guy **who's**[3] only five years older **than**[4] me – I really like him. I am having lots of **interesting**[5] experiences and I really enjoy **talking**[6] to the costumers here – their Yorkshire dialect is lovely to listen to! **Everyone**[7] is so friendly to me.

Yesterday something really extraordinary **happened**[8]. I was standing behind the counter when all of a sudden I saw my old friend Traudi next to the Folk Music section. Just imagine – she's got a job as an au pair in a family in Sheffield. It really is a small world! She had never mentioned to anyone back in Kronach that she **would**[9] go to England to improve her English! She seems **to be**[10] quite happy in her 'new' family: The children she looks **after**[11] are very nice. She is usually so busy with the kids that she doesn't have **any**[12] time to go shopping in Meadowhall. So we were really lucky to have met! Anyway, she likes the family so much that she is thinking of staying there for another six months. If she **stays**[13] so long, her English really will be good! Well I must stop now, and get my beauty sleep! **I'll write**[14] to you again when I have more time next weekend.

Very best wishes,
Stefan

---

1 Vergangenheit, „said" nicht, weil in Zusammenhang mit einem direkten Objekt
2 Signalwort „since" braucht present perfect
3 Relativpronomen + Verb „is"
4 „than", nicht „as" bei einem Vergleich
5 Adjektiv, da Bezug auf das Nomen „experiences"
6 „enjoy" + Gerundium
7 „Everyone", nicht „everything", weil es sich auf Personen bezieht. „All" geht hier nicht, weil kein Nomen danach steht. Zum Beispiel: „All kids like ice-cream."
8 Signalwort „yesterday" braucht simple past.
9 „would", nicht „will", wegen Vergangenheit. Da kein „to" danach steht, geht „wanted" hier nicht
10 „seem" + Infinitiv des Verbs
11 feste Verbindung „to look after" = aufpassen auf

12 „any", weil der Satz verneint ist. Hier passt „no" nicht, weil sonst eine doppelte Verneinung entstehen würde.

13 Bedingungssatz „Conditional 1" (If + simple present, will + Infinitiv)

14 Signalwörter „next weekend", deswegen „will future".

2 Gap filling

Hinweis: Aus diesem Text wurden Wörter entfernt, die nun wieder eingesetzt werden müssen. Du musst Wörter von der „wordbank" einsetzen, die den Text sinnvoll und grammatikalisch korrekt ergänzen. Obwohl der vorgegebe Text nicht komplett ist, solltest du trotzdem den Text durchlesen, um einen Überblick zu bekommen. Diese Strategie bringt den Vorteil, dass du so eine bessere Vorstellung davon hast, worum es geht und sie hilft dir passende Wörter zu finden.

What to do in and around Sheffield

Sheffield is a great place to be! You'll **certainly** *(Adverb, da Bezug auf das Verb „love")* love our parks and woodlands. We're only five miles from the wonderful scenery of the Peak National Park! You'll also enjoy our exciting events and great **attractions** *(„exciting events and great" + Nomen)*. No matter what your **choice** *(Possessivpronomen + Nomen)* is we're sure you'll have a great time – as so **many** *(Bezug auf ein zahlbares Nomen)* people have before you!

To get further information, please call +44 (0) 114 221 1900. The service is available Monday to Saturday between 9.00 am and 5.30 pm. An answering service operates outside of **these** *(Bezug auf ein Nomen im Plural)* times for ordering brochures.

You can also e-mail us at visitor@sheffield.gov.uk. We aim to reply to email requests and **recorded** *(„recorded", nicht „recording", da passive Bedeutung ausgedrückt wird. Zum Beispiel: "The messages are recorded by the callers".)* messages by no later than the working day after the one on which they are received.

Part C: Productive skills

Hinweis: Vorschlag I (Task 1: Writing a formal letter + Task 2: Writing an informal letter) oder Vorschlag II (Task 1: Telling a story + Task 2: Writing a formal letter) Freie Textproduktion ermöglicht viele verschiedene richtige Lösungen. Vom Kultusministerium werden deshalb Bewertungskriterien festgelegt, die von allen Korrektoren angelegt werden sollen. Dazu dient das auf Seite 2007-23 stehende Bewertungsschema, das – in Anlehnung an die Notenstufen – die zu erwartenden Leistungen sechsmal abgestuft definiert und diesen Definitionen eine bestimmte Bandbreite von Punkten zuordnet.

*Die Definitionen charakterisieren jeweils die schriftliche **Gesamtleistung,** die sich im Wesentlichen aus den folgenden Einzelaspekten zusammensetzt:*

– Ausführung der gestellten Aufgabe (task achievement),

– sprachliche Korrektheit (accuracy),

– Wortwahl und Angemessenheit des Ausdrucks (range and appropriacy).

Vorschlag I

1 Jumble sale notice

Hinweis: Hier ist eine E-Mail zu schreiben. Halte dich genau an die Liste mit den Angaben, die dein Schreiben beinhalten soll. Nur so kannst du die volle Punktzahl erreichen.

Hi. My name is Stefan and I've been living in the area for a while. Last week I got a job in Meadowhall and need a bike to get to work. I'm looking for a used bike in good condition. I don't care how old it is, but I'd prefer a silver or black one. I don't earn a lot at the moment so I can't spend more than 30 pounds on the bike. The tires, lights and brakes should work well. I can pay cash and can pick up the bike as I live near Sheffield myself. You can contact me by phone on 0049178765765 or by email stefan@t-offline.de. Please call after 7 pm, otherwise leave a message – I'll call you back.
I hope to receive a reply soon.

2 Application

Hinweis: Hier ist ein Bewerbungsbrief zu schreiben. Wichtig ist, dass du die Anzeige und die Aufgabe genau durchliest, damit dir klar ist, an wen du schreibst und wofür genau du dich bewirbst. Um die maximale Punktzahl erreichen zu können, musst du nicht nur Angaben zu jedem Stichpunkt machen, sondern auch den Brief höflich anfangen (Bezug darauf nehmen, wo du die Anzeige gesehen hast) und beenden (Hoffnung ausdrücken von ihnen bald wieder zu hören).

Dear Ms Banks

With reference to your notice on the bulletin board in the Meadowhall Shopping Centre, I would like to apply for a part in your film.
I am 17 years old and live in southern Germany. At the moment I am doing my final exams at a business school in Rosenheim.
My reasons for wanting to take part in your film are because I would like to meet other young people from all over Europe and to improve my English skills. As I have been a member of the school drama club for 3 years and have experience in films, I think I would be a suitable candidate.
Could you please send me information about wages, accommodation and working times?
I look forward to hearing from you soon.

Yours sincerely

Vorschlag II

1 Personal letter

Hinweis: Auch hier ist ein Brief zu schreiben, allerdings von persönlicher Natur. Da das Treffen erst im Sommer stattfindet, sind die Zeiten besonders zu beachten. Du solltest einen freundlichen Anfangssatz und Schlusssatz nicht vergessen.

Dear Tony

Thanks for your letter. It's great that you are going to visit me in summer. I have been thinking about our tour through England. In my opinion we should travel by bus because it is not as expensive as the train and we will be able to see more. I think that youth hostels are the best kind of accommodation because they are cheap and we will meet other young people. We could start in London and see some of the famous sights like Big Ben and Tower Bridge. Then we could travel to the north of England and go hiking or mountain biking. What do you think?

Please write soon.

Best wishes

Stefan

2 Formal letter

Hinweis: Bei formellen Briefen ist auf Sachlichkeit und Höflichkeit zu achten. Wichtig ist es, alle Angaben gründlich durchzulesen und dir zu überlegen, wie der Auftraggeber die Sätze und Fragen formulieren würde.

Dear Mr Fuller

We would like to confirm our telephone order placed this morning and make a small change. Could you please send 100 posters of the group "The Beauties" instead of 50. The demand is bigger than expected.

If you grant us a volume discount of 10 %, we will be prepared to place large orders in the future. Punctual delivery is very important because we have already received orders from customers. Please deliver by 20 August at the latest.

The terms of payment, as agreed, are 30 days after receipt of invoice or 2 % cash discount within 10 days.

We hope that this order will also be carried out to our satisfaction and look forward to hearing from you soon.

Yours sincerely

Christine Eder

Punkte	Definition der Leistung
Task 1/2: 18–16 Task 1/2: 12–11	Die Aufgabe ist vollständig gelöst. Der Text ist sofort verständlich und flüssig lesbar. Orthographie und Strukturengebrauch sind überwiegend korrekt; Wortwahl und Redewendungen sind dem Anlass gemäß gewählt und im Wesentlichen idiomatisch verwendet.
Task 1/2: 15–13 Task 1/2: 10–9	Die Aufgabe ist vollständig gelöst. Der Text ist verständlich und erfüllt seinen Zweck. Zwar wird der Lesefluss gelegentlich durch kleinere, aber nicht sinnstörende Fehler unterbrochen. Ein vielfach erfolgreiches Bemühen um situationsadäquate und idiomatische Ausdrucksweise wird deutlich.
Task 1/2: 12–11 Task 1/2: 8–7	Der Text erfüllt seine Hauptfunktionen, auch wenn die Aufgabe nicht in allen Einzelheiten vollständig ausgeführt ist. Orthographie, Strukturen- und Wortgebrauch sind nicht fehlerfrei, erfordern aber kaum Rekonstruktionsleistung vom Leser. Ansätze zu situationsadäquater idiomatischer Ausdrucksweise sind erkennbar.
Task 1/2: 10–9 Task 1/2: 6–5	Der Text kann seinen Zweck erfüllen, auch wenn die Aufgabe nicht ganz vollständig ausgeführt ist. Er enthält gelegentlich den einen oder anderen sinnstörenden Fehler. Aber auch nicht sinnstörende Fehler treten gehäuft auf und verlangsamen die Lektüre. Ansätze zu situationsadäquater idiomatischer Ausdrucksweise sind kaum zu erkennen.
Task 1/2: 8–6 Task 1/2: 4–3	Der Text erfüllt seinen Zweck kaum mehr. Eine hinsichtlich Wortschatz und Strukturen stark von der Muttersprache geprägte unidiomatische Ausdrucksweise behindert den Lesefluss erheblich. Das Gemeinte ist an etlichen Stellen nicht verständlich und muss vom Leser mühsam rekonstruiert werden.
Task 1/2: 5–0 Task 1/2: 2–0	Der Text erfüllt seinen Zweck nicht mehr. Er enthält, wenn überhaupt, nur rudimentäre Satzstrukturen und/oder ist nur noch mit Fantasie vom Leser zu entschlüsseln.

Notenschlüssel

Punkte	Note
100–85	1
< 85–70	2
< 70–60	3
< 60–50	4
< 50–33	5
< 33–0	6

Ihre Meinung ist uns wichtig!

Ihre Anregungen sind uns immer willkommen. Bitte informieren Sie uns mit diesem Schein über Ihre Verbesserungsvorschläge!

Titel-Nr.	Seite	Vorschlag

Die echten Hilfen zum Lernen ... **STARK**

17-VW9

Bitte ausfüllen und im frankierten Umschlag
an uns einsenden. Für Fensterkuverts geeignet.

Zutreffendes bitte ankreuzen!

Die Absenderin/der Absender ist:

☐ Lehrer/in in den Klassenstufen:

☐ Fachbetreuer/in
Fächer:

☐ Seminarlehrer/in
Fächer:

☐ Regierungsfachberater/in
Fächer:

☐ Oberstufenbetreuer/in

☐ Schulleiter/in

☐ Referendar/in, Termin 2. Staats-
examen:

☐ Leiter/in Lehrerbibliothek

☐ Leiter/in Schülerbibliothek

☐ Sekretariat

☐ Eltern

☐ Schüler/in, Klasse:

☐ Sonstiges:

Unterrichtsfächer: (Bei Lehrkräften!)

STARK Verlag
Postfach 1852
85318 Freising

Kennen Sie Ihre Kundennummer?
Bitte hier eintragen.

Absender (Bitte in Druckbuchstaben!)

Name/Vorname

Straße/Nr.

PLZ/Ort

Telefon privat   Geburtsjahr

E-Mail-Adresse

Schule/Schulstempel (Bitte immer angeben!)

Sicher durch alle Klassen!

Faktenwissen und praxisgerechte Übungen mit vollständigen Lösungen.

(Bitte blättern Sie um)

Abschluss-Prüfungsaufgaben

Mit vielen Jahrgängen der zentral gestellten Prüfungsaufgaben an Wirtschaftsschulen in Bayern, <u>einschließlich des aktuellen Jahrgangs</u>. Mit vollständigen, schülergerechten Lösungen.

Mathematik

Abschlussprüfung Mathematik
Wirtschaftsschule Bayern
1998–2006: Mit vollständigen, leicht nachvollziehbaren und schülergerechten Lösungen – zur selbstständigen Kontrolle und gezielten Vertiefung des Wissensstands. Im Format A5.
■ .... Best.-Nr. 91501

Deutsch

Abschlussprüfung Deutsch
Wirtschaftsschule Bayern
1998–2007: Jede Aufgabe mit vollständiger Gliederung, Musteraufsätze zu ausgewählten Aufgaben. Hinweise zu den prüfungsrelevanten Aufsatzarten Erörterung und Textanalyse sowie Tipps zur Texterläuterung. Thematisches Verzeichnis der Prüfungsaufgaben. Im Format A5.
■ .... Best.-Nr. 91541

Ratgeber für Schüler

Richtig Lernen
Tipps und Lernstrategien 5./6. Klasse
Schülerband: Äußere Arbeitsbedingungen; Anlaufschwierigkeiten beim Lernen; Arbeitseinteilung; Lernen und Gedächtnis; Lernrezepte für jeden Stoff; wie ich Zutrauen zu meinem Können fasse.
Elternband: Wie Sie Ihrem Kind helfen können; optimale Arbeitsbedingungen; typische Probleme bei den Hausaufgaben.
■ .... Best.-Nr. 10481

Richtig Lernen
Tipps und Lernstrategien 7. – 10. Klasse
Vermeidungsverhalten ab-, Motivation aufbauen; Arbeitseinteilung und Arbeitsorganisation; wie unser Gehirn Informationen auswählt und speichert; aus der Trickkiste der Gedächtniskünstler; Lernaufgaben erfolgreich meistern; das Können auf dem Prüfstand.
■ .... Best.-Nr. 10482

Englisch

Abschlussprüfung Englisch
Wirtschaftsschule Bayern
2000–2007: Mit vollständigen, schülergerechten Lösungen mit vielen Hinweisen und Tipps. Dazu Übungsaufgaben zu den Bereichen Leseverstehen, Sprachfertigkeit, Textproduktion und mündliche Prüfung sowie eine systematisch aufgebaute Kurzgrammatik in deutscher Sprache. Im Format A5.
■ .... Best.-Nr. 91551

BWL/Rechnungswesen

Abschlussprüfung BWL
Wirtschaftsschule Bayern
Original-Aufgaben der Jahrgänge 1995–2007 mit vollständigen, leicht nachvollziehbaren Musterlösungen – zur selbstständigen Kontrolle und gezielten Vertiefung des Wissensstandes. Als zusätzliche Übung eine zusammenhängende Fallaufgabe im Stil der Abschlussprüfung. Im Format A5.
■ .... Best.-Nr. 91575

Abschlussprüfung Rechnungswesen
Wirtschaftsschule Bayern
Enthält die zentral gestellten Prüfungsaufgaben der Jahre 2000–2007 mit schülergerechten Lösungsvorschlägen. Zusätzliches Übungsmaterial anhand einer Musteraufgabe im Stil der neuen Abschlussprüfung 2007. Mit Kontenrahmen zum Ausklappen. Im Format A5.
■ .... Best.-Nr. 91571

Natürlich führen wir noch mehr Titel für alle Schularten. Wir informieren Sie gerne!

Telefon: 0 81 61/179-0   **Internet: www.stark-verlag.de**
Telefax: 0 81 61/179-51   **E-Mail: info@stark-verlag.de**

Die echten Hilfen zum Lernen ...

STARK

<u>Bestellungen bitte direkt an:</u> STARK Verlagsgesellschaft mbH & Co. KG
Postfach 1852 · 85318 Freising · Tel: 08161 / 179-0 · FAX: 08161 / 179-51
Internet: www.stark-verlag.de · E-Mail: info@stark-verlag.de